HEAL T

Surprising Secrets to 21st Century Healing of Mind Body Spirit and Relationships

By
ANAN RISING

Copyright © 2019
pimrosebooks.com

i

DEDICATIONS

I have been truly blessed to be surrounded by loving and caring people throughout my years.

To my kids. We learn from each other every day. You helped me discover what true love is.

To Emily for showing me what loving with reckless abandon feels like.

To Mary & Troy for taking in a young knucklehead and helping to shape a young man.

To John for showing me where power and raw grit and determination can take you.

To Stefan for helping to show me what growing into manhood looks like.

To Clem and Alfred for showing me what spiritual and family growth look like when you live a life serving others.

To my nieces and nephews. It's been a true joy and honor watching you all grow and develop into the outstanding people you are today.

To Keenan, Rory and Rich. Keeping the mind sharp as well as the silver tongue. Thanks for always keeping me honest.

To all the lovers out there spearheading the campaign to spread the religion of love.

LOVE IS MY RELIGION

ACKNOWLEDGEMENTS

To the Most High! Whoever or whatever you are thank you.

INTRODUCTION

There are millions (probably more) of books on the market touting how you can save time, life hack, bro hack, instant this, instant that and algorithm your way to a better, happier, healthier you. I would like to start off straight away by calling bullshit as should you.

We are extremely complex beings of infinite consciousness residing within a complex biological organism which resides on a mosaic plane(t) of immense beauty.

We work and live out our lives inside of an incredibly sophisticated and dangerous social and emotional construct that we have been born into that we must navigate every waking moment.

We've been navigating these treacherous waters for many years and we all have been left with scars be them physical, spiritual, emotional or all the above.

With that perspective in mind do you really believe in your gut that you are going to get a drive thru instant gratification fix for what ails you? I sincerely hope your answer to that question is a resounding NO!

Wherever you find yourself now at this moment consider that it has taken you years to get to this place in your life. It took years of progress (and neglect) for us to beat ourselves down mentally, emotionally, physically and spiritually (with the enthusiastic assistance of our social construct) so I'm here to let you know that it is going to take time to recognize and disperse these things in our lives that no longer are welcome. This is not a 4-hour fix all or a 7-minute ab routine. Time is not linear as we perceive it so even considering achieving your goals by X date within X amount of time is pretty silly when you get right down to it.

I like "life hacks" as much as the next person BUT this is a journey into the very nature of who and what you are. It's your own unique journey and, the words, thoughts and emotions entombed inside of this book can only assist as a guide on your journey. You are the navigator of this great adventure and the hope is that this book can act as a companion to assist where possible. The true spiritual guide is inside of YOU and we label it in human terms as intuition or perhaps God, YHWH, Buddha, Allah, Uranus, Atum, Anshar, El, Shiva, Jah.

As your journey grows and you start to break away from the fake social construct you will start to become in tune with your inner voice of nature, your intuition. Don't fight it. It knows what you want and how to provide it for you.

You cannot find what you truly seek via a computer algorithm or a life hack. You must let go of your perceptions of reality and recognize that you have been programmed since birth to believe the lies of the social construct. You will need to dive down into the deep waters of your own internal realities. At the start you may dive very shallow or even just dip a toe into the great depths of your inner consciousness but as you continue your journey you will find that you will start to dive ever deeper into a wonderful cacophony of discovery and power. Sometimes these waters will be icy cold but know and understand that your conscious will not hurt or harm you. Sometimes you must be shown things that are difficult for your programmed mind to accept. You will likely find yourself experiencing past childhood traumas at some point during your healing. In these moments understand that you as your now maturated, wiser self can embrace the inner hurt child. You can hug and love and care for that inner hurt child in a way no one else can. This embrace can open the bounty of true love inside of all of us. You are your own best medicine and you will need to embrace this concept to move properly through these writings.

Embrace the difficult as you would the fantastic and let the healing begin.

Live2Luv2Live

TABLE OF CONTENTS

LEGAL NOTES

No stealing, we've got lawyers.

The thoughts, ideas and beliefs expressed in this book are those of the author and should not be consumed, imbibed, inhaled, licked or rubbed without adult supervision. If no adult is available you, the consumer, agree to conduct yourself in an adult manner to the best of your ability.

I am not a doctor and this content is in no way representative of allopathic medical butchery. The information expressed in this book are based on personal experience of the author and is not intended as a medical manual and should not be used for diagnosis or treatment. Professional health care should be consulted prior to attempting any treatment on yourself or others.

These writings will seek to honor healing modalities that rarely have a cost in terms of dollars associated with them. Instead, these are time honored modalities that have existed for many years and in many cases, have been suppressed for various reasons but usually for money, power and control.

CHAPTER 1. BREATHING

Y ou do it every waking and sleeping moment of your life. It's interesting to consider that you can't live without breathing and you're doing it right now without having to actively think about it, which is great but also can be problematic.

There isn't necessarily a wrong way to breath per-se but the way we currently breath is not the most efficient and because it's auto regulated we are rarely aware of our breathing patterns, depth of breath which means we lose the opportunity to breath in a more efficient manner.

All of us for nearly our entire lives breath in a very shallow manner taking air into the top of our chest but never into our bellies. Nearly all breathing techniques utilized for healing have a key focus on breathing into our belly's. The importance of this lies in the fact that the breath of life serves not only the physical purpose of exchanging air in and out of the lungs.

There is a deeper level of cellular activity taking place within our bodies when we inhale. We have so many cells in our bodies that there is no scientific consensus on just how many on average there are in the human body. The best they have come up with is over 37 trillion cells based on an estimate of how many cells make up each organ.

These trillions of cells work tirelessly within our bodies and need a continuous source of energy. The foods we eat are converted into energy for our bodies, but this fuel must be converted into the proper form for the individual cells to use.

When we are shallow breathing into the upper lungs only, we are using a mere fraction of the amount of air and this oxygen rich air is responsible for nourishing every cell within your body. With the simple act of mindful concentrated breathing you can better nourish your entire body bringing an incredible amount of health benefits for your overall physical body as well as your mind.

I am free, I am free, I AM FREE

There are many breathing techniques, and each can serve our bodies, brains and yes even our spirits. The Healing Modalities chapter presents several breathing techniques, the potential dangers, why you are being presented the technique and when to use the breathing technique.

How Breathing Works

Quick overview of what is happening on the physical "mechanical" side of things when your breathing. There is plenty of medical jargon available to us, but we purposely do not want to overcomplicate an explanation of the basic act of breathing.

Respiration:
Something most people don't consider is that every cell in your body is breathing which makes your entire body part of the respiratory process. Air is delivered to every cell not just your lungs. Each cell brings in oxygen and expels carbon dioxide. Without this oxygen our cells cannot produce the much-needed energy our bodies require.

The automated system for breathing is controlled by the autonomic system. To simplify, this can be broken down into two parts.

The sympathetic and parasympathetic nervous systems.

Sympathetic System:
Think of the sympathetic system as your fight or flight response system. The sympathetic system prepares the body for sudden stressors in your environment and controls breathing, the heart and adrenal glands.

Parasympathetic System:
The parasympathetic system is the opposite of the sympathetic system. Its primary purposes are to allow you to rest and digest your food for extracting nutrients.

Are you already starting to understand the importance of breathing and how taking time out of your day for focused breathing can have an impact on your entire body, mind and spirit?

Breathing, the basics.

You inhale air through either your nose or mouth, it travels down your trachea which divides the air into two different passage ways (bronchial tubes) for your right and left lungs. The air passes through yet smaller passages called bronchioles. The end of the journey takes place at some little sacs called alveoli. The body has over 300 million alveoli and they are important.

There is a mesh network of capillaries covering the alveoli which allows for the air to pass through the alveoli to be delivered into the blood. The blood then heads out of the lungs and makes its way to your heart. Your heart then pumps this oxygen rich blood to the cells of your organs and tissues.

With this basic understanding we can realize that by simply super-charging our inhalations of air and pushing it deep into our bellies instead of the top of the lungs we can have a positive impact on our entire bodies by increasing the oxygen input into our bodies.

Specific techniques are outlined in the healing modalities chapter but for now let's press on to that other all important element water.

CHAPTER 2. WATER

T he elixir of life or perhaps more accurate the great supporter of life or yet even better…. LIFE!

Water is life for these bodies we inhabit? Air, water, food in that order of importance are essential in sustaining the human lifeform.

Water seems obvious right? Most of us are fortunate enough to have been born and raised in a society that has indoor plumbing and irrigation that is important in two ways.

1. Getting cleanish water into your living spaces.
2. Extracting the dirty water from your dwelling helping to ensure a cleaner living environment and helping to avoid disease (the Archimedes Screw).

Since water is an everyday part of our existence, we tend to pay no mind to the extraordinary life-giving substance nor to the fact that many of us have easy access to cleanish water sources.

In the forthcoming water chapter, I will be reviewing many aspects of water and the role it plays in our lives. The dangers some of these waters possess and how to best utilize the water you have readily available in order to attempt to improve the overall health and wellbeing of our bodies and perhaps our spirits.

Much to discuss so let's get right into it and start with one of the most readily available sources of water in American and European households. It came from the tap!

5

I am free I am free I AM FREE

TAP WATER

Distillation

Most of your tap water started out as distilled water thanks to good ol' Mother Nature.

The lakes, rivers and streams are heated up by the star of our young Milky Way galaxy, the sun. This causes these bodies of water to have large portions vaporize and begin their journey into the Earth's upper atmosphere.

While in the atmosphere it starts to cool off and then will condense back into water. It then falls back to Earth in a cycle that is seemingly continuous and allows for a natural way of cleansing water. Unfortunately, we run into a bit of an issue particularly within our modern industrial reality. Our atmosphere has been heavily polluted mostly by the manufacturing industry and by "human ingenuity". This natural distilled water now accumulates many man-made toxins from the atmosphere as it makes its majestic journey back to the Earth and its human inhabitants.

When some portions of this water lands on mountains it will work its way down to level ground as water always seems to. Along the journey it will glide and maneuver over under and through various rocks and other items and will pick up inorganic minerals from the rocks, dirt and silt. It's also picking up various microbes from things like carcasses of dead animals along the journey.

As the water moves along the soil it will pick up billions of bacterium, parasites and various viruses. If you consider for a moment that nearly every mammal, insect and reptile that has ever existed has decomposed and become part of the soil a better understanding of just how many impurities are being picked up by this natural water source can be better understood.

Companies will scoop up these waters, run them through filters then sell it as mineral water, or spring water. Part of the selling point is the fact that this water is full of minerals. Yeah, your body wants minerals. What companies don't tell you and what most people don't know is that these are inorganic minerals that your body absolutely

6

I am free, I am free, I AM FREE

does not want any part of. Arthritis anyone? Calcium deposits accumulating within your joints are largely attributed to inorganic minerals.

Water absorbs and transports just about everything that it comes into contact with and there is a whole host of toxins that water will accumulate prior to getting to your city's treatment plant. But hey why even think about that. After all your hard-earned tax payer dollars are going towards those treatment plants so it's all good. Who cares if the treatment plant can't souse out all the crude, after all your refrigerator has a filter on it so once again all good brosif. If this is your current line of thinking you may not be too psyched about what you're about to read next.

The Treatment Plant

Ah the treatment plant. The panacea of cleanliness. How could it not be, after all its sole purpose for existence is to cleanse the city's water coming from various sources to ensure it is safe for consumption. But alas our treatment plants are going to expose this already dirty water to a battery of toxic chemicals in an attempt to "clean" the water and make it safe for human consumption.

You can probably already understand the issue here. Let's clean the water with chemicals that are toxic to humans because we have a federal mandate to ensure we meet a standard of cleanliness. Part of the issue here is that pathogens become more and more resistant to the chemicals, so the municipalities are going to continue to implement additional chemicals in an attempt to limit the number of pathogens that are retained by the water. These chemicals will cause cancer and death by continued consumption. Not pulling any punches here people. We are only a couple years removed from the Michigan water incident which permanently injured a large number of children and if you really want to dive deeper into the insane machine roll your calendar back to the 80's and do just a little bit of research into the various water wars and death water that was being delivered to various communities on the west coast of the United States. But the water wars of the 80's is a bit too deep of a dive for our intentions here and besides water wars continue all over the world and will likely be coming to a city near you very quickly. Let's get back to the discussion of cancer-causing water supplies.

What kind of cancer we talking?
Urinary Tract Cancer
Colon Cancer
Bladder Cancer
Prostate Cancer

The UT, colon, bladder and prostate are the locations within your body that water is going to migrate to first consequently these areas of your body will have the longest duration of exposure to these cancer-causing elements within the water you have consumed.

I am free, I am free, I AM FREE

Let's not forget that wastewater is also collected from homes and businesses. That's pretty nasty to think about but one should also consider the fact that it's not just poop that goes down those toilets.

<u>Toilet Thoughts</u>

Trash
Baby wipes
Used tampons
Used condoms
Various drugs and needles

All kinds of insanity go down toilets not to mention the city sewers.

Many treatment plants work in phases to attempt to clean or "purify" the water.

1. Hits the sedimentation tanks first. This separates solids from liquids. This first stage is to extract large chunks of physical matter from the waste water.

2. Next it's off to secondary treatment. This process will consist of adding oxygen to create a "biological treatment". Oxygen will activate the living microorganisms such as bacteria that will then chomp, chomp, chomp away the organic material that was not separated in stage 1.

3. Off to be disinfected after stage 2. After disinfection it's back into the environment the water goes.

What the heck is being utilized to disinfect the water? Wish I could tell you but through all my digging I couldn't turn up this answer.

Another thing to consider is how industry plays a role in the water coming into your home. Unfortunately, many people drink tap water, cook with tap water and most of us shower and bath in it.

I am free, I am free, I AM FREE

Industries you may not consider play an important role in dumping MASSIVE amounts of manufacturing byproducts into your city's water supply.

Industries such as breweries and wineries can contribute thousands of pounds per day which can account for a substantial percentage of the overall waste coming into the treatment plant.

Is your water treatment area near any airports? I hope not. Something as simple as deicer being used on the planes are going to create a large amount of poisonous run off directly into the soil and this same poison will be introduced into the water chain.

What are other toxins that can enter the water supply via industry.

Dentist offices: Mercury

Fast food: FOG which stands for Fats, Oils, and Grease oh my!

Automobile shop: Various oils and deadly metals

You also have companies that are licensed and permitted to utilize septage for discharging industrial and commercial wastewater.

The following is a list of some of the toxins your cities treatment facility is attempting to minimize.

Arsenic
Cadmium
Chromium
Copper
Lead
Mercury
Nickel
Silver
Zinc

Here's a pretty graph of a waste treatment plant close to my dwelling. It shows a 4-year average on how much based on percentage they are able to remove. Notice the very low numbers on Arsenic then consider what Arsenic is.

I am free, I am free, I AM FREE

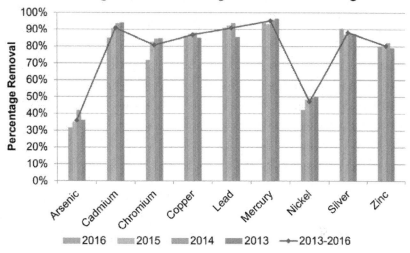

South Treatment Plant Annual Average Removal
Percentage vs. 4-Year Average Removal Percentage

11

I am free, I am free, I AM FREE

Your money is being extorted from your paycheck before you see it and a portion is going to things like a water treatment plant. How much of this water is being contaminated by industry and how much by you and your fellow neighbors' households?

Let's get back to the path this water will take to get to your home.

After leaving the treatment facility it will be carried to your home or business via pipes. Really old pipes. REALLY OLD PIPES often made of lead and other toxic metals. Aside from the material the pipes are made of can you imagine what has accumulated inside of those pipes when you consider the numerous amounts of years these pipes have been in place?

If you think that filter on your refrigerator is going to filter out the massive amounts of toxins residing in your tap water, you are wrong.

To give us further insight into how polluted this tap water can be I turn to my handy, dandy water tester or TDS meter.

These are cheap little gizmos that you can place into water and it will provide a reading on the number of impurities in parts per billion. Those impurities could be anything.

I had a trip planned for Mexico coming up and knew I had a stopover in Los Angeles so decided to pack the pocket-sized meter and conduct readings from water directly from the tap in three locations along the west coast.

Pacific North West: 33 PPB
Los Angeles: 309 PPB
Mexico: 635 PPB

This is very telling. In the more northern areas of the map which tends to produce lots of mountain water via snow/ice run off and using the local municipalities water treatment plants we see an extremely low 33 PPB reading from the tap. This low number is rather extraordinary for a city of any size.

As we move into the extremely densely populated area of greater Los Angeles, we see a massive spike when compared to the PNW. At 309 PPB this has got to be some hard water that is further taxing on

12

I am free, I am free, I AM FREE

your body and if drank directly from the tap seemingly would cause potential health risks.

Moving further towards the equator and further away from larger scale treatment plants we see another massive jump in PPB as the number more than doubles compared to the LA area which is already incredibly high.

Don't be fooled by the low 33PPB in the Pacific Northwest. In late 2018 a woman died from improper use of here Netipot. Using tap water filtered through a Brita filter in the Seattle area she managed to contract a brain eating amoeba. While nasal douche can be a great healing modality and one I'm likely to add to this book it's critical that you utilize distilled water as often as possible for consumption and cleansing.

The international standard states that any number higher than 40 total dissolved solids (TDS) is the critical point for the purity of the water. Keep in mind this is JUST reading the actual solid-state particles which does not speak to other risk factors such as bacteria which could be deadly in any amount.

We live inside of a chemical world. Chemicals permeate just about everything in our 3D reality and we knowingly eat and drink these chemicals as well as rub them all over our bodies and brush our teeth with them.

The best way to clean these toxins out is via water but you better make sure it's the correct type of water. Using anything except distilled water isn't going to be much help and could actually have the opposite affect you are attempting to achieve.

Okay we learned a bit about consuming water now let's move into some other uses for water we tend to take for granted. That's right it's time to strip off your clothes (took long enough) and jump our bare buns into the beauty that is cold showers.

COLD SHOWERS

Who in their right mind seeks out cold showers when you can simply turn a knob slightly in one direction and find yourself basking in the glory of 21st Century ingenuity?

Why YOU silly!

Let me tell you, in the past I was the last person I can think of that would seek out cold. In the past I HATED the cold. I don't like the word hate but seriously I hated the cold. I would go to great lengths to avoid even the hint of cold entering my sheltered cocoon of warmth. After spending a year doing cold showers, I can happily say that I now find the cold to be my friend. Where I once saw a nemesis, I now understand that this cold was presented to me to allow me to become stronger on many levels on my journey towards higher self.

I recall that first miserable cold shower. I will present you with a couple of options on how to start cold showers but for me often I prefer to dive head first into things. I'm not sure if that's an ego thing or just the way I prefer to function on this plane of reality. Regardless day one I turned my shower to the coldest setting, gave myself a steely eyed glint in the mirror, flexed my guns a couple times then jumped in.

YOWZA!! DOWZA!!

It was SOOO much colder than I imagined. I could barely breath and felt like I was going to hyper ventilate from quickly sucking my breath in and out. I figured I could settle down and accept the cold, but it just wasn't happening. I was shivering like crazy and could barely hear my own thoughts over the clattering of my teeth.

Thankfully I had set my timer to a meagre 2 minutes. After the 2 minutes I jumped out of the shower and felt fantastic. My energy was way up, and I had conquered something inside of my own head. My auto-pilot voice that always said I couldn't handle the cold was now only partially correct.

The first 5-6 days of the daily morning cold shower was fairly close to the same but after about the 5-day mark, I started to become a

14

I am free, I am free, I AM FREE

bit calmer and was able to remain under the water for the full 2 minutes. By week two I was no longer shivering (much) and by the end of week two the cold showers started to feel amazing! I went from fearing my morning shower to looking forward to it with great enthusiasm. And a funny thing happened along the way.

At that time, I was going to a kickboxing studio after work with my boys. It was a fantastic studio with a great owner and a family friendly vibe. I had gotten to the point of full contact sparring but even though I had many techniques and lots of pad work under my belt too often I would freeze up and consequently get lit up during full contact sparring. When I would spare with people that had size, speed and technique advantage over me whenever I got blitzed with shots I would cover and turtle up which would result in many painful bruises particularly when getting kicked in the ribs.

It had been a couple months since I sparred, and now cold showers were very enjoyable. One day in class the main instructor asked if I could work in rounds for a sparring session to prep someone for an upcoming fight. An interesting thing happened during this sparing session. I was calm. SO calm! Oddly calm. Whenever I would get blitzed with combos all that external force coming at me had very little effect on my spatial awareness. I found I could easily parry, dodge, slide, counter and I had total breath control. After the session I was kind of scratching my head trying to figure out how I had improved so much when I hadn't been sparring. The realization didn't hit me until my cold shower the next morning. As that external force of the cold water bombarded my body and I stood under the water calmly breathing and focusing on warming my body internally I realized the calmness I had discovered in the eye of the storm.

Although you will not find scientific studies into cold showers, I can tell you from experience that the welcome calmness it can bring into your life is a joy.

But alas as often is the case there is yet another reason you should consider cold showers that I've never heard anyone bring to discussion.

From the earlier tap water chapter, you have gained a better understanding of the potential high volume of poisons coming out of your tap. When you are standing under the warm water pouring out of your shower head your pores open which is going to allow for

15

easier introduction of poisons into your system. Multiple studies have been conducted which have shown that disinfectant chemicals (you know the aggressive ones they utilize at the water treatment plants) can be absorbed into the skin and lungs.

Annual report by the 'Presidents Cancer Panel'
https://deainfo.nci.nih.gov/advisory/pcp/annualReports/pcp08-09rpt/PCP_Report_08-09_508.pdf (you will be doing yourself a favor by reading the entire report as it delves into many hazards present within our daily lives).

This report on page 56 has the following:

People are exposed to DBPs through consumption and through inhalation and absorption through the skin during bathing, showering, and swimming in chlorinated pools.267 Relatively little research has been done on DBPs and cancer; the strongest data show increased bladder cancer risk with long-term (up to 40 years) exposure to DBPs, particularly among men.

Your body is packed with lymph nodes. There is a nice little collection right under those hairy pits you should concern yourself with. See the healing modalities chapter to start creating your own easy to use natural deodorant so you can stop self-poisoning your body.

Let's move along to a comprehensive list of benefits.

I am free I am free I AM FREE

Cold Shower Benefits

Weight loss: Brown fat vs. White fat, ready FIGHT!
White fat is to store fat as emergency energy rations
Brown fat is to generate heat to warm up your body.
So, what's going to happen when you take a cold shower?

Your brown fats get activated to generate heat for your body.
Get a slight caloric burn here but you also get a huge energy boost.
For additional information regarding fat check out the
Intermittent Fasting chapter which goes into a bit more detail.

Circulation:
Stimulation of the circulatory system is brought about because
your heart now must start pumping harder to ensure blood is flowing
through the entire circulatory systems including the extremities.

Improved Immunity:
How important are white blood cells? Extremely if you want a
strong immune system. White blood cells are those little guys
responsible for fighting disease amongst other things. Studies have
shown that taking cold showers on a regular basis allows for more
abundance of white blood cells compared to taking warm showers.

Lymphatic System (lymph nodes):
The lymph system tends to get very little mention when
compared to your immune system however the lymph system has a
HUGE responsibility for helping to protect the health and overall
well-being of your body. The lymph system carries waste out of your
cells so pretty darn important job there. Your lymph system also
allows the heart to not work as hard as the lymph's pull blood
throughout your body. When your lymph system has blockages, this
can cause all sorts of issues but in a relatively healthy person this can
lead to colds, sore muscles, aches and pains. For those with less
healthy systems you're potentially creating a huge negative impact
and blocked lymph nodes can act as a catalyst towards creating a dis-

eased body. It's important that you utilize the hot/cold 30-40 second transition exercises to help flush any stagnant fluids out of the lymph nodes. You should be doing the hot/cold therapy at least once a week to help flush the lymph nodes.

Breath Control:
When you first start cold showers, you are going to be panting and probably like me wondering what the hell you're doing standing in this cold shower being assaulted by this cold water! BUT if you have been following along in earlier chapters than you already have several types of different breath work you can do to calm your mind and focus on the sensation with control.

Muscle Recovery:
You have heat to relax the muscles and apply cold to help build immunity and recover from an active lifestyle. Ideally you would want to have total body submersion into a still body of water that is at around 55 degrees Fahrenheit. You could also opt for a cryochamber if you want to spend the money, but if you want a quick, easy and cheap DIY use that cold shower my friends. You can do a straight cold shower or also use the hot/cold method. This will allow the heat to draw the blood to the surface of the muscle then let the cold go to work. The primary reason for the muscle relief is the ability for the hold/cold to flush lactic acid build up from the sore muscles.

Healing:
That's rather all encompassing. What I'm referring to is something I don't hear anyone mention when speaking about cold showers. Your local municipality likely has water that is full of all kinds of toxins. You should take the time to track down the annual reports that your local municipality makes available online. You can invest in a shower filter but when I tested my shower filter, I found it was not very useful. My TDS meter moved only 2 parts per million lower when my shower water was running through the shower filter. When you take a 15-minute warm shower your pores are going to open up and you are going to make your body more susceptible to any toxins carried in the water supply. Also, to note you're have lymph nodes in areas that will absorb like crazy.

Depression:

I'm told that cold showers can have a significant impact regarding depression. I know for me cold showers fire me up and get me going in the mornings and later in the day after my workouts. In my journey I was able to help a friend during a difficult break up he was working through. I put him on a week of guided meditation via an audio therapy session I created and had him finish all his daily showers with a 30-40 second cold water shower. I would love to say that the next day we sat down over a lovely conversation and he told me how great this all was but as it was, he texted me the next day telling me how much better he felt.

That's rather antidotal and doesn't exactly carry any long-term study information to support the claim that cold water immersion will help with depression. I can't say for certain that it will, however in my research this is a claim made by many.

To note tracking down scientific studies regarding cold showers is no small feat my friends. Hydrotherapy has been around for many years and bathing in cold waters to boost strength (mental, spiritual as well as physical) is as old as time immortal. Applying these same concepts to cold SHOWERS is different. Cold showers right now in the main stream will fall under bro-science and with some of the crazy things being said about it it's not surprising. With that said cold showers have had a huge impact on my life in a positive way particularly when I meshed it with changing my eating habits. I was able to find one study from the US National Library of Medicine National Institutes of Health (easy for you to say) from 2014. This was a study titled "Scientific Evidence-Based Effects of Hydrotherapy on Various Systems of the Body". It was pretty awesome reading, but their conclusion left a lot to be desired. Let me paraphrase.

"And in Conclusion: This is awesome son! It helps in so many various ways especially with improved immunity and it's been around like I don't know.....UH...FOREVER! Also, hey look all these evidences are scientifically based so BAM there you go. Oh, but also, we don't know how it works when applied directly to individual diseases so maybe it's all bullshit too?!? Give us a grant and we will conduct some more studies"

19

I am free, I am free, I AM FREE

Ok, are you convinced yet? NO!?! Convinced or not we're moving along so to find information on the how to's grab your rubber ducky, loofa and toy boat and head on over to the Healing Modalities chapter for some splish, splash fun in the shower.

I am free I am free I AM FREE

Distilled vs. Alkaline

Hey, are you still here? Well hey good to see you and thank you for sticking around after a round of cold showers.

Okay let's rewind the clock just a bit and take a step back into the world of water quality.

I started this chapter speaking about the water coming out of your tap. It should have been eye-opening information if you are not already spending time digging into this world of fake manufactured madness. But as typically happens I paired that information down a bit to make it more digestible and now that we are on the other side of incorporating some physical practices let's dive back into the wonderful world of well mostly confusion and misinformation.

Often, I read two different viewpoints regarding distilled water vs. alkaline water. Which is better, safer, etc.

It can be confusing. After all, if you keep your body (blood) at just over 7.0 pH on the alkaline table it's known to keep your organic body in a healthier state and make you much less susceptible to dis-ease.

Distilled water tends to get a bad rap for leaching minerals from your body which many say will hurt your body in the long run.

I have listened to many in the health community decry the sinister nature of distilled "dead" water. This is important so pay attention as we pull back the curtain and peer into the abyss of water science.

Distilled water does in fact leach minerals out of your body. What most people either don't know or purposely leave out is the fact that distilled water is only able to leach inorganic minerals from your body. Inorganic minerals come from rock deposits which come inside of things like spring water.

Your body does not want or need these inorganic minerals. They are bad for your body in many ways. What your body does need are organic minerals.

Distilled water cannot remove or leach organic minerals and vitamins from your body because it has the same ion charge as organic minerals and vitamins. Like cannot attract like but positive

21

I am free, I am free, I AM FREE

ions do attract negative ions such as inorganic minerals. Therefore, distilled water can work to repair your bloodstream.

Another thing to consider is that absorbing minerals via water is extremely inefficient compared to consuming minerals via food.

Most minerals absorb efficiently when attached to a protein molecule which is not what is happening when attempting to do this through water alone. It cannot attach to the intestines for proper absorption especially if it is competing with minerals which are riding on a protein molecule. Plant sources already have the minerals attached to the heme biomolecule hence they are able to more easily attach to the intestines for better, faster absorption.

You should simply look to get your various minerals and vitamins from the closest thing you can get to raw organic foods such as fruits, vegetables, legumes, nuts and grains. If necessary, you should take specific supplements such as a liquid form of B12.

Did you recently go out and purchase an Alkaline water machine? I know several people who have and well when you do the research it seems to make sense but as you perform a deeper dive everything starts to fall apart. So, if you put some money into one of these get ready to smack your forehead and possibly look to resell it.

What is alkaline water and how you were convinced that it's good for you and you should drink it.

We should all know by now one of the most important items within our bodies is our blood. The cleaner the medium the blood resides within and the easier the blood is able to flow throughout the body in general the healthier the overall organism.

The blood likes to be oxygenated and likes to be alkaline as opposed to being acidic. When your blood is in a high acidic state it increases the probability of the blood getting tainted and causing a whole host of issues throughout the living organism of your body.

If you can get your pH levels more alkaline and you can oxygenate your blood levels, you're going to be in danger of greatly improving your overall health.

With that in mind it's easy to see that alkaline water seems to be a great option for achieving a higher alkaline state for your blood. At least that is what the manufacturing companies producing these bad boys are telling you.

Here's the rub (don't act so surprised you knew it was coming).

22

I am free, I am free, I AM FREE

One of the primary reasons our bodies become more acidic and thusly more toxic to the surrounding tissue is taking place at a cellular level. Peoples alkaline reserve minerals become depleted or deficient usually due to their poor eating habits. Unfortunately, alkaline water does nothing to resolve this issue.

Alkaline water does not help your mineral reserves instead it can often have the exact opposite effect. Sounds weird right? Can that be right? I mean alkaline is right in the friggin name of the thing. It's labelled in bold, colorful letters right on the bottle. The problem is if your body is tricked into believing it has the correct amount of alkalinity within it then it can start to dump its reserve alkaline minerals. Oops!

BUT WAIT THERES MORE!

Sorry dudes and dudetts but things only go downhill from here. Alkaline machines have a whole host of issues. They often replace minerals with lead and arsenic along with other toxic metals found in tap water.

In nature water generally becomes mineralized by running down mountains or high points and running over rocks and other items and picking up minerals from the rocks along its journey to flat land.

These machines attempt to mimic this behavior which doesn't work out too great for you. We should consider the fact that they will be using machined parts from a manufacturing plant and the resources they will utilize while attempting to mineralize the water will be far from what nature is able to achieve.

From a manufacturing stand point that means using metal plates that pass along platinum and titanium into the water before that water hits your glass.

You might think it stops there but it gets worse.

To also purify the water, the water will pass over a series of filters which is not going to benefit the water. I know it seems like filters would be the best option, BUT carbon filters remove very few toxins from your tap water. They can also become breeding grounds for bacteria as this organic material starts to decompose. It's damn

I am free, I am free, I AM FREE

near equivalent to just drinking straight out of the tap. Don't believe me? Here's a neat trick.

Go out and purchase a low-cost water tester. Fill one clean glass with your regular tap water and another clean glass with your filtered water from your alkaline machine. Now using your tester check the difference between the parts per billion of contaminants in both glasses. For certain the filtered water will have a lower number, but it won't be much lower and even that lower number is still allowing an incredible amount of truly harmful toxins into your water. What type of toxins?

Fluoride
Chlorine
Lead
Mercury
PCBs
Arsenic
Perchlorate
Dioxins
DDT (see section on vaccines for a special note regarding DDT and polio)
HCB
Dacthal
MtBE

Okay that's the short list. But buyer beware there are loads more.

In 2016 a study led by researches from Harvard T.H. Chan School of Public Health and the Harvard John A. Paulson School of Engineering and Applied Sciences (SEAS) found that over SIX MILLION Americans have unsafe levels of toxic chemicals found in the drinking water. Why is it even still marketed as "drinking water"? How about "death water" or "cancer water". Not as catchy I suppose but much more accurate.

The study was published August 9th, 2016 in Environmental Science & Technology Letters.
https://pubs.acs.org/doi/pdf/10.1021/acs.estlett.6b00260

Since PFAS's (polyfluoroalkyl and perfluoroalkyl substances) have been in use for roughly 60 years in commercial production they have been linked with many forms of cancer as well as hormone disruption. The chemicals most easily are passed along to humans and animals via drinking water.

An alkaline machine is an expensive way to take in calcium tablets and potentially introduce your human organism to a whole host of other toxins you don't want roaming around in there.

Distilled water on the other hand is 99.98% devoid of any impurities making it the purest water you can obtain.

When a company is selling you on mineral water there is something very important, they are leaving out of the sales pitch.

Your body is most efficient at assimilating minerals via your food intake not via water.

You can purchase your distilled water in plastic 1-gallon jugs from your local store. You can also invest in a machine that can be placed on your countertop for at home distillation.

The drawback to purchasing any water in 1-gallon jugs from the store is the potential for the chemicals from the plastic container to leech into your water.

Side note: C'mon admit it your starting to dig all these side notes.

When a plastic container is labelled BPA free it's just a bit of sleight of hand. The entire point to being BPA free is to help ensure that the chemical compounds don't leech into whatever liquid you place into the BPA free container. Well not really from the perspective of the manufacturers. After they started receiving backlash with regards to BPA toxicity, they needed to find a way to ease the concern of the consumer.

Enter our friend BPA free.

Many and most manufactures did in fact stop making their plastics with BPA and can now slap that BPA Free sticker on their plastic bottles. What no one is telling you is that they simply slightly change the chemical compound. Yeah, it's not BPA anymore but the change they made didn't make it any less dangerous it just changed it enough so at a chemical level it's no longer BPA.

The new chemical compounds used are BPS and BPF. Additional testing needs to be done on how these truly effect the body

25

I am free, I am free, I AM FREE

but judging by the historical record of chemical manufacturers, they are likely just as bad as BPA. They are still willing to poison you for profit. As much as is reasonable get those plastics out of your household. Do NOT store consumables for your ingestion in plastic.

Water is SO cool. We've visited our taps, the city's systems to attempt to purify our waters, the health benefits of having cold water assist your mind and body on its pattern of growth. What are we leaving out? Oh yeah that next level shiz. Come along as we journey into the strange world of water and intentions.

I am free I am free I AM FREE

Rice Water Testing
Water is life. We've all heard it before. If water is life and 75% of the plane(t) is made of water AND roughly 60% of adults are made of water then really how important is water to you, to me, to humans as a species? Pretty important.

Often what is overlooked regarding the importance of water is how energy can positively or negatively affect water. You can research for hours, days, weeks in a futile attempt at finding the correlation between energy and water or you can try the following experiment yourself within the comforts of your own domicile. It's easy and you don't need much to get this bad boy going.

Items needed:
2 cups uncooked white rice
2 clear jars rinsed out with available lids.
Distilled Water
30 days
Marker
Paper
Tape
Intentions

Grab your two clean jars, take the lids off and place them on your counter.

Place one cup of rice in each jar.

On a piece of paper write the words "I HATE YOU". As you write these words really feel it. Really put some rage into the words onto the paper.

Relax for a bit.

On another piece of paper write the words "I LOVE YOU". As you write these words really feel it. Really pour your love onto the paper with great joy and passion.

27

I am free, I am free, I AM FREE

Tape the I hate you, paper to the front of one of the jars.

Tape the I love you, paper to the front of the other jar.

Fill the rest of both jars with water. 1 or 2 cups of water will do.

Put the lids on the jars.

Place the jars somewhere in the house out of the way.

I placed my jars in the kitchen out of sight and out of mind.

In 30 days check your jars.

The outcome of my experiment is shown in the images.

I am free I am free I AM FREE

I am free I am free I AM FREE

Water is life.

The average adult male is 60% water.

The average adult female is 55% water.

The amount of water in the human heart and brain is 73%, lungs 83%, muscles and kidneys 79%, the skin 64%, and the bones around 31%

As humans we are mostly a water bottle made of living organisms. It is crucial to keep the water (blood plasma) in a healthy state to keep the organisms from putrefying.

Your thoughts and intentions can make your internal rice rotten or healthy. Keep your thoughts about yourself full of love and then pass it along so we can all keep healthy body rice.

Your energy and intentions have a direct impact on your water of life. Your blood. You are walking around all day with thoughts, intentions and behaviors that have a direct impact on your physical well-being. If you are in your head beating yourself up or creating stress, then you will infuse your life blood with these intentions which will in turn rot and mutate your cells.

Your cells need healthy blood to keep you functioning properly. Many already live in a social construct that presents immense amounts of external poisons that our body's beautifully work to cleanse. DO NOT self-sabotage yourself with your own reckless thoughts. Above I mention stress, but stress is not real. It's not a tangible thing that exist but instead is wholly manufactured by YOU! If you say "Man, I am so stressed because of this guy, or this amount of work" or whatever you should recognize the fact that you are lying to yourself. These outside stimuli are not creating stress because they cannot create something that does not exist. You manufacture stress within yourself based upon your interpretation of this external stimulus. When you are feeling overwhelmed and something inside of you feels like it is going to spill over.

STOP!!!

I am free, I am free, I AM FREE

Take several deep breaths (see chapter on breathing techniques and ensure you are breathing safely). Find one of your favorite memories. Feel it, taste it, touch it, smell it. Be there once again and breath. You are power. You are infinite consciousness and this so-called stress in this blip of time does not define you. You can decide right now to be happy or just.....be.

CHAPTER 3. FOOD

F ood! Isn't it the greatest!?

I've felt for many years that good music and food can heal and work to bring people together in ways other social methods cannot. Alcoholic lubrication can of course help to bring people together in more ways than one but since we are focusing on being a bit more health-conscious let's leave the spirits to their ill wills.

Why are food and music so good at bringing us together? I believe this is due to several factors but primarily because we humans living in today's society tend to place deep seated emotions into both the music we listen to and the foods we eat. Often, we don't even realize we are doing it.

Have you ever heard a song you haven't heard since you were a kid and suddenly get an overwhelming emotion of joy or sadness? At some point in your life you attached this emotion to this song probably without even realizing you did it.

Likewise, with food we tend to unwittingly create extremely powerful emotions with our foods and food like products. Then we can rollercoaster up and down, round and round the land of fad diets wondering why we feel emotionally drained just from cutting out this or that type of food. I think most of us don't take the time to reflect on the emotional connection we have with our foods.

For me it's easy to understand. As a youth I spent many years in an abusive household. The lady of the house had not learned her polities. She was a bit of an overbearing, obsessive insane person to the point of putting a chain and lock on the refrigerator, so we could only have access to food when she made it so. Reflecting on what that must have done to my young mind it probably created a sort of twisted love/hate relationship with food (or at least the fridge).

I was always a skinny kid and when I matured into adulthood and decided to bulk up and put on some serious muscle, I started to

32

I am free, I am free, I AM FREE

reflect on how I had chosen to eat up until that point. I realized I had a really distorted emotional relationship with food and didn't even realize it.

Aside from the oddball relationship I had with food I had my 20's. Man, in my teens and 20's I could eat anything, anytime, anywhere and wouldn't feel even a tiny bit of consequence physically for my actions. Copious amounts of fast food and greasy burgers were consumed in my lust for flavor and ignorance of all thing's nutrition based.

After years of study and plenty of trial and error in my tiny kitchen I have found a much more comfortable landscape for consuming nutrients, vitamins and minerals through foods whilst maintaining a robust palette of flavors and excitement in the foods.

We will begin our food discussions around addiction and will include some options for ideal times to consume calories to better allow the good doctor (your amazing body) to do its job in the Healing Modalities chapter. We will discuss fat and fat loss, a quick jaunt over to some additional information regarding best practices when eating then straight on to the food creation portion.

FOOD ADDICTION

It's a real thing and many studies have been conducted. Let's take a short glance at how food like products are put together (almost always in a lab) to trigger food addictions some as powerful as addictive drugs.

In a study conducted in 2015 which is publicly available here: http://hdl.handle.net/2027.42/109750
it shows which foods are the most addictive and the roles of processing fat content and the glycemic load.

They performed two studies, the first with 120 volunteers and the second with 384 participants. They used 35 foods with varying nutritional content and created a "forced-choice" for the participants.

The study is worth a read but here is a very brief showing of some disturbing numbers.

- Persistent desire or repeated unsuccessful attempt to quit.
  - Group 1: 97.1%
  - Group 2: 91.7%
- Substance taken in larger amount and for longer period than intended.
  - Group 1: 11.7%
  - Group 2: 15.1%
- Food addiction diagnosis (Three or more symptoms plus clinically significant impairment or distress).
  - Group 1: 6.7%
  - Group 2: 10.2%

Considering that these test's took place within a controlled environment likely does not do justice to what we would see in a normal social situation. If you're out for a drink and everyone in your peer group is throwing down on some chicken wings, it's easy to move in that same direction.

I am free, I am free, I AM FREE

If you just got off a busy day of work and you are not looking forward to cooking dinner for the hungry masses in your house it's easy and quick to pull into a drive-thru or purchase from the frozen food sections of your local grocer. A simple solution is food prepping every week and cooking enough for easy to reheat leftovers.

Millions of dollars are spent to get just the right flavor, mouth feel and create just the right amount of dopamine hits to keep you coming back for more. These millions can be spent on one single product like a potato chip. Extrapolate that out to fast food and the super market and you can start to realize that billions of dollars are being generated to make you addicted to foods that will lead directly to poisoning your body.

Stacked on top of these sugary, salty, umami flavored food stuffs are subliminal and not so subliminal advertising as well as peer pressure from peer groups. From this point of view, it's easy to see why so many living inside of "civilized societies" are eating themselves to death. Not so easy to understand is why the other half of the world is starving to death?

Let's push along oh fellow addicts.

I am free I am free I AM FREE

EATING

Since we are already looking at the consumption of calories for energy, this is a great place to drop some knowledge on other ways to masticate your foodstuffs in a more efficient manner.

Mastication:
What is it and how does it work? The process of mastication begins once you place food into your mouth hole. There is a lot of focus and you can find a plethora of writings which will investigate and discuss the digestion process, but many leave out the start of the process which is within the mouth.

It's a shame this information is not presented more often because if you have the knowledge of how your entire organism is working to break down food stuffs into energy you will be better equipped to eat in a more efficient manner.

Have a seat at any food court USA and have a look around and watch people eat. It's a weird thing to watch as people nearly swallow their food whole and hardly bother either tasting or properly chewing their food.

Before we discuss eating more efficiently let's take a quick look at what the body is doing inside of your mouth when that food gets dropped in.

Saliva. Yep, spit. This stuff is great so long as it's not used as a projectile weapon coming from an angry camels' maw. Saliva is a key component in assisting the body in breaking down foods. When that food first goes into your mouth your brain is triggered to start up the saliva machine.

Saliva like many things inside of our bodies seems simple and direct but has many layers to how it works as well as having a layered purpose. Let's keep it simple shall we.

Saliva has two primary purposes when it comes to helping you break down your food. It creates a substance called salivary amylase that begins the job of digestion by breaking down complex carbohydrates.

Second it forms a lubricant around your food called mucin. This surrounds your food to create a sort of shield to help reduce acidity. It

36

also helps to kill germs and acts as a slippy slide for the food chunks to be able to more easily make their way further down the digestive tract. Not to be outdone saliva also helps to break down food particles into smaller pieces for easier digestion.

Your teeth are another part of this process and are hard workers that unfortunately put in very little work for most people. The grinders are instrumental in tag teaming with saliva to really break down that food to get it ready to pass along. Remember the exercise of sitting at a food court and watching others eat? You will notice people just don't seem to chew much. Most people will take HUGE bits of food but chew less than 10 times before swallowing. OUCH!

The longer you chew your food per bite the longer the saliva and molars have to properly break down the food to ready it for the rest of the journey. On top of the saliva obviously the more time your teeth have to grind the food the easier it will be for your stomach to handle the incoming food.

Proper chewing allows your food to be broken down prior to getting further down the digestive track which will help your stomach get some additional rest. Perhaps eating this way for a couple of meals will not have a large impact however this small incremental change implemented on a regular basis can add up to a much healthier, happier digestive system.

A secondary benefit to eating in a fashion in which you take smaller bites and chew more is that it takes longer to eat. This is of great benefit to anyone looking to cut down on portion size per meal. It is said that it typically takes the brain in the stomach 20 minutes to notify the brain in your head that your full. Your stomach is surrounded by these kinds of sensors that when they stretch a bit they signal to your head brain that you are full. This is also the reason why drinking plenty of distilled water while fasting can help squelch hunger pangs. The sensors surrounding your stomach that trigger the full response don't know the difference between food or liquid they only know full or not full. By drinking plenty of distilled water and taking your time while eating you can help to ensure that the brain in your head is triggered with the full response before you devour an all you can eat buffet.

"Healthy Eating"

It's great to be eating foods that have higher nutritional value. Spending more of your eating time masticating organic nutrient dense whole foods is wonderful BUT there is something you need to be aware of.

Most of the nutrients from your foods are absorbed by the small intestines since the small intestines are a long labyrinthine maze and is the longest portion of the digestion process. It's divided into three sections and does most of the breakdown and absorption work with little help from other organs.

Part of the issue with purchasing the more expensive but healthier nutrient dense food options lies in the fact that your rectum and intestines are likely a sewage pit from years of abuse and non-cleansing. This makes it difficult for your body to properly absorb all those beautiful nutrients you are putting down your mouth hole.

I did not include it within the healing modalities section of this book however you should consider weekly enemas using properly heated distilled water only. It is a brilliant healing modality when done properly and home kits are cheap and easy to use. The only reason I did not include it within these writings is due to the potential dangers surrounding a perforated colon if done incorrectly. There can be some dangers with enemas for those that become addicted to them and those them attempt to use them as a means of shitting instead of using it as a tool for cleansing.

There's lots to discuss in the realm of food but alas we have come to the finish line for this chapter. With all the craziness our bodies and minds must combat within this environment one item you have TOTAL control over is what you decide to put directly into your body. This isn't relegated to food only. You decide what foods, liquids, pills, antibiotics, shots, etc. you put into your body.

The most important factor is to be actively aware and present regarding what you put into your body to attempt to maintain and sustain homeostasis.

Let's move along to timing our meals.

INTERMITTENT FASTING

The holistic healing modality of fasting has been around since time immortal and is practiced by several animals within the kingdom, not just us humans.

Intermittent fasting can be utilized for weight loss to help build your physical body towards better overall health and well-being but can also be utilized to help heal the physical body of many current or potential future ailments.

I constantly hear people say calories in and calories out for weight loss as though it were that simple. But much like most things we interact with in our lives there are multiple layers and levels to the simple act of eating foods and food like products.

Not all calories are created equal so simply applying a most basic math equation of consuming less calories than you burn is inefficient in the extreme. Example.

Person A consumes 2,500 calories today.

Person B consumes 2,500 calories today.

Both person A and person B have relatively the same metabolism and have the same level of activity throughout the day.

By the simple equation of calories consumed vs. calories burned both person A and person B should be relatively equal in weight and body composition.

The problem here is that we are looking to address healing holistically, so the type of calories consumed within the day is very important.

If person A consumed 60% of their calories from protein sources, 20% from complex carbohydrates and 20% from fat their body holistically would perform and react completely different from person B if person B consumed 40% from complex carbs, 20% fiber, 20% protein and 10% from fat.

If one person is consuming many daily calories from preprocessed "foods" and sugary sports drinks vs. another who is consuming many from wholefoods and prepping their meals by hand

I am free, I am free, I AM FREE

they are likely to have wildly different outcomes to their body compositions, weight gain, mental fatigue and much more.

These become two entirely different worlds of calorie consumption which have a massive impact on the overall health and wellbeing of the body.

The how to guide for implementing IF into your lifestyle can be found in the healing modalities portion of this book. For now, let's go visit our good friend fat.

FAT

Seems like fat is straight forward and if someone asked you for a definition of fat you could probably come up with a satisfactory answer quickly. You wouldn't even need to utilize a search engine or notin.

But hey, I took the time to write this here book and so long as you didn't work the 5-finger discount, you paid for this content so here comes some gristle for you to metaphorically chew on.

Here's the first thing about fat that is rather odd to think about. It's an organ. You read that right. In our general knowledge of fat, it's widely regarded as unhealthy, unsightly gooey nastiness BUT if you poke your head around the scientific community the consensus is that fat is an organ (mostly consensus anyway).

This puts fat into an entirely new light. In the immortal words of Johnny Castle.

"Nobody puts fat in a corner"!

Wait that's not right.

Why has the girl that couldn't get a prom date suddenly become the bell of the ball in some scientific corners? Leptin that's why. Turns out fat produces leptin a rather important hormone that communicates with the brain and amongst other things helps to regulate the body's energy levels. Fat you sexy thing you. Who knew?!

Not impressed yet? Well, researchers also found that fat helps to protect bones, protect organs, regulates the immune system and helps in managing women's reproductive systems.

BUT WAIT THERES MORE!

There are two primary types of fat.

White fat and Brown fat.

41

White Fat:

Okay so we here in the 21st century aren't big fans of white fat, certainly not excessive amounts of it. Aside from it assisting in leading to a host of health problems it just isn't as sexy as a six pack of abs (unless you come up with something like "dad bod" to convince the masses that excessive white fat on a body is a good thing). A reasonable amount of white fat on your body is not only good it presents health benefits as well. It stores readily available energy and produces hormones which are released into the bloodstream.

The skinny on the fat is that when not in excess on your body it acts on our behalf to make us less susceptible to diabetes and heart disease. I know your skeptical but small fat cells produce a hormone called adiponectin. This guy helps make the liver sensitive to insulin which in turn lowers the risk of diabetes and heart disease.

Brown Fat (brown adipose):

Who? What? Yeah for real there's a whole nother type of fat you've got on your body called brown fat. Kind of weird that our social construct dedicates so much time to white fat yet speaks nothing of brown fat. It's weird because brown fat is magic for your body.

When you are born you are born with a nice layer of activated brown fat located primarily just under your neck around your collar bone and upper chest. You are provided this brown fat primarily (but not exclusively) because it acts as an insulator of heat. More to the point it allows you to generate your own heat. For years scientist have decried brown fat as worthless nothing fat and are just now starting to realize the potential power of the brown fat.

The problem we tend to have is that as we have gone through our lives, we seek greater and greater comforts particularly from the cold. So much so that we bundle our bodies with shirts, sweatshirts, scarves, jackets, coats, furs and so on. Because of this too comfortable lifestyle our brown fat atrophies and simply stops firing up and starts to lose its ability to perform as intended. In studies it has been seen repeatedly that adults have nowhere near the same amount of brown fat as children.

I am free, I am free, I AM FREE

Brown fat is more like a muscle as opposed to being considered an organ like white fat. In fact, brown fat can and does burn off white fat. Your body has much more white fat compared to brown fat however the little bit of brown fat you are carrying on your body right now is likely lying dormant because it does not get activated as nature intended.

It is estimated that when your brown fat is activated even though it accounts for such a small amount of overall fat on your body it can burn up to 300 to 500 calories a day which equates to roughly a pound a week.

Activating your brown fat is yet another reason to hop in that cold shower ASAP.

Other fats to mention to round out the conversation.

Visceral Fat:

This is the stuff that can help put you 6 feet deep. This is deep fat that wraps around your inner organs. If you have a large gut, chances are you've got too much visceral fat which can lead to increased risk of diabetes and heart disease. Just as white fat can help with insulin visceral fat has the opposite effect. It is thought that visceral fat plays a role in insulin resistance which greatly increases risk of diabetes.

Subcutaneous Fat:

This fat lives on the surface or rather they are directly under the surface of your skin. This fat in general is not considered to pose too much of a health risk throughout the body apart from subcutaneous fat on the belly. This belly fat when combined with large quantities of visceral fat on the belly can spell bad news. If you've ever been to a health fare those cheap calipers, they pinch your arms and belly with is measuring your subcutaneous fat.

Belly Fat:

As indicated above belly fat is both subcutaneous and visceral fat making it a double dose of cringe worthy health risks. According to most expert's belly fat is considered the most at-risk surpassing thigh and butt fat. Since there is no way currently to spot loss fat stores you must put in some work on the overall health of your body to reduce this deadly belly fat.

Why the belly anyway? Ever consider why so much fat accumulates in the belly? Aside from the fact that there are many organs located just under this area the body itself is built in a fashion that our legs are much like pistons. Moving our frame through the world one step at a time. It makes sense that when storing extra energy stores in fat that the body would choose to locate this extra weight directly over one of the strongest portions of the body, the leg pistons. This is exceptionally useful when walking, jogging or running. Can you imagine if all that extra fat took up residents in your forehead or feet instead? That would be awkward and very inefficient for locomotion.

Thigh and Butt Fat
Sir-Mix-A-Lot gave us a lot to consider with his chart topping, enigmatic hit "Baby Got Back". Turns out that big butts aren't considered nearly as dangerous as belly fat. The main reason is because this fat is the less dangerous subcutaneous fat and not the more dangerous visceral fat. Unfortunately, studies have shown that as most women of particular body shapes hit menopause fat stores start to shift from the thighs and butt to the gut which is bad news for Mix-A-Lot and those looking to live a longer, healthier life.
Enough about fat. Let's do an abrupt 180 in the mostly opposite direction.

I am free I am free I AM FREE

To Vegan or Not To Vegan

A question for the new age whiner am I right?

I'm not a fan of the term vegan primarily because it tends to elicit different emotions usually negative within people.

Some are going to immediately be standoffish towards those who identify as being vegan or being part of the vegan lifestyle and culture which I understand from my own background. I always thought that vegans were pretentious douche bags at least that was my overall feeling towards every self-identified vegan I had ever met at that point in my life. I now realize that a large portion of it was how I perceived people in a very stereotypical way. Prejudice is defined as the act of prejudging an individual or group of individuals based upon preconceived notions. That's what I used to do with vegans and vegetarians and we all know that there is a portion of the population that feel and act the same way I used to.

When I was consuming charred flesh, I was eating it at nearly every meal. Part of the reason was because I was what most people would call a gym rat and I had subscriptions to a couple popular workout magazines and much like the fish on the hook I was completely bought it to the protein myth. I knew that I needed an abundance of meat particularly boneless, skinless chicken breast to stay strong, stay healthy and have enough protein to build muscle and have enough energy for my workouts at the gym. To take it a step further I also felt that as an American it seemed incredibly stupid not to eat meat. Part of my stance was; you live in a country where you have access to a plethora of readily available meat. So many other countries and people around the Earth are starving to death and would kill to have the opportunity to be able to eat meat at their leisure. So, to me I felt like you were a complete moron if you didn't eat meat. Not only are you a moron but you're basically un-American. I mean what's more Americana than firing up the grill and tossing some steaks on that bad boy?!?

45

I am free, I am free, I AM FREE

High quality proteins can be found in many vegetables, beans and legumes it's simply that meat provides a small package allowing for the complete amino chain of proteins. If you do not consume meat you can easily obtain proteins, you simply need to ensure to mix your protein sources to ensure you are getting all proteins within the complete amino chain.

This gets into another line of thought regarding food in general. Before we journey any further together, we have to get on a somewhat level playing field in terms of understanding our deep seeded relationship with food and food like stuffs. We should all admit regardless of how Earthy or healthy our food intakes are that we are all addicted to food. You're addicted my friend, and just like the pill popping crazed zombies looking for another hit so are you. I suppose the only people you could argue are not addicted to food are breatharians, but I've never met one so at this point of my journey I have no idea if that's even possible for the current class of humans roaming this plane of reality. It's important to understand this deep-seated love affair with our food and fake food stuffs that we harbor within ourselves.

Often when people first jump off the meat wagon, they tend to steer into finding vegan/vegetarian friendly foods that look and taste like the meats they used to consume. This make sense on many levels. I was eating meat for roughly 40 years so within that time there are so many fond memories associated with the terrible eating habits of a typical American diet. Some of my favorite memories are family bar-b-ques. It's a strange thing how the old factory senses work. I can smell some BBQ ribs and my brain can instantly take me 20 years into the past to a happy memory of tossing the ol' pig skin (Americana baby) around with my brothers or nephews while the wafting scents of BBQ came off the grill to smack me in the nose and gut. Giving up things in your life that you associate as part of your personality is difficult enough but when you start tying in the deep-seated love affair, we have with food things can get dicey quick.

I often hear people berate individuals new to the meatless game. "Hey man, how come you're always trying to eat foods that are just like meat?! Just eat the meat damn it!!"

46

I am free, I am free, I AM FREE

There are many ways to address this type of negative input from someone but the key to remember in my opinion is that we are ALL addicted to food. Whether we are eating meat or passing on the meat and dairy it's not really our place to judge unless you're a breatharian in which case Judge us oh mighty purveyor of the great Prana!

My point is you shouldn't judge others on what they decide to put on their plates and you shouldn't take it personally when others judge you for what you decide NOT to put on your plate. Define your own set of ethics regarding what you're comfortable with putting into your body and leave it at that.

When I first stopped eating meat it had nothing to do with ethics. I really didn't care whether animals lived or died; after all I had spent my entire adult life eating meat for almost every meal. After I challenged myself to go a week without meat the ethical part of it starting to kick in. First, I went a week without eating meat but then I thought....that wasn't much of a challenge let me go two weeks without eating meat.

Two important facts to point out here.

1:

I tend to meal prep on Sunday for the rest of the week. This always sets me up for success which I'm a big fan of (setting myself up for future success that is). The meal prep work on Sunday allows me to ensure that I am never hungry (a new vegan's worst enemy in the initial crave phase) and that I always have foods prepared by my own hands ready to go.

2:

I heavily researched non-meat/dairy based nutrition BEFORE going down the meatless path. Too many vegans/vegetarians don't attempt to further their understanding of nutrition. In my experience I have met many vegetarians that have zero sense of nutrition but most vegans I have met are pretty read up on the subject. With that said I highly encourage you to do some research in this regard. Some content will be in these writings but there is SO much information out there that I will simply be grazing over some of the larger risk factors to be aware of. Keep researching people it's your health on the line.

I am free, I am free, I AM FREE

Cooking is one of my passions in life. I don't get paid to do it, but I truly enjoy the process. I was fortunate enough to have a big brother (big shout out to bro T-roy) that taught me the ins and outs of getting some delicious homemade meals on the table. One thing he told me on several occasions was that his secret ingredient was love. At the time in my capricious youth I thought he was talking out of his ass but as I grew and started to create my own meals, I soon found the importance of energy, particularly positive energy when cooking. So why the heck am I yammering on about love and energy regarding food? You should consider where your food comes from and how it got to your table. Aside from the various trade acts and our military might's support of the petrol dollar cycle through the shipping and receiving of food and fake food goods we should also consider the actual vibrational energy of foods.

When an animal is slaughtered it's likely not going to have highly positively charged vibrations going on during the slaughtering process. I would hazard to guess it's in a state of massive vibrational panic and pain (so much so that now some farmers are getting their livestock high as a kite to attempt to calm them before the slaughter). When you consume this charged flesh, you should consider what is happening to your vibrational energy. It was Nikola Tesla who stated: "If you wish to understand the Universe, think of energy, frequency and vibration."

As we are beings of infinite consciousness it's important to understand that you can change your vibrational energy by simply stopping the consumption of meat and following a couple of other simple steps. When you consume this flesh, you are creating a heavy vibration for your spirit (or whatever you want to call it) and that has the potential to hinder or slow your growth towards finding your true self.

When I first tried to cook some chicken again after having stopped eating meat for a couple weeks, I was completely disgusted by it and I couldn't do it. I really didn't expect that I would care about chickens, cows, pigs so for me ethics didn't play a role until AFTER I had stopped eating meat for a couple of weeks. At the time it was kind of a bummer as I stood over my chopping board in my woefully too small kitchen staring at some bone in chicken thighs realizing in that

48

I am free, I am free, I AM FREE

moment that it was not possible for me to manipulate these neatly packaged animal parts for consumption.

Aside from the ethics of being a self-described vegan, keep in mind that there are many levels to being vegan. That's another reason why I don't label myself as a vegan. I still have leather belts, leather shoes, etc. Veganism takes on many different looks and feels and emotions for individuals (although at times the vegan community acts as emotional thugs towards meat eaters which is damn silly). So just one person calling themselves vegan doesn't necessarily represent or mean the same thing to somebody else who's going to also identify as a vegan. Personally, I identify as a person that is attempting to eat nutritional foods that will help my mind, spirt and body.

When one considers consuming foods for physical health, I believe there is room for most human bodies to consume animal flesh, eggs, fish etc. Although over consumption of these items has proven to be dangerous to most human bodies and has led to an abundance of health issues amongst a large portion of the human populace. The types of meats you consume also play a large role as the current manufacturing process of animals is rift with bacterial dangers amongst many other (anti-biotics) dangers presented before that hunk of flesh makes its way to your plate.

While small amounts of meat may seem wise since loads of complete proteins and nutrients can be found in a very compact vessel the current dangers around how animals are raised for slaughter and what and how they are being fed, the vaccines they are being injected with, and so much more does pose a potential health risk to your physical body. It's when you start diving a bit deeper into the realm of spirituality that consuming the flesh of other worldly animals from my perspective seems to have a greater negative impact.

If you're considering going down the path of veganism, I would also encourage you not to necessarily speak about veganism unless you are very confident and ready to have some passionate conversations sometimes with close family and friends who will not mind telling you how wrong you are for not eating what they think you should be eating. In my opinion it makes more sense to simply do what is right for you and avoid applying labels to it.

I am free, I am free, I AM FREE

The rise in the popularity of veganism is both a blessing and a curse.

On the one hand with more non-meat options available at grocery stores and restaurants even heavy meat eaters may start to eat just a bit less meat which could help their physical bodies and may lead to a bit less slaughtering of animals.

On the other hand, now, we see in grocery stores packaged meat alternatives that are so full of preservatives and other little nasties that from a physical health stand point your probably just as likely to damage your body whether you're eating meat or these meat alternatives. This is showing itself at chain food restaurants now as well. Just for giggles let's do a small dive into this, so you can better understand what I'm rambling on about here.

Let's move along for a very short stint in the world of vegan friendly faster food vs. typical tried and true fast food staples.

PLANT BASED FAST FOODS

When considering eating healthy someone who has made the decision to attempt to eat cruelty free often will believe by the simple act of not eating meat and dairy that they will be on board the train to healthy and nutritious eating.

This is far from true as it is often much more difficult to get all the necessary nutritional needs in the necessary quantities if you are no longer consuming meat. Although consuming meat can be harmful from an energetic and spiritual standpoint, we are talking physical health here.

Now we are seeing vegetarian and vegan friendly fast food chains popping up primarily on the west coast of the United States and all-over various parts of Europe. One might assume that by ordering from a vegetarian/vegan menu that they will be eating in a healthy manner.

One day while on a trip to Los Angeles I found myself at Veggie Grill and having not eaten in 18 hours I was rather famished and decided on ordering a burger and fries. Whilst thoroughly enjoying the burger and fries I decided to pop onto the Veggie Grill website and look up the nutritional information for the foods I was currently consuming.

What a mistake or perhaps a blessing.

Some of the numbers were so insane that I decided to start comparing them to some of the tried and true fast food chains such as McDonalds and the like.

Below is a chart I whipped together showing the "healthy" Veggie Grill numbers vs. the unhealthy McDonalds and Burger King options. The menus are not identical as they don't serve the same types of burgers, but I did attempt to line the menu up with similar options.

Veggie Grill

VG Beyond Burger

Cals	Fat	Chol	Sodium	Protein
620g	37g	0	1420mg	25g

McDonalds

Quarter Pounder with Cheese

Cals	Fat	Chol	Sodium	Protein
530mg	28g	100mg	1110mg	

Burger King

Spicy Crispy Chicken Sandwich

Cals	Fat	Chol	Sodium	Protein
700	42g	65mg	1140mg	25g

As we can see the cholesterol is zero in the VG option which is great for marketing your food as a healthy alternative. The issue lies in the fact that the fat and sodium levels are through the roof.

When you are looking at most prepackaged vegan/vegetarian friendly goods at your local grocery store you are going to find the same insane numbers not to mention the "foods" being loaded with preservatives.

So, what's one to do? Start cooking your own meals as often as possible. By home cooking we're talking about moving away from prepackaged death and moving towards actual whole ingredients. Other benefits of home cooking.

Nutrition:
You can control the nutritional content of the foods your cooking but when you're eating out especially fast food you are going to be consuming high amounts of sugars, salts and fats. Not only do you get the benefit of reducing the intake of these items by cooking at home you also help to retrain your palate to become more sensitive to the intake of high amounts of these items.

Food Safety:
Plenty of danger with the simple act of getting food at home or on the road but with home cooking at least you are in control of the environment and the cleanliness.

Family Time:
If you have children, creating a dedicated practice of sitting around the dining table enjoying home cooked food and each other's company is an important dynamic to create and one that your children are likely to continue into their adult lives with their children. You can create an environment in which you can have your children help and you can teach them in a fun-loving way how they can prepare their own healthier, tastier meals. Too often we get caught up in the fake perception of time and we rush to get food to the table. Choose one or two days out of the week and take your time cooking a meal while allowing your kids to assist. You can make this a fun

I am free, I am free, I AM FREE
interactive experience for your kids instead of creating a hectic time crunch in your head space.

Cheaper:
There have been many studies done that show eating at home is more cost effective when compared to eating out on a regular basis. If you really want, you can also buy in bulk and find other ways to keep your food costs down. Your likely to skip trips to the white coats as well which can save some serious cash.

Portions:
Seeing as you will be creating the meal you get to decide on the total volume of food and how much is distributed on each plate. Portion control can be slowly scaled back especially if you struggle with overconsumption or someone else within the household has this struggle. This coupled with slower eating can greatly cut down on total volume of calorie consumption per meal.

Food Sensitivities:
If you or someone in your family has a food "allergy" or rather is sensitive to certain herbs, spices or other fare you are in control and can ensure that these items never make it into the prepared foods.

Childhood Obesity:
Not only has there been countless studies showing the health benefits in helping to curb childhood obesity with home cooked meals, but this also plays into something we mentioned earlier. This family time helps to create a stronger family bond which in turn helps to create a better sense of self-worth for your children.
    Also, to be clear making nutritionally valuable home cooked meals doesn't just mean avoiding restaurants and fast food chains whenever possible. It also means staying away from the frozen food sections of your local grocery store. There may be some prepackaged items you purchase to cut down on food prep times but buying a frozen lasagna compared to prepping your own healthier version is not going to be very helpful. Frozen pizzas, burritos, lasagna etc. are not nutritional based foods and the amount of preservatives and fillers

54

I am free, I am free, I AM FREE

added will have a negative impact on your overall health and well-being.

You can read all day about the various health benefits and the how to's, but your best bet is to find time to get into that kitchen and start prepping some meals. Just like anything else with time you will get better. And the good news is that cooking is much like art. You can play around and have fun and as you continue the practice the better you will become at it and before you know it you just might start to enjoy yourself.

I tell you what. Just because I love you all SO, SO much, I have added a chapter about Meatless Mondays. Let's start simple guys. Don't start the race focusing on the finish line. One foot in front of the other and one step at a time. Let's look at implementing one day of no meat a week and making sure we make that meal by hand.

So, c'mon put a smile on your face turn the page or electric page? Let's go visit Meatless Mondays.

MEATLESS MONDAYS

I keep seeing this stuff pop up all over the place about Meatless Mondays. Videos and books galore. You would think this was a newfangled fad but alas no my dear readers there is a bit of recent history to Meatless Mondays and it's rather fascinating.

Let's take a little ride in the way back machine and travel to the year 1914ish. This was the time of the World War also known as the First World War or The Great War (naming a war great seems odd).

This was a "Great" war that started in Europe and involved France, Russia, Britain, Italy, Austria-Hungary, Germany, Japan and eventually the United States.

Due to trench war fare the death toll was staggering. Estimates put the military combatant's death toll at NINE MILLION and the civilian death toll racking up a sickening SEVEN MILLION deaths due directly to the conflicts. Unfortunately, as if that wasn't enough madness there was also multiple recorded genocides as well as the Spanish flu (which oddly enough didn't start in Spain). The Spanish flu itself is estimated to have taken somewhere between 50 to 100 million human lives globally. To put that into perspective at that time that equated to an American citizens life expectancy to drop off by 12 YEARS!!

This pandemic went Captain Insano for a couple of reasons. The environment for one. People were largely malnourished making their bodies susceptible to dis-ease and some lived in squalor and filth. Add a bunch of sick people into overcrowded medical camps without properly keeping the areas free from filth and Biggity Bam! The other problem was why it's named the Spanish flu in the first place. In areas such as the United States and the United Kingdom the various media outlets (the papers) downplayed the epidemic within these geographical locations and instead focused on Spain as being a particularly hard-hit area taking focus away from areas such as France, Germany the UK and the US. This campaign of misinformation created an environment that did not allow for people to properly prepare for the seriousness of this epidemic.

I am free, I am free, I AM FREE

That's painting a bit of gloomy picture but there you have it. That was the reality of the early 1900's and can you imagine sitting by the homestead attempting to prepare food for the family? Now imagine you're the head of the household for one of the allied families such as France or Belgium. Many of the citizens were starving because war was on their doorstep. Their crop fields had transitioned into war fields. Their farmers put down their hoes and picked up rifles.

Herbert Hoover prior to becoming the 31st President of The United States was brought into the fold as the head of the newly created Food Administration. The year was 1917 and Hoover took the reins of leadership for this newly formed seat of power.

Food will win the war.

That was the slogan they ran with and they plastered this message everywhere. The campaign started around April and by November somewhere between 11-13 million American families signed a pledge to take part in Meatless Tuesdays and Wheatless Wednesdays (it was titled Meatless Tuesdays before it changed to Mondays). But that's not all. New York city hotels had managed to save 96 tons of meat by November 1917. Europe was fed much of these foods and we see that the original efforts behind Meatless Mondays was to ration foods to help feed people in war torn regions on the other side of Earth.

Fast forward to 2003 and America is at it again with the Meatless Monday slogan. This go around a gentleman by the name of Sid Lerner a former ad man turned advocate for healthy living started this campaign anew. Things are much different in 2003 compared to the early 1900's. The average American is estimated to consume 75 more POUNDS of meat each year compared to past generations. Many reasons factor into this staggering figure but one of the crucial elements of Meatless Mondays is to snap some of us out of this zombie state of meat consumption.

It seems everyone's jumping on the once a week no meat train. Households, schools, hospitals and restaurants are cropping up globally in support of Meatless Mondays.

I am free, I am free, I AM FREE

So, what are you waiting for? If you eat meat everyday sometimes 2-3 times a day give your gut a break one day a week and see how you feel. If someone gives you shit about it just give them a backstory about The Great War and how the Meatless Monday shenanigans actually started. If nothing else, you will sound more like a purveyor of educated information instead of just someone who hoped on the Meatless Monday's bandwagon because they saw it on social media or worse read about it in some new agey book (DOH!)

Let's lob up what's in store next. Your gut. One good reason to cut back on meat is to help digestion and your gut. C'mon you can't be on the internet more than 2 minutes without seeing some sort of story or pop up regarding probiotics and gut biome so let's journey forth and find out a bit about this stuff.

I am free I am free I AM FREE

GUT HEALTH AND MODERN AGRICULTURE

Let's start this off speaking to one simple item you can cheaply and easy create in your own home laboratory.

Kombucha.

Kombucha was a wonder drink for me to allow me to move away from the sugar laden and deadly soda's I was consuming on a daily.
   Then a funny thing started to happen. As it gained in popularity store bought kombucha started to get expensive. Very expensive, especially when compared to the price point of a 16 oz. can of soda.
   Typically, within a given industry as they become more well established, they're able to lower their price points due to several factors such as
   Lowering manufacturing costs.
   Fully paid lines of credit for initial business startup.
   Lower cost wholesale purchasing for goods.
   Larger distribution channels.

One would assume that the prices would come down in the world of store bought kombucha but that certainly is not what we as consumers are seeing. To the contrary the prices move only in a northerly direction.
   I also realized that many of the flavors I would try were not palatable and after dropping $4-$5 bucks on a single bottle of kombucha I felt like it just wasn't worth it. But alas I did not want to continue to be soda's bitch but still craved the tantalizing tingling pleasures of a carbonated beverage dancing across my tongue.
   Being curious and frugal (the polite term for a cheapskate) I chose to seek out brewing my own kombucha. The first time I brewed the bouche it wasn't difficult, but it was a bit intimidating. From the second batch on it got easier and easier and then you start to experiment with various flavors during the second portion of the fermentation process.

I am free, I am free, I AM FREE

So, let's talk about kombucha, what it is and why you should consider both brewing your own (it's cheap and easy) and consuming it on a regular basis.

Benefits of Kombucha.

The primary benefit for you in consuming kombucha is the beneficial probiotics that can be introduced to your system to help promote better gut health. This can be a particularly positive win if you, like former me are drinking a can of soda a day or more. It was kombucha that helped me kick that bad habit as the second fermentation process allows the bouche to bubble up nice and fizzy much like a soda. For some reason the combination of the sweet with the carbonation had me hooked.

By brewing your own kombucha you can control the amount of sweet and the type or choose not to sweeten it at all. But I digress. Let's get back on track here to determine some of the additional why's when it comes to consuming kombucha.

In a word MICROBIOM

There are 100's of TRILLIONS of microbes within each of our 27 feet of Gastro Intestinal Tract.

That's a lot of zeros and to put it into perspective that represents 90% of the entire human structure. The cells of our bodies make up the other 10%

We are 90% microbes which is pretty important information to know.

Now we must dig just a bit deeper to figure out what this means. What are these microbes? Are they good, are they bad?

Can I control which microbes go into my body and if so, do I want or need to?

First, we must dive just a bit deeper kiddos. That's the only way we are going to get to some sort of "truth" regarding the highly chemical and processed diet that has taken over our eating habits and consequently our gut biome in the last 30-40 years.

Our subject matter regarding microbes must take a bit of a back sit for just a tick as we dive into the wonderful world of agriculture.

60

I am free, I am free, I AM FREE

You're probably getting a bit annoyed with reading the following line but to be consistent: The subject matter of agriculture and the history of could very easily consume several large volumes of written work. As such we are taking more of a shallow dive into this history to give us a baseline idea of how and why our food sources are so jacked.

Let's begin our discussion with laws because heck there just aren't enough laws out there governing our minds, bodies and movements.

The first law of thermodynamics is at the core of this information.

Inside of an isolated system the totality of energy is constant. We cannot add nor remove energy, energy can simply be transformed from one form to another.

That's an important concept to conceptualize and hold onto with regard to agriculture considering we use food as a source of energy for our human bodies.

Solar (sun) is energy and specific crops (as well as petroleum) are excellent mediums for transporting energy.

All animals within the kingdom including humans eat plants and or other animals (who eat plants) for the consumption of solar energy. This is the Earths food chain which is essentially plants turning sunlight into stored energy in the form of carbohydrates. This means that photosynthesis through plants is the only true source of this fuel of life for us humans. Currently there is no alternative to plant fuel which keeps all us funny little creatures alive and kicking.

As mentioned earlier energy cannot be created or destroyed however it can be concentrated and as alluded to above certain plants are quite exceptional with their ability to store this energy in a very compact manner.

Corn, wheat and rice (soy aint so bad either).

Because these plants have the unique ability to store this solar energy in a very compact manner, they have essentially taken over the agriculture landscape in the last 10,000 years or so.

This is important because what you choose to eat and feed your family is mostly based on these staple plants. It's also very important because natural agriculture has largely been eradicated to ensure these

61

three crops inundate our dinner plates. It's an incredible source of wealth for a small few but has led to the destruction of our topsoil which is bad for all us little creatures of the plane(t).

Many parts of the heartland of America at one time were full of prairie land that has all but been wiped out and replaced with artificial farmland. This destructive process has radically changed the natural process of wiping out portions of the topsoil to create a blank slate which is important in the natural order of organic matter and microbes.

Without these prairie lands we lose an incredibly important system. Prairie land use to convert energy to flowers, roots and stems that eventually die and pass back into the topsoil as organic matter. That energy rich topsoil in turn creates a robust pool of energy for new growth of energy rich plants. This goes back to the fist law of thermodynamics regarding the transfer of energy.

Once the prairie land was mostly wiped out by farmland the destruction began as the farms are used to plant seeds for human food consumption. Although a prairie can create a robust rich area of biomass it cannot produce plants that can consolidate energy in the same way that farmlands can and more to the point not nearly as well as corn, wheat and rice. And thus, the destruction of the American topsoil and the destruction of the natural food supply for human consumption.

If we think back just a couple years in the past the American prairie lands would have been full of bison and other animals that would have been consuming the energy of the prairie grasses, stems and roots. Humans that chose to consume their solar energy through the consumption of animal meat could have hunted bison and the like and the topsoil would have continued along its merry way. Instead we mostly just slaughtered all the bison and other furry creatures for sport and pelt and for the money grab aka the American Dream. That dream unfortunately had the terrible side effect of creating nightmares such as the dust bowl which was not some natural event that suddenly started to happen as is typically written. Humans came along and removed and displaced the natural bank of energy from the grasslands with wheat for human consumption in those regions which lead to the unfortunate changes such as the dust bowl.

I am free, I am free, I AM FREE

That's a wrap on the destruction of the topsoil. Let's get back to the gut.

Where to get your probiotics?

Probiotic labeling standard

Probiotic supplements and such are popping up all over the place but the wild world that is supplements is not regulated so much like a box of chocolates you never know what you're gonna get.

Unless you read below which breaks down in easy to digest (see what I did there) terms the Probiotic Labeling Standard (see you probably didn't even know that was a thing).

What matters when choosing?

The selection of the material used for the probiotic
How they are produced
Where they are produced
How they are shipped
How they are stored

Much like our friend fish oil supplements, probiotic supplements are very sensitive and if not handled correctly during any one of the above-mentioned steps they are not going to perform for you.

Pretty much anything sitting on a shelf is probably crap and isn't going to do much if anything for you and could potentially do you harm.

Head to the refrigeration aisle and MAYBE you can find something in a dark glass jar that MIGHT help a bit.

Whatever organism is listed on the label should have listed a guarantee of potency. If it lacks this information, then it's likely that the potency is very little and is useless for you.

This is the colony forming units through an expiry date. Most companies selling these probiotics are simply out to make a buck (or many bucks) and largely have no clue what they are doing.

I am free, I am free, I AM FREE

Most of the time you're just going to see a bright eye-catching label that will list all these microbes within the product and you're going to think. Sounds good to me. It's probiotics so it must be good.

And to be fair how the hell would you know what is good vs. what is bad microbes?

It's difficult to understand much less trust what you can purchase at a local grocery store or online when it comes to probiotics to promote positive gut health so let's look at one way, we can do this ourselves. We started this chapter talking about kombucha so for further details check out the Healing Modalities chapter and journey with me to the land of kombucha brewing. It's super easy, tasty and requires a minimal investment in terms of required tools.

For now, let's turn to the also confusing world of organics.

Organics

Let's decipher some of the mystery because not all organics are created equal.

<u>100% Organic</u>:
This stuff only has organic ingredients.

<u>Organic</u>:
95% organic. The other 5% can only consist of approved items from the USDA.

<u>Made with Organic Ingredients</u>:
Has at least 70% organic ingredients. The other 30%????

<u>Natural</u>:
This is a meaningless marketing term. Natural can mean anything. For example, it's likely that the vanilla extract you have in your cupboard right now has "natural" ingredients on the label. The natural ingredient is excretion from a gland located on beaver sphincters. In other words, it's beaver ass juice which does come from nature.

To further complicate the Organic labels is the fact that items shipped from outside the US may or may not have been inspected. Some countries are self-regulated, so they can just slap an organic sticker on anything and there is no 3rd party testing to make sure it's organic. If you're in the US many of your stuff will likely come from Mexico which does have proper inspections, but you should attempt to buy as local and in season as possible. I would highly recommend local farmers markets if you have any in your area.

SUGARS

In Vegan cooking high quality maple syrup is used often as a natural sweetener, but which sweeter brings the most healthy benefit whilst also bringing banging flavor?

Which sugar is the "healthiest'?
Sugar isn't exactly a health food as we all are aware however some forms of sweeteners can at least offer some nutritional contribution beyond simple calories.

Let's take a moment to compare nutritional data for 1 ounce of maple syrup, agave and dates (technically dates are not sugar but people tend to use them a lot to sweeten vegan desserts). Honey was not included because the health benefits of honey varies by brand and location based largely on its microbial properties.

Maple Syrup:
73 calories
19 grams carbohydrates
17 grams sugar
46% daily value for manganese
8 % zinc
28 milligrams omega-6 fatty acids
2% daily value for calcium, iron, and potassium.

Agave:
80 calories
21 grams carbohydrates
20 grams sugar
No significant other nutrients

Dates:
78 calories
21 grams carbohydrates
19 grams sugar
2 grams fiber
6% DV potassium,

5% copper,
4% manganese, magnesium, and 2% Niacin, B6, Pantothenic acid, phosphorous and calcium.

VERDICT:
I tend to use maple syrup (the darker the better) as my sweetener of choice when cooking. When making desserts I tend to lean more into the large Majool Dates.

Maple syrup while not healthy will provide the highest volume of nutrition per calorie when compared to agave and dates. The addition of the zinc is a nice little bonus for our immune health. Dates for sure provide the additional fiber and the Agave provides essentially no nutritional value as it mostly sugar.

Artificial sweeteners found in items like diet soda do not help you lose weight. On the contrary they stimulate bacteria in the gut that predispose us not to lose weight.

Artificial sweeteners carry less calories than "real" sugar so that's a great win for a marketing team. Hey, look here buy this no calories it's great for you.

What's really taking place however is that the artificial sweeteners are doing just as much damage to your gut biome as standard sugar with some having links to various deadly health issues.

I am free I am free I AM FREE

Plenty of people put themselves into one of two camps when it comes to consuming fresh vegetables. Either eat them or juice them. Let's review and toss in the good ol' blender as well as this one is usually just passed off as No Bueno.

But first let's talk fresh veggies.

Plenty of long-term studies done on this topic so I'm not going into detail regarding the studies themselves, but we should at least have a basic understanding of the super fantastic health benefits we can gain from consuming fresh vegetables (preferably organic, local and in season).

The U.S Department of Agriculture recommends consuming two to three cups of vegetables a day. This recommendation is made because vegetables have been seen time and again to provide essential nutrients as well as the key factor of phytochemicals/phytonutrients, which have been found to protect cells from damage and help stave off dis-ease. These phytochemicals/phytonutrients have been found to prevent and fight against many and several diseases such as diabetes, cancer, and heart disease.

68

JUICING

People in the juicing camp often will state that juicing is healthier than eating your vegetables. For you see juicing extracts the juice from the flesh of the vegetables which is fantastic for ease of consumption. These same proponents will also say that this is better because it allows for better absorption of the nutrients and provides for additional water intake compared to directly eating your vegetables.

Although it does make sense that you can consume a larger volume compared to eating your vegetables only, I have not found any studies to suggest that extracting the juice allows for better or healthier consumption.

There is the additional benefit of your digestive system not having to kick into overdrive to break down and digest the fibrous content of vegetables. If you have problems digesting vegetables or eating them then juicing could be a good friend.

There are a couple of caveats regarding juicing.

When you heat up your vegetables, they tend to lose the enzymes present that are key to the health benefits. If you go with a cheap juicer you run the risk of spending lots of money on fresh vegetables but heating them up to the point of killing much of the health benefits provided by the enzymes.

If you really get into juicing those bad boys tend to get pricy so make sure it's worth it for you.

I have found that most juicers are a serious pain to clean as well.

EATING

Eating fresh organic raw local vegetables is one of the greatest things you can do for your overall physical health. Again, there are SO many studies done on this topic that I won't get into the details because you can easily find peer reviewed long-term studies spouting the many and varying benefits.

I am free, I am free, I AM FREE

As great as these veggies are, they are much less healing once you start cooking them down. You might think you're doing something great by consuming your veggies but if your pouring oil over them in a skillet and cooking them down your killing nearly all the beneficial enzymes.

Eating can be better than juicing with regard to the fiber intake. Those in the juicing camp will taut the benefit of not having to consume the flesh of the vegetables but the fiber can be good for you as well.

BLENDING

This is really juicing vs. blending which seemingly are alike but actually are very different.

When you juice you are separating the liquid and removing the flesh. When you blend you are smashing everything up and creating a smoothie.

The biggest difference here is the absence of most of the pulp when you juice whereas when you blend you keep that pulp. When you blend you still get the fiber but much of it has already been broken down for you making it easier for your body to absorb. Blending is going to be much more robust and filling compared to juicing. A blended drink can act closer to a meal replacement whereas a juice is more like an energy booster.

When you blend you also have many more options with regard to what you can toss into the blender.

A juicer will take most fruits and vegetables but does not do well with the following:

Figs
Bananas
Avocado

When creating a smoothie in a blender you can include the following to allow for a wide range of nutrients.

Fruits and Vegetables
Nuts
Oats
Seeds
Non-juiceables such as figs, bananas and avocado.

This not only allows for a wider range of available nutrients to be absorbed by the body but also allows for slow absorption as the body must work to break down the fibrous content. This also gives you a very wide range of experimentation to find the right combos of vitamins, minerals and nutrients for items outside of the vegetable world only.

I am free, I am free, I AM FREE
!!DANGER WILL ROBINSON!!

When creating either a juice or a smoothie take it easy on the
fruit. They have their own sugars (fructose) and it can be easy to
quickly overdo your sugar consumption which can cause your blood
sugar to rise.
   Good options for adding fruits to your smoothie that have less
sugar content
   Bananas
   Strawberries
   Blackberries

The final thing that is nice about blending vs. juicing is that if
you already have a quality blender for prepping foods and sauces you
do not need to invest in new hardware such as a juicer. Juicers vary
in type and style but the most important is centrifugal and
masticating. Masticating being more expensive in general but as it is
a slow processing juicer it tends to not heat up the juice keeping as
many of the VITAL nutrients intact prior to consumption.
   As there are so many options available for both a blender and a
juicer here are the key factors to be consider.

   Blender
   Reputable name brand
   Extended warranty availability at low cost
   Powerful motor
   Plenty of attachments and multi-use such as being accompanied
by a food processor
   Ease of use
   Easy clean up
   Pitcher size (plus additional one size serve cups)

   Juicer
   Reputable name brand
   Extended warranty availability at low cost
   Slow speed juicing
   Space: I've seen some massive juicers on the market especially
some of the mastication juicers.

Conclusion

If you are already investing in the pricier organic vegetables, you want to ensure that you can absorb as much as possible. A combination of eating and either juicing or blending tends to provide the best overall health benefits. The more often you eat fresh vegetables without cooking them down the more nutritional value you will receive.

Alas we move away from food and start our journey into something that should speak to all of us. We are after all light beings so why should we not gravitate towards this next chapter touching on light? Come along star children as we make our way through the labyrinthine maze of light.

CHAPTER 4. LIGHT

It's everywhere except when our eyes are closed, I suppose but even then, photon light exist and permeates our entire visual perception of our 3D reality. In the absence of light, we see via the pictures we form within our own minds which is important information we will be touching upon in just a bit. For now, let's try to figure out what light is and why it's important to humans?

The spectrum of visible and ultraviolet light is but one spectrum of reality that we perceive but without it we do not SEE objects that we interact with inside of this reality. 3D objects are a bit of an oddity. They don't exist as solid objects, but rather are atoms vibrating at various rates of speed. The specific vibrational velocity dictates the solidity of said object that we perceive via light photons reflecting off the object. We perceive these objects because photon light reflects off the objects and entering our retina forms a visual representation of the object. In the absence of light, we are forced to visualize the 3D world we live inside directly from our own interpretation of perceived solid reality. Which is interesting considering that we all interpret the 3D world we all live inside of differently. You and I can be looking at the exact same object yet "see" vastly different objects. This is largely due to all of us having our own BS coursing through brains. BS meaning belief systems (and the obvious as well).

No doubt you have heard the sayings amongst various peoples that we humans are beings of light or light beings. Usually they are looked at as wackadoo's or new age hippies that have toked the bong a little too long.

If we are patient and wait long enough eventually the scientific community starts to catch up on some of humanities instinctual knowledge that has existed for millennia. With this in mind we can start down our path of mindful meanderings regarding light.

I am free, I am free, I AM FREE

There exists a type of light particle that is emitted by all living things. We humans are not sensitive enough to these Ultra-weak Photon Emissions (UPE) to detect them or rather our two eyes are not sensitive enough.

Laboratory experiments are starting to show that UPE's are stored inside of cells and can traverse through the nervous system which is the highway of information giving UPE's the ability to transfer both energy and packets of information riding on this energy throughout the human body. These experiments are further proving that our DNA is a strong source of UPE's potentially making the DNA helix literally created from light.

Biophotons are emitted from within the human body and can be released through intention.

It was Thomas Edison and Joseph Swan who brought humanity a proper thin filament within a vacuum bulb that utilized a small amount of electrical current which helped to shuffle into our reality the basis for the common light bulb that held strong for many years up until the recent creation or expansion of light bulb tech.

LED (light emitting diode) technology has been hailed as a triumph of a more cost-effective energy saving way to light up the 3D reality we humans journey through.

Before we get too far into the reality of artificial light which is the light bulb, I feel it's a great time to side step this conversation to mention just some of the dangers that come with the technology that is the LED. Not just to freak you out but to help you understand how your health is being compromised in the name of efficiency (which in reality means a more cost-effective way to produce artificial light for greater profits all while eliciting an emotion within the populace to help save the world by usurping less energy and helping to save the planet).

On paper LED is fantastic. It doesn't use mercury and utilizes much less energy to keep the artificial light available to reflect off 3D objects within our reality giving us more "daylight" and a lower cost of moving energy from one place to another.

The downside to you being led (BOOM!) to believe that you are saving the world one light bulb at a time is the fact that LED bulbs are extremely dangerous to your health. They contain lead, arsenic and at

I am free, I am free, I AM FREE

least a dozen other potentially dangerous substances to the human (and other animal) form.

There have been several studies with regards to various types of LED lights including their use in car lights, Christmas lights, traffic lights and street lights.

UC-Irvine researches found back in 2010 that some of the worst offenders were low intensity red light emitting diodes which were found to contain up to eight times the amount of the neurotoxin which we call lead. In fact, when there are traffic accidents it is recommended that the clean-up crew wear protective clothing and treat the cleaned-up material as hazmat material. This is because LEDS are used within the majority of automotives and within traffic lights. Further there is a recommendation that if an LED is to break within your home you should treat it as hazardous material and go so far as to dispose of the broom and sweeping pan utilized to clean up the material.

Municipalities throughout the United States and the UK now outfit as many street lights and traffic lights with LEDS as possible. This makes total sense when you are sold the reality that these LED lights consume less energy therefor, we will be saving the planet by the simple act of replacing all bulbs with these more energy efficient sources of light. What they fail to mention is that these same LEDS have been linked to cancer. Yeah you read that correctly.

In the United Kingdom they have switched out hundreds of thousands of street lights with LED bulbs likely because it's a nice cost savings initiative. The problem lies in the fact that a recent study showed that in Spain when they performed an analysis of 4,000 people living in 11 separate regions they were able to establish a link between heavy amounts of LED exposure (think it's in my house, it's at work and it's in every street light I walk under) and what they termed as a "strong link between the technology and prostate cancer". You read that correctly. Long exposure to specific LED lights show a link to a greater chance of prostate cancer. This study also found that within this group of 4K there was a 1.5 times higher chance of breast cancer.

This specific study means that the researchers cannot make a direct link between LED lighting but can prove a causal link. This is because they believe that the blue light emitted by the LED's could be

I am free, I am free, I AM FREE

acting as a disrupter to the body's natural circadian rhythm, which changes the hormone levels within the body.

The birth of artificial light allowed for factories to remain running on a 24/7 cycle. This further allowed for an expanded global work force which is simply the transfer of human energy into work (national pride/national currency). The larger and more productive the workforce the more value is applied to the strength of the dollar applied to each country.

This artificial light has allowed for the greater use of your life energy to be applied to made up fiat currencies.

STARCHILDREN

I'm sure you've heard it before. We are Star Children! That is, we are made up of the same stuff as the rest of the Youniverse.

Our brief overview of biophotons shows us that our very DNA is itself created from light. But if I know you your still not amazed enough. Fine let's step this up a notch.

We are made of light, we emit light and light information travels through our bodies. If that's not cool enough for you then consider this.

We can affect light with our thoughts alone.

In a study subjects were given the task of visualizing a bright light while they were placed in a dark room. It was discovered that all participants biophoton emissions increased significantly which shows that our intentions have a direct effect on light itself.

This short chapter to lead up to get us on to the talking points of our natural circadian cycle/rhythm and how it has dramatically been changed and manipulated over the last several centuries to create a human form that does not function properly within the confines of artificial light.

I am free I am free I AM FREE

CIRCADIAN RHYTHM

As humans we are naturally active during the daytime when the sun is raining down beautiful energy and, in the evenings, when the sun is down, we are less active (at least historically) This is deemed our natural circadian rhythm. In fact, all plants and animals have their own naturally occurring circadian rhythm. What is circadian rhythm anyway?

The hypothalamus located in the forebrain holds and helps to regulate your bodies internal clock (circadian system, circadian oscillator). This is your own natural clock that takes cues from various external stimulus (light/dark) to help regulate many internal processes.

The word circadian is rooted in Latin and means "about a day".

The circadian rhythm is the measurement of the Earth's 24ish cycle and our own internal cycle is supposed to be linked to this naturally occurring light/dark cycle of the Earth.

Due to human progress however, we have managed to introduce light sources other than the sun (see info on LED's) which has thrown off the proper governance of our built-in circadian system.

Our built-in circadian clocks regulate many functions but some of the most important are cell regeneration, hormone production, body temperature regulation and the all-important melatonin. Melatonin is produced within your pineal gland and it appears that its primary function is to help regulate body temperature and tiredness/alertness.

The melatonin hormone activates at night in the absence of light. Melatonin levels are kept very low during daylight and ramp up over the course of the evening hours.

Early research led the scientific community to tell humanity that humans are not like other diurnal organisms and that we simply take our cues from society about our circadian systems. They believed this because they incorrectly believed that humans are not sensitive to light.

Although mice aren't men scientist tend to perform studies a great deal on mice. It's been known for many years prior to these studies through the 1950's – 1970's that cell division inside of the body follows a circadian rhythm. We know that the circadian rhythm is affected by light. Studies performed on mice have shown that when exposed to unnatural light patterns the mice tend to develop problems with their cell division. If exposed to this unnatural light repeatedly they develop long term health issues.

Humanities exposure to unnatural light has skyrocketed in the last several centuries. The places we live, work and play are inundated with various sources of unnatural light that moves through the various spectrums with blue light being one of the most hostile to us humans.

Blue light wavelengths are the most detrimental during the evening hours after sundown. Exposure to this unnatural light suppresses the secretion of melatonin which some early stage studies link to an association with cancer.

In the evening hours spend less time on your cellphones and more time looking at people as you converse with them.

Keep your circadian rhythm healthy and don't spend an overabundance of time around disruptive unnatural lights especially after sun down. Harsh lights emitted from electronics are some of the worse. Get as much natural sunlight during the day as possible.

It can be difficult living inside of this social construct to simply remove yourself from unnatural light during evening hours. Over time you can train yourself and others you communicate with via cellphone to stop usage during late night hours. You can turn off the TV and computer monitors and focus on direct human connections and communications as opposed to tech enabled communications.

Because I didn't have room to fit in a chapter on body language it was left out but if you spend less time with your face buried in your phone and more time directly interacting with your human companions you will find that the most powerful form of communication is body language, facial expression and tonality. None of these subtle communication ques come through over tech mediums even video chat. As we journey further into raising generations of humans dependent on electronic communication devices the further we remove humanity from true human experience and connectivity.

The next time you're at a social gathering or just hanging out with some family friends or colleagues make it a point not to check

I am free, I am free, I AM FREE

your phone until after you have left their company for the evening. A game that some friends of mine play from time to time is everyone putting their cellphones in the middle of the table and the first person to pick up their phone to check it pays for a round of drinks. You can make creating "good" habits fun if you think outside of the box and make it all inclusive.

We have touched on many topics within these writings regarding dangers in our environment that can lead to cancer. Let's wander into the not so happy land of cancer because there is much to discuss on this topic

CHAPTER 5 CANCER

The sandy shores of circadian rhythm is a great place to visit but I think it's fine time we battle the powerful waves of that all too horrendous beast we call cancer.

I wander into this realm of cancer with great trepidation as so many have and are currently hurt by this cellular predator.

Every time I walk by a marketing campaign that is raising money for child cancer, I wonder why we even have the term "child cancer" as part of our personal and social lexicon (sadly it's a term that's been around for much longer than most of us realize).

But alas this is the reality we find ourselves in. Attempting to protect our loved ones and ourselves from this scourge that seems to touch most of society in one way or another.

Aside from attempting to keep your internal organism and blood in good shape we also are dealing with many outside influences/poisons within our environment from the obvious poisons we freely purchase and put into our dwellings to the unseen high powered various wireless and many other frequencies gliding through our atmosphere, bodies and brains.

Living, working and playing inside of any city and or suburban landscape predispositions us to many external outside influences on our body, minds and spirits working to weaken us on many levels.

Although none of us can claim a cure for cancer we can view some of the conditions from afar and sues out that our unnatural environment plays a key role in creating cancer cells. Viewing the Gearson healing modalities for treating cancer shows us that removing a person from their environment and aggressively cleansing the internal body can and does have a large impact on the ability to recover.

It seems strange that we accept without question that an individual gets cancer, battles through chemo and successfully eliminates the cancerous cells but is then forced to continue business

I am free, I am free, I AM FREE

as usual to fund the payments for all the treatments and medications necessary to battle the cancer cells. After recovery most individuals will slip right back into a business as usual learned modality to allow continued survival within the social construct but will continue to predisposition their cells to future cancer forming cells.

Working and living within these same mental, emotional, spiritual and physical environments can and unfortunately often does reproduce additional cancer cells in the future.

Although we cannot always change our physical environment, we can change our mental, emotional and spiritual environments.

I often hear the term "there is hope" but hope alone is meaningless. We need more than hope we need a paradigm shift in our mental, emotional and spiritual states.

CANCER REALITY

Cancer

That's a scary word. There's so much pain and heartache associated with a single word that can carry the scythe of destruction and death.

Unfortunately, I like far too many others have experience with this cellular predator.

It was a bright and beautiful Saturday in the Pacific Northwest. The sun was shining, and I was in a particularly upbeat mood.

I had family in town and the night prior I had a conversation with my wise if not a bit randy older brother. We discussed many topics as we are both worldly travelers with diverse backgrounds. I was talking about brewing kombucha and cleaning your colon and he was talking about what I have titled Soul Gazing.

Ok, so I totally stole the term Soul Gazing from a novel series I used to read back in the day. The way the author utilized the term was about an adult wizard working in Chicago. Said wizard had a special gift as all other wizards did where he could lock eye contact with another person and dive deep into their heart/soul to find out the true nature of the person. The problem with this gift was that it was also a double-edged sword as it worked both ways. While the wizard gained knowledge on the true nature of the person he was Soul Gazing the recipient also was able to peer into the heart/soul of the wizard.

It seemed like a cool concept when I was reading about it in this novel and it immediately clicked in my head when my brother started telling me about mirror gazing.

For this setup you create a quite relaxed environment and you stare into a mirror for an hour. It's an amazing experience and one you should practice (with a new mirror).

On this Saturday in question I decided to give it a shot. I put my phone on silent, setup my spot and started my mirror stare Soul Gaze. It was profound, amazing and well strange and wonderful.

Once the hour was up I was feeling amazing and was looking forward to chewing up some pavement on my mountain bike to work

I am free, I am free, I AM FREE

off some of the burning energy that was coursing through my mind and body.

Looking at my phone I noticed that I had missed several calls and text from my sister who was also in town.

I called, and she was already on her way over because she had some important information to lay down.

As we are sitting in my back patio enjoying the comforts of both each other's company and the sunshine she lays it on me. She's got breast cancer.

BOOM!

It would have been difficult enough to ingest this information but just after finishing my first Soul Gaze it felt like a Mike Tyson uppercut followed shortly by a Bruce Lee one-inch punch to the face.

I didn't take it well and although I wanted to be strong for my sister I broke down like baby. I was still a bit distant from my own body due to the Soul Gazing and it felt odd to look down on the scene as it was happening and see my sister comforting me. But that was the reality of the situation and that made cancer much more than a statistic it made it a reality in my world.

I found that you learn a lot about the content of one's character when a scary monster like cancer comes crawling out of the shadows and shows up at your doorstep. My sister's daughter was 19 at the time and even with the shock of the information and the situation I was struck by her calm demeanor and nerves of steel. She was a lightning rod of support for her mother and up until that moment I had no idea that my niece was such a wonderfully powerful person.

There's something to be said about the strength of healing via your head and heart. I have had acquaintances that got cancer and decided they were done with life and that's exactly what happened. Their hearts, minds and bodies rapidly wasted away. They exhibited no hope and put up no fight. Once they got the word from the doc's they allowed their minds to hasten the process of what the cancer was already doing.

On the other side of the coin you have your fighters. Fortunately for our family my sister is nothing if not incredibly feisty. My brother called it "another blip in our lives" which I assume to mean since we

85

I am free, I am free, I AM FREE

had already struggled through so many other painful situations in our youth that something like cancer was merely a blip in the timeline of our lives.

My sister successfully fought through her rounds of chemo and good thing for her she has a beautiful head because she looked amazing with her bald head and bold attitude. She had a great support structure and systematically worked through her treatment protocols and physical therapy amongst so much more that one has to deal with.

At this time, I was already deep into a lifestyle that included cruelty free eating (at least with regards to animals) amongst many other things such as meditation, yoga, breath work, physical exercise, etc. With the shock of what my sister was going through I started to dive deep into the subject matter of cancer. My focus was fourfold.

One:
Can one avoid getting cancer and if so how?

Two:
What is it? How do cells mutate into cancerous cells and propagate?

Three:
If you have cancer are there holistic ways of healing that work?

Four:
How do you mentally/spiritually deal with cancer whether you have it or if someone you love and care for has it?

With that in mind please read on. I hope this research can in some way help you or others along your journey.

I am free I am free I AM FREE

Some Ways To Avoid Cancer

1939 Cancer Act

Due to the act above I cannot say there is a cure for cancer which is not something I would claim anyway.

BUT perhaps you should switch to an alkaline diet and move your body away from an acidic diet. If your body is not acidic and you have plenty of healthy oxygen flowing throughout your body how will your cells become cancerous?

Remove unnecessary stress from your life. There are micro and macro stresses and we are so out of touch with our own mental state living within this social construct we tend to not even register these micro stresses that are occurring on a regular basis within our day to day lives.

Something as simple and entertaining as watching a scary movie can trigger a massive amount of stress responses within your mind/consciousness which in turn will create a stress response within your body. A single hour and half scary movie can trigger your fight or flight response several dozens of times. That is the specific response that the movie maker is attempting to trigger to fully engage you into their storyline and make you want to come back for more. Like mini hits of dopamine to keep you addicted and wanting more.

Now extrapolate this concept out to watching the news, reading the newspapers with its emotionally charged content. Your day to day conversations with negative energy persons in your life that consistently trigger negative emotional responses within you. The social macro emotional stressor that is simply amazing to witness to me as I write this is regarding the current sitting American president. So many American citizens are creating massive negative impacts inside of their own minds, hearts and bodies due to the words and movements of a single human. They also are collectivity creating a negatively charged reality for everyone living inside of this construct. It's amazing to me the amount of self-created venom and hate conjured in the name of freedom. People are SCREAMING that their freedoms are or have been taken away because the person they wanted as President of The United States did not win that seat of office. The incredible irony in this fashion of thinking is that they are

I am free, I am free, I AM FREE

arguing that having some other person dictate and lord over your natural freedoms equates to freedom but having someone else lord over their natural freedoms is not freedom. The absurdity of arguing that my slave master is better than yours is completely lost on these individuals because they are fully amerced in the fake reality social construct.

It's time to put on your big boy pants (or big girl panties) and wake up to who and what we all truly are. We are NOT slaves to be bullied and kowtowed into a slave mentality. Voting for your slave master is not freedom it is the illusion of freedom and we seem to fall for this sleight of hand and smoke and mirrors repeatedly. Your only master is inside of you screaming to be let out of its cage, so it can dance, sing and breath true freedom and love into reality.

And on that sour note let's look at trophoblastic cells.

I am free I am free I AM FREE

T-CELLS

Trophoblastic cells and cancer.

Cells that form the womb wall during pregnancy are incredibly fast and efficient at their job.

These trophoblastic cells need to form quickly to form the womb wall for the creation of a protective environment for the fetus. According to Dr. John Beard's research, cancer cells are made up of these same trophoblastic cells.

Dr Otto Warburg

According to Dr. Otto Warburg historically the primary purpose for cancer becoming prevalent within the human body was as a healing process. If the cells of the body were low on oxygen these cells, then often became cancerous attempting to save the cells. That is the cells rapidly propagate to survive within this low oxygen environment.

One way your cells become low on oxygen is when your body becomes overly acidic. When your body is too acidic this overly acidic environment stops your cells from being able to properly take in oxygen.

Cancer is your body's attempt at a last-ditch effort to keep that part of the body alive that is suffocating due to the lack of oxygen.

Just as the rapid formation of the womb wall for protection of the fetus these self-same trophoblastic cells are now forming around your oxygen deprived, acidic cells to attempt to rescue them.

By the way although Dr. Otto Warburg has a name that sounds like a Bond villain, he is a Noble prize-winning doctor taking away that honor and distinction in 1931.

Dr Ernst T Kraigs or Krebs

Estrogen is also a key player in this mystery cancer production machine. When you injure yourself your body pumps large amounts of estrogen to the site of the injury.

When the estrogen encounters certain stem cells, those stem cells are triggered into turning into trophoblastic cells. How estrogen combining with certain stem cells turns into these trophoblastic cells is a mystery.

We should all understand that most of us live, work and play within environments that are inundated by electromagnetic radiation. If you start looking around your neighborhood and the various environments, you spend time in you will see a massive amount of cell towers going up (hello 5G). They are on rooftops, at parks, next to schools, playgrounds, next to and mounted to water towers. These cell towers are constantly zapping you with deadly electromagnetic radiation, and when you have your cellphone on not only is the phone creating potentially deadly radiation, but the real kicker is when you are driving down the road.

As your phone moves at a high rate of speed it is constantly attempting to reconnect to various cell towers, so you are getting mega zaps on that cellphone and as a result to your body as you drive down the road. Turn that cellphone off as often as reasonable.

Dr Bruce Lipton

According to Dr. Bruce Lipton under the electromagnetic radiation we are all under the cells of our bodies start to become stressed which starts altering hormones.

Especially estrogen!!!

Now you have the catalyst for mutating cancer cells to start to form and propagate.
 One thing you can control is what YOU decide to put into your mouth. If you are eating highly acidic foods on a regular basis as SO many humans do, then you are helping to create the foundation necessary to create cancerous cells. That's not even to mention that some meats according to the CDC are class 1 carcinogen. Put it all together and you have a highly acidic diet that many humans partake upon.
This potentially lays the foundation for cancer.

If you have a standard American diet you have been born and raised into having the precursor for cancer by default.
Now if you injure yourself in some way: smoking injures your lungs, breathing bad air injures lungs, heavy alcohol injures liver.
 Whatever injury your incurring your body is now to the rescue so it's going to pump heavy amounts of estrogen to the injury site to take care of repairs.
 Now you have stresses of everyday society and your body is basking in an electromagnetic cesspool then the estrogen is triggered into turning those stem cells into cancer.

A multi part biological almost invisible weapon.

Was this deliberately engineered?

Were you born into a reality and social construct that mass produces and makes highly available extremely acidic foods which leads to an unstable cell structure which in turn creates an internal environment of self-destruction of your body's cells?

I am free, I am free, I AM FREE

This so-called food is purpose built to be HIGHLY addictive as mentioned earlier in the food chapter.

Was this engineered on purpose to lower our frequency and slaughter not only our body's but our minds and spirits?

Or is this simply capitalism on steroids? A system that once put into place created a necessity to put the needs of quarterly and annual earnings and profits above all else including the lives of all sentient beings from cows, chickens, goats, pigs, and yes humans as well.

Once your industry creates an environment of wholesale slaughter of all other sentient beings on the plane(t) it is then an easy leap or rather small step to the death of humans for profit. We have been born into a social construct that puts quarterly profits above the lives of you and everyone you have ever known or cared for. By the late 1980's but likely much earlier these industries which are merchants of death knew the link between their products and massive pain and suffering and injuries created in the human species and consciousness.

They will have you believe that their goals are altruistic while attempting to feed the masses, but this is untrue. If this were true, there would be no need to create packaging aimed to hook your children at the earliest age possible to insist on buying cookie cereal and the like. This may sound like an alarmist overstatement but it's not overstating by saying you are at war with these companies. They are spending billions upon billions in research dollars to find ways to circumvent your children's conscious and to hook them with their imagery. There would not exist the need to infiltrate the human senses with dopamine type responses to snare you into the non-nutritious terrible calorie consumption trap if not purely for profit. It's a true oddity that people can gain massive amounts of life threating weight while simultaneously miss out on nearly all necessary nutrients.

Fix your acidic body and you have removed the primary precursor for cancer.

Alkaline diet:

Get your body closer to 7.0 – 7.5 alkaline and avoid the creation of acidity within your body.

Stress:

I am free, I am free, I AM FREE

Turn off your TV which creates artificial stress or at least stick to positive themed content.

Stress:
Make meditation a daily practice (or as often as you can).

Stress:
Turn off your cellphone as often as is reasonable.

Stress:
Make sure to set time aside to spend with those you love.

Stress:
LAUGH, LAUGH, LAUGH

Stress:
PLAY, PLAY, PLAY

Stress:
Get out in nature often and safely.

Stress:
Find your inner child and allow the child to dance and play.

Stress:
Get out of your own head.

Stress:
Do not judge yourself just be.

Stress:
Let go of the past and future and be in the present moment often.

Stress:
Make passionate health positive love often.

Stress:
Breath

I am free, I am free, I AM FREE

Stress:
Breath some more with intention.

Let's look at how cancer is currently studied to lift the vail on one method that does not work to serve humanity efficiently.

STUDYING CANCER

One thing we rarely think about is how cancer is currently being studied within a laboratory setting.

There are five primary ways to study cancer
Clinical trials
Human studies
Observational studies
Meta-analyses
Laboratory studies

Let's kick the tires on laboratory studies as applied to cancer research.

Laboratory Studies:
Within a controlled environment using cells from animals and/or humans or animal models.

Cell cultures are kept in sterile environments and within test tubes or petri dishes which in and of itself is a good thing and doesn't pose an issue. The issue is regarding the culture media utilized for growing cells which is likely nothing the public thinks about or considers. But we should because it's important to the data output which is the information that is spread to the masses and repeated and propagated as truth.

An American physician by the name of Henry Eagle was the first to present the world with "Eagle's minimal essential medium (EMEM). Henry mixed together the most basic cocktail necessary to grow human and other animal cells within. His formula consists of:
Amino acids
Sugar
Salts
Vitamins

Henry Eagle came up with this concoction in 1959 and it is still in heavy use today. This is mostly due to the ease of commercial use

I am free, I am free, I AM FREE

and not having to put in the money, time or effort to create a new medium that is closer to what human and other animal cells experience outside of laboratory settings.

The EMEM medium is the most basic medium that is used which means that most of these laboratory studies have no basis for what is really happening outside of the laboratory.

Nearly 90 percent of cancer research papers are using two or three commercially available media.

The outcome of the output data will reflect information based directly on the medium in use.

There are some biomedical researchers that are mixing their own media which consist of additional material that is closer to the reality that our cells experience on a daily.

These studies being done with the EMEM lead to a massive outpouring of misinformation which is critical when allopathic doctors are working with a patient to attempt to put their cancer into remission.

How do they know how sensitive cells are to chemotherapy drugs if nearly all the testing is done in such a basic media that does not reflect reality?

The next time you're reading a headline or a research paper with regard to a new cancer fighting drug dig deeper and find out additional background on exactly how they studied and determined the effects of the drug.

I am free I am free I AM FREE

Dealing with Cancer

It's difficult to imagine receiving the news that you or someone you dearly love has been diagnosed with some form of cancer. The severity and aggressiveness of said cancer will also play a large role in how you accept and decide to move forward with treatment.

With that said these writings will provide a short list with details on how to deal with this unwanted destroyer of cells when it makes its way into your life.

When you first start treatment options you will be inundated with medical terms and information. So much so that it will be overwhelming and difficult to process. You will feel lost and confused. This is the time to take a deep breath. Your entire life you have just been you but now you are told that you are a cancer patient and when all this information is being thrown at you the words that will stick out the most will be CANCER PATIENT and DEATH. Do not allow the word cancer to own you. A single word does not define you and cannot take your power from you.

Now is a good time to begin your own personal medical journal as early in the process as reasonable. This can work as a great companion as it will be your own voice in the writings to allow for better overall understanding and absorption of medical information that can be overwhelming, confusing and scary. It can hold all relevant information related to treatments but can also be fun and playful and full of your own special inspirational quotes, pictures, doodles, etc. I have created a cancer journal that is available online. I attempted to create something that I believe can be truly helpful during the process of dealing with this new reality.

The loss of control accompanied by the lack of knowledge of how to properly treat your specific form of cancer is scary and can strip away your power. This new diagnosis is a hammer blow to your psyche and you should take the time to realize that it can take years to fully accept the diagnosis. Just because your super mother, brother, father, sister, uncle, worker etc. doesn't mean you should ignore the potential for deep emotional blowback from this news. Being strong is great, however being willfully negligent to yourself can create more harm than good.

Your brain and emotions may lean in to the why and how. Even those of us who take painstaking efforts to keep our minds, bodies and spirits in relatively good shape can still be attacked by cancer. Now is not the time to curl into the fetal position and hide from this monster. You will need all your wits and wisdom about you moving forward to tackle the emotional upheaval of having to directly deal with your own mortality.

There will be many and varying decisions to make in a relative short period. You will need to be hyper aware and not allow fear to push you down a path that one doctor is pushing if it does not feel like the correct path for you. The more grounded and centered you are the more likely you are to make proper life altering medical decisions for yourself.

It's a terrible thing to think about and accept but in our current reality sickness is big business and that includes cancer treatments. The doctors and nurses you choose to utilize will become part of your team. It's important to ensure you are shopping around for the right team. It's also recommended to investigate non-traditional, non-Western medicine options. This is a point in your life where focusing on holistic, full body/mind/spirit healing should be front and center. If the first words out of your doctor's mouth are "let's cut out some of those organs and see what happens", it's a good time to start looking at 2nd and 3rd opinions. It's always a good time to look at 2nd and 3rd opinions even if you are very comfortable with your current doctor.

Things to consider when choosing a doctor.

1. How many patients with your specific condition have they successfully treated and what are the typical treatment options?
2. What is their reputation within the medical community?
3. Asking the doctor that first diagnosed you a question like: "Who are the top 2-3 doctors YOU would send a loved one to see?"
4. Bedside manner. In the days, weeks, months and years to come you may start to feel very strongly with regard to bedside manner when it comes to your treatment.
5. Are they board certified? Not all doctors who are specialist are board certified.

I am free, I am free, I AM FREE

Most or all the people you love that surround you will be freaked out as well and concerned for your wellbeing. There is no "one size fits all" option for how you progress with treatment so the best thing you can do for yourself is attempt to be centered within yourself to make the best decisions possible for your cancer survival journey. Most everyone is going to have an opinion on how you should move forward but only you can make the proper decision for you.

Now is the time to narrow your focus on what matters most. Do not allow yourself to be defined as a "Cancer Patient". You can still go out and enjoy life and live fully in the moment. Too often we allow our brains to focus on the past or projected future events. This is the time to put away the past and remove the projected future. The desire to fix everything and have everything put in place and ready to go in a structured manner should be set aside. Take time to live in the moment.

Create a special space

Create a piece of real-estate in your house that is setup as a special space just for you. It might contain soft pillows, soft music, candles, photo albums. Whatever items are special to you. This can act as a sacred safe space where you can go to breath, relax and speak to yourself in a gentle and loving manner. It should be established with other house members that this is a safe space for you and no one should enter unless you allow it at any given time.

Find your mental helper

This may be in the form of a professional psychologist or psychiatrist or even a family member or very close friend. Whatever form this takes ensure that you are treating your mental health as well as your physical. Along with the mental is the emotional partner(s) needed to assist.

Breaking the news

Aside from acceptance telling the people you love that you have cancer is no small feat. It doesn't get easier each time you tell another family member, loved one or close friend. Most people take their ques from how you are dealing with it and how you deliver the information. Most people will not know what questions to ask or how

I am free, I am free, I AM FREE
to move forward with helping without showing feelings of sorrow or
pity. It may be that you find yourself comforting others as you give
them this information, however if they continue to be an emotional
succubus you will need to create space from them. Now is not the
time to spend too much emotional currency on helping others even if
that is what and who you are before the diagnosis.

It's a strange balancing act of considering their feelings when it's
you that is dealing directly with the diagnosis and the pending cell
battle. At this point it should be all about you but we as humans are
funny creatures and too often in our attempt to make sense of difficult
situations we lose sight of other people's emotional states. You know
your people the best, so you will know how to let them know while
attempting to protect yourself and their emotional state. It's a rather
strange place you find yourself where you need to deliver this
information that is difficult for you to deal with and speak about and
at the same time cater to other people's emotional state.

It may sound a bit strange and silly, but it may help to dress up a
bit when having these conversations. If you look good you're going
to feel good which can help to make these difficult conversations just
a bit easier to manage.

Insurance
Now is a good time to make sure you have a nice tribe of helpers
and to start delegating tasks. One such task is to have someone within
your tribal cancer group to help you navigate the labyrinthine reality
that is medical insurance. You MUST know what type of insurance
you have and what is covered and what is not covered. For those
things that are not covered what are your options?

If you receive information on a bill such as "This procedure is
not covered by your policy". Understand that you have the right to
see this in writing and further you should ensure that the specifics of
this policy were in place when you started the policy and did not get
written in later.

Finding your voice
Now's the time to find something inside of yourself that you
have kept from doing for various reasons. Perhaps you have always
wanted to be a painter or play an instrument, plant a garden. Put time

101

aside to cultivate one or more of these desires which can help act as a healing element for your mind and spirit.

Keep in mind that a hospital is not the only place to go for care. Many things discussed in earlier chapters such as yoga, meditation, proper breathing, getting into nature, eating whole foods for nutrition, drinking plenty of distilled water are all part of a natural healing process for your body mind and spirit. Figure out what makes the most sense for you to help you fully recover and kick cancer right in the ass! The most important factor is your mindset. You have had many challenges in your life and this is yet another challenge. Do not attempt to be so rigid and stiff that you allow the fear of the diagnosis to break you. Instead of being the mighty oak tree that eventually cracks and breaks under the high winds be like the bamboo that will ebb and flow with the wind and after the high winds have subsided will continue to grow in strength.

I have also created a cancer journal to help you along this new reality. Many and most items discussed in these pages are included in the journal which will guide you on the journey. Please see the end pages of this book to find the title and location of the journal.

Stay strong and stay in the reality of love not fear. You can still be loving and playful living in this new reality.

Let's move this discussion along to the wonderful world of sound.

I am free I am free I AM FREE

Things not to say to someone that has informed you that they
have cancer (or their loved ones in idle conversation).

A pity party is usually the last thing someone wants. They may
need your support, but pity is usually not wanted. Saying things like:

"Oh, you poor, poor dear"
"How long do you have to live?"
"Hey, my best friend had cancer and she just died"
"Fuck those doctors just juice oranges man!"
"Maybe you shouldn't have done so much X because it was just a
matter of time".

Things you can do for that someone you love that has a
diagnosis.

Assist with specific tasks.

Generic offers of help are just that and someone dealing with a
new diagnosis doesn't have the time or energy to guide you on how to
help. Instead come up with targeted tasks that can truly help.

Targeted Tasks Ideas:

Make healthy home cooked meals.

Food prep for them.

Purchase meal delivery gift cards.

Grocery shopping trips.

Chauffer for a day (or week).

Laundry duty.

Shopping outing (when they have the energy both physically and
emotionally).

I am free, I am free, I AM FREE

Never underestimate the ability to be a good listener to those in need.

Take the kids for a day or weekend.

Don't constantly talk about cancer.

24/7 conversations regarding the persons diagnosis will quickly become tiresome and emotionally draining for them. You can still touch base with everything else that is going on in their lives. Cancer does not define them it is their cells' acting in a distinct state at this given moment. Don't make their entire reality about cancer.

That's a wrap on the cancer front. Come and listen as we speak about sound and how it influences so much of our reality.

CHAPTER 6. SOUND

Sound. What is it and why is it so important to our existence here in this reality?

Seemingly it makes the most sense that we can hear sounds for survival purposes. After all we have been taught that we evolved into this human flesh and at some point, we crawled out of the oceans and gained the ability to hear sounds. This would be tremendously beneficial for our ancestors as they hunted and as they worked to protect themselves and their living environments.

Here's an important question. What is sound?

To journey down that road let's first ponder a question that has been pondered for many a moon.

If a tree falls in the forest and no one is around to hear it does it make a sound?

I know you've heard this one before, but have you ever really sat down and thought it out?

To do so would take you upon a journey into the inner workings of the various components that make up sound and how they work with and within us bi-pedal humanoids. This could become a deep dive into the inner workings of various components but let's keep it light and get some of the basics down.

Sound is comprised of vibrations moving at a specific frequency. Sound is a transmission of vibrations in any frequency.

Frequency:

Frequency is measured in Hertz aptly titled so in honor of the 19th Century German physicist Heinrich Hertz. Frequency is simply a means of measurement. In this instance frequency is used to measure the number of waves that pass a fixed location in a given amount of time.

Regardless if someone is in the forest or not when the tree falls no sound is truly heard because sound does not exist, rather we as individuals interpret this thing we designate as sound. Even if someone is in the forest and see's the tree fall, they do not actually hear a tree falling. Weird, right?

Sound is an illusion. A pretty good one to boot. Sound is a *concept* that takes place within your brain/mind. Objects within the physical 3-D reality we find ourselves do not and cannot make a sound. Everything is completely silent within the 3-D reality we live. When we "hear" our brains are interpreting vibrational waves and my interpretation of these vibes will often greatly differ from yours. This is in small part why we can both "hear" the same thing but have wildly different interpretations of what was said or heard. Not only is it necessary to have a central nervous system to even be able to detect these vibrations and interpret them as sound but the history of our programmed minds also dictate how we interpret these sounds and how we ultimately react and interact with these sounds.

Physical objects in the "real world" create compression waves in the atmosphere around various other objects. The energy waves propagate outward (not as you have been taught, more on that in a second) and eventually reach your fuzzy little ear hairs. The tiny ear drum then vibrates, then these tiny little bones within the ear move just a bit, this then hits the cochlea which sends electrical pulses to your brain where your brain then interprets this thing called sound. That brings us full circle back to electricity and the electric body.

Regarding how sound propagates it's important to note that this energy does not travel in the classical sine wave formation we have been taught. Sound propagates spherically from its point of origin. Sound travels as complex geometric patterns not as flat, straight moving energy, frequency.

This can be partially proven out by looking at the study of cymatics. What? Cymatics that's what.

Read on.

106

I am free I am free I AM FREE

CYMATICS AND HEALING WITH SOUND

Cymatics has become one of the latest crazes in the world of the healing arts. That is working to heal the entire "person" holistically. It's easy enough to take part in cymatics to keep it sufficiently trendy but not so trendy as to have the unfortunate faux pas of posting to social media about your Tibetan sound bath and appearing out of date on the latest healing fashion.

Before we dive into cymatics let's discuss the topic of specific frequency Hertz and their meaning and potential healing or negative impacts they can have on you.

Everything is moving energy atoms (vibrations) and as they move, they resonate to a specific frequency.

With that in mind we should further note that it makes sense that the planet Earth itself should have its own resident frequency. This is part of the reason why you have healers that tout walking in the grass barefoot to ground yourself. With its ability to discharge some of your pent-up energy it also can help to reset your own residential frequency. Much like a tuning fork used to reset your frequency in various parts of your body (and beyond) so too can simply walking barefoot on the Earth.

The Earth's frequency is measured to be 432Hz and in good ol' yesteryear recorded music around the world was recorded at 432Hz.

In ancient Greece instruments associated with Orpheus (the God of music) were tuned to......YES! 432Hz.

Ananda Bosman found that many instruments excavated from Egyptian sites were tuned to...... any guesses? Anyone? No? 432Hz (probably just a coincidence).

This probably has to do with the Schumann Resonance which German physicist Winfried Otto Schumann re-discovered in 1952. Schumann found that electromagnetic resonance existed within the cavity of the Earth's surface as well as the inner edge of the ionosphere and were excited by lighting (by the way this is the same concept that Nikola Tesla was using when he created man made lighting at Pikes Peak lab to excite the ionosphere to create free wireless energy for all of humanity).

I am free, I am free, I AM FREE

The 432Hz frequency resides in the top end of the Theta range and the beginning of the Alpha range. This is why many binaural beats utilize this frequency. The brain is conscious but in a relaxed near sleep state.

"If one should desire to know whether a kingdom is well governed, if its morals are good or bad, the quality of its music will furnish the answer".
-Confucius

The famous Italian composer Verdi and that most famous composer Mozart tuned their music to 432Hz because of the musical theory that 432Hz is mathematically consistent with the Universe. They understood (or stumbled into the truth) that by tuning their music to 432Hz they could change the vibrational frequency of their audiences to make them more attune to and to feel and become part of the music. This is because the audience would have collectivity started to internally resonant at a subatomic level with the music being played at 432Hz.

Verdi was so enthralled by 432Hz that he along with various physicists and scientist pushed to have the Congress of Italian Musicians (that would have been a big deal before the advent of moving pictures) set 432Hz as the standard tuning which was approved in 1881.

In 1936 the American Standards Association recommended that the A above the middle C be tuned to 440Hz.

Why? Why change the resonance of the pitch from 432 to 440?

In 1940 the 440 Hz was introduced by the United States for the entire world.

By 1953, 440 Hz had become the ISO 16-standard meaning everything in the world is now recorded and produced at 440 Hz. It's interesting to consider that nearly all music today is recorded at 440Hz which is out of sync and harmony with the laws of the Universe. But hey if most of the chart-topping music consist of ass shacking and titty smacking (did I get that backwards) then I suppose it makes total sense.

440 Hz is the removal of the healing properties of nature's 432 Hz. Dr. Leonard Horowitz writes:

I am free, I am free, I AM FREE

"The music industry features this imposed frequency that is herding populations into greater aggression, psycho social agitation, and emotional distress predisposing people to physical illness."

Aside from harsh noise pollution of city's that work subtly to destroy your body you can witness a barrage of 440 Hz being directly implanted into the ears of adolescents and adults alike. Headphones (some priced at over $200.00 a pair) are connected to the multitude of electronic slave masters as our children and often we ourselves believe we are listening to "good" music.

To further bombard our own frequency, we live in a world of 24/7 bathing of multiple frequencies from items such as Bluetooth, Cellphones, Wi-Fi, radio and microwaves to name a few.

In 1905 Albert Einstein presented to the world his theory that matter, and energy are interchangeable and interconnected.

This means that our physical bodies our energies and our vibrational frequencies all share the same substance. We are part of the entire cosmos and we exist as one universal pool of energy that manifest itself in many multiple ways including as a physical human body.

It was Einstein's famous equation $E=mc2$ that helped to spawn the theory of relativity. Broken down in an incredibly simplistic format this is the world of vibrations. It is odd to consider that the solid world around us is not truly solid but rather a collection of "invisible" atoms vibrating at variable rates to create the illusion of solid states of matter. All physical matter in our 3D reality is composed of vibrating atoms.

Let us consider that resonance allows for two vibrational frequencies to come together. That is, if one frequency is vibrating lower and another higher, resonance allows for the lower frequency to modify its vibrational patters so it's frequency can climb to meet the higher frequency.

This can be witnessed when someone tunes a piano or uses the healing arts of tuning the human biofield via cymatics. When a tuning fork of a specific frequency is struck then held near a piano string the piano string then changes its vibrations to match the frequency of the tuning fork. A similar process is utilized when a

sound therapy practitioner uses various tuning forks to tune the
human biofield.

The reason why this concept is of importance to us is because
we all have our own biofield surrounding our body's and we have
various portions of our human biofield vibrating at specific
frequencies. When a sound therapist works on an individual's biofield
they are often working on frequencies in areas surrounding the body
that have existed for many years. A practitioner can then utilize
various tuning forks to manipulate the vibrational residence of the
human body field to heal various traumas that you may have been
carrying around for far too many years.

There is a subatomic world of constant and consistent movement
that takes place beyond the vision of our eyes. The book your
holding, the chair your bum is keeping warm right now. They may
appear to be lifeless stationary objects but on a subatomic level they
are constantly moving and at play. This is the world of pure energy
and your body is no different. If you consider this subatomic world
then we can realize that nothing is ever at rest. Energy is always
moving and flowing. Energy never dies, and new energy is never
created. Energy simply migrates from one location to another in a
never-ending cacophony of vibrational movement which creates
various frequencies. If you take the time to tap into these energy
fields via breath work, MO work, or various body movements such as
Yoga or Isometrics you will find that in a small way you can
manipulate and control the movements of these energies within your
physical body.

Presented is another example of resonance and the concept of
one lower state of vibrational energy rising to meet a higher state of
vibrational energy.

You have been in a social situation where the overall mood and
ambiance is rather subtle and low key. Until in walks someone with a
wide smile on their face, greeting everyone with genuine interest and
a palpable attitude of love and joy. When this occurs some or many
of the lower frequency individuals at the gathering suddenly perk up.
Their energy levels step up a notch or two. This is a social example
of resonance at work.

You have yourself experienced this same feeling. You don't
want to go out for the evening because you're a bit tired and you

I am free, I am free, I AM FREE

don't feel up to being social. You force yourself out anyway perhaps to ensure you don't hurt someone's feelings by not showing up to their important gathering. Once you're out and at the social event your suddenly much more vibrant and joyful. This is because your vibrational frequency effects your energy which directly effects the physical world your living in. This can also be chalked up to the power of resonance.

When you are feeling fear which often manifest itself as self-loathing, anger, grief etc. on a subatomic level this is vibrational energy and frequency vibrating at a low and slow frequency. Once you get into the social situation and you let go of fear and embrace love which often manifest itself as joy, happiness, freedom etc. to our physical senses suddenly you are switched on and feeling wonderful.

What changed? Did all your various fears and life issues suddenly disappear while you were at the social event? Kind of but also once you were around people that had their energy vibrating at a higher frequency your frequency rose up to match, allowing you to enjoy yourself while fully committing to the moment?

Therefore, it's important to ensure you do not spend your energy currency in the company of low vibe people. You know what I'm talking about because you either have some in your life now or you did in the past. You should be spending as much time around high vibe people that live inside of love and not fear. If you spend your energy with people living a life of fear within fear, you will lower your vibrational energy and spend your precious energy currency living in fear. If you watch the news for 30 minutes you can immediately feel and understand that they are emoting fear to bring you out of love and into fear which manifest itself as hate.

As you take your time to learn and grow within the reality of physical, mental and spiritual healing your vibrational frequency's will shift and migrate from a low slower state to a faster higher state (thus the colloquialism "higher state of consciousness")

TIPS FOR RAISING YOUR FREQUENCY

Love 2 Love:
Let go of the fear and embrace the love.

Tune Out:
Do not let other people's lower frequency bring your frequency down. Including those within the realms of social media and so-called news outlets.

Thought Control:
You are what you think. When you have internal dialog chattering about in your head stop and listen for a bit and try to figure out just who the hell is that talking anyway. If that voice is speaking ill of you give it a good laugh a hug and send it about its way.

Spiritual Embrace:
It's easy to lose track of the fact that we are spiritual light beings of infinite consciousness having a human experience at this point of perceived time. We live in a materialistic world and it's easy to get caught up in the wave of consumerism. Take a break from spending, take a break from consuming (even content such as television, movies, music, books, etc.) and spend time creating and/or focusing within.

Dependence Power Up:
Take a break from depending on others even the ones you love and care for. Take small breaks from using other people's energy as a crutch. Bask in the joy of empowering yourself.

Judge Not:
Decide to take an hour, then a day, then a week of working to not judge others. Even in your own head.

Judge Not:
Decide to take an hour, then a day, then a week of working to not judge yourself. Even in your own head. ESPECIALLY IN YOUR OWN HEAD!

Believe:

Take time to believe in the power of self. Living and loving our families and friends is truly a blessed and beautiful thing, however it can be difficult to truly love others if you have not figured out how to love yourself. It is further difficult to tell others how you expect to be loved if you do not understand how you love to be loved.

Play:

PLAY!! It seems far too many of us "grew up" and forgot how to play. Relearn the natural skills of being at play.

Nature:

Take time to go outside and connect to the physical world and nature with all your perceived senses. Even if it's just for a couple of minutes a day go outside and smell the air, feel the breeze on your skin, lick the.....uh well maybe we leave taste out of this one. Hopefully you know what I'm getting at. Take time to appreciate the "little things" (little things like the Earth, trees, bees and clouds).

Meditate:

Hey, I gave you an entire section on meditation yo. It can be difficult when you first start to attempt to cultivate meditative practices into your lifestyle, but you WILL feel and BE better with regular meditation as your partner.

Give:

Not necessarily money or physical objects. You can give time to go to an old folk's home and listen to some stories. You can give time to read books to kids. You can give sincere compliments to strangers you pass on the sidewalk. Give doesn't necessarily mean to give material objects or money. The gift of giving love without the expectation of a return on investment is the best giving you can give (that's kind of a weird giving sentence).

Negativity Shut Down:

I am free, I am free, I AM FREE

If you have someone in your life that is consistently bringing you down mentally, spiritually or any other way you may consider removing them from your life.

Higher Vibrations.

Seek to spend time with those that resonate at the same or higher frequency than you.

Laugh Smile Love:

You are energy and every moment you are awake and conscious you can make the conscious decision to live a life of love. Even if the perception of your reality is not what you wish it to be. You create your own reality and how great can your personal reality be when full of laughter, smiles and love?

I am free I am free I AM FREE

Why A Sex Chapter

The upcoming chapter may seem at odds with the rest of the content of these writings, but it does play an important role for several reasons.

This chapter is full of content that some may deem vulgar, but rest assured there is a reason for its inclusion. Provided is a simple bullet point list as to why I chose to present this content in these writings.

- There are many healing modalities available via sexual energy.

- Young men in the United States in troves have stopped having sex or rarely participate in sexual pleasures (the statistics are staggering).

- A lack of sexuality is driving many young men into deep depression with some lashing out with physical violence and acts of vile aggression.

- Releasing or migrating and utilizing sexual energy can help many young men move away from tension, pain, guilt and a sense of loneliness bringing a sense of control and power into their lives.

- Many men of a slightly older generation now rely on pharmaceutical companies to gain and maintain an erection and (un)healthy sexual energy. Too many men have not been taught nor taken the time to learn to cultivate sexual energy for better overall health for their physical bodies as well as for their mental strength. A man losing his libido can be a crushing blow to his ego and consequently all his personal relationships in his life.

- Far too many women are unsatisfied with their current love life on many levels including between the sheets. For men,

I am free, I am free, I AM FREE
learning some of these modalities in a non-pressure
environment such as these writings will 100% create a
stronger more powerful and longer lasting relationship with
everyone in his life but most importantly with the love of his
life.

- Learning to cultivate their own sexual knowledge and
  prowess before seeking validation from an outside party.
  Way too many young and old men seek approval from a
  woman based solely on her physical appearance and whether
  they determine her to be aesthetically pleasing. This shallow
  view generally infests a young man's mind and continues to
  grow and manifest as men age.

- Creating and maintaining a healthy sexual relationship with
  yourself and your lover is important to overall health and
  longevity.

- Too many men are weak and powerless under the spell of a
  beguiling woman that is more concerned with his bank
  account than the nature of the man. Learning these
  techniques allows for the maturation of inner strength over
  one's own sexual desires.

- After becoming MO a man becomes much more attuned to
  himself allowing him to become more attuned and connected
  to his partner which in turn greatly strengthens the
  relationship both physically and spiritually.

- Some of these practices are thousands of years old but are
  mostly unknown and therefore not taught to western cultures.
  Gaining wisdom from those that came before us may enrich
  our lives and our perceptions in ways we never knew were
  possible.

CHAPTER 7. SEXUAL KUNG-FU

And now we journey into the land of something totally different. If you are sensitive to conversations involving overt sexuality, then you will want to skip this chapter which is heavily focused on channeling sexual energy for healing. As such the language and stories within this chapter are inundated with sexual context that may not be suitable for all. You have been warned.

WARINING!!

T his chapter is NOT about sex, intercourse, coitus, making

whoopy, or fucking. No wait it's totally about that. Well actually it's mostly about that. It's also about controlling and moving energy and the way you have been programmed to believe a fallacy.

What fallacy might that be you ask? Man's ability to be Multi-Orgasmic.

It's considered general knowledge in the western world that women can and often do have multiple orgasms, but this wasn't always the case. In modern history it's only within the last 50 years or so that it's become common place for women to be Multi-Orgasmic. It is claimed that since the 50's women's ability to be Multi-Orgasmic has skyrocketed from 14% to 50% (Hartman and Fithian, Any Man Can, Page. 157). So why the drastic increase in such a small window of time one might ask (I know I did).

117

I am free, I am free, I AM FREE

I turn to an oft overused example for my monkey see monkey do analogy (or perhaps a better theory of our unseen but often felt connection via the aether). Roger Bannister.

It's May 6th, 1954 and you're a 20 something English chap in Oxford doing your med school thing. In 1954 the collective knowledge of humanity had an understanding, which was "Aint no way no human can run a mile under 4 minutes". And up until that point as far as our knowledge goes in modern history our collective agreement was true. No human could run a mile in under 4 minutes.

Bannister, running for the Amateur Athletic Association won the mile race that day in 1954 clocking a time of 3 minutes 59.4 seconds. YAZAA!! Our entire collective agreement of knowledge on this subject now must shift which is an odd thing considering SO many athletes had tried and failed to break that record. His world record in the mile did not hang around very long. As it turns out once our collective human consciousness agreed that humans can run a mile in under 4 minutes it started happening repeatedly until a sub four mile became rather common place amongst elite athletes. Over time running conditions changed such as shoe tech, track tech, timing devices, ways in which athlete's train, etc. At the time of this writing it's estimated that roughly 10-20 American men break 4:00 for the first time each year.

How does the sub 4 tie into our subject of discussion? In the west our collective consciousness has agreed that when men ejaculate they orgasm and that's that end of story. I'm here to tell you all those foolish people are running a 5-minute mile in the bedroom. That reference isn't just to be cheeky via my track analogy above but also a bit of a dig to dudes chasing the nut and busting in 5 minutes.

With the techniques outlined in the following chapter you will learn to be Multi-Orgasmic which, once well practiced will allow you to ejaculate on your terms or not to ejaculate at all. Not to worry the whole blue balls thing is not a thing once you learn to control your sexual chi. For the uninitiated a simple translation of chi is energy. I think I know what most dudes are thinking reading this right now. What's the point if I don't ejaculate? You will still orgasm but in a different more powerful way and once you increase your control and

I am free, I am free, I AM FREE

abilities you will lean more towards the multiple orgasms without ejaculation as opposed to what you have been doing your entire life.

Before we move on I would like to clarify a couple other important items regarding this chapter.

First, this is going to be a brief overview of a deep topic. Think of this as cliff notes not the greatest works of William Shakespeare (who by the way couldn't spell his wife's name, couldn't spell his own name, didn't own a single book or manuscript, whose parents couldn't read or write and whose daughters couldn't read or write. I guess being the world's greatest literally genius skips generations).

When I stated in the opening that this chapter is kind of about sex what I mean is that I will be briefly discussing how you can bring some of these learned skills into your bedroom to better please your partner and greatly enhance your sexual connection. I will only be briefly skimming this portion of being Multi-Orgasmic as my primary focus is for you to learn to recognize your sexual energy and move it into other portions of your body to utilize in multiple ways as opposed to simply allowing it to explode out of the tip of your cock. Yes, I said cock. Were all adults here and were about to talk about cocks, shafts, testicles, masturbation, etc. If the word cock offends you recognize that you have been programmed to be offended and skip this chapter. If on the other hand you recognize that cock is not a bad word and can be a great turn on when whispered in your partners ear, then please continue.

I am free I am free I AM FREE

Rules

Hey you made it! Thanks for not bowing out during the whole cock talk back there in the intro.

Welcome! Welcome! I'm very happy you're here because much like Santa Claus, I have gifts to share.

For most of you reading this you should relax and forget everything you have ever been taught about sex and how your cock works. There are millions of self-help books and I can't imagine how much money is being generated by dick pills on an annual basis. The good news is that you don't need any of that bullshit. What you do need is time, patience and commitment. I want you to make a promise to yourself now that you will be patient and kind to yourself and make a commitment to learn how to properly masturbate and have powerful sexual encounters. The techniques I lay out here are going to be a challenge for some. It was for me when I started partly because I had to put aside what I thought I knew and had to open myself up to accepting one of my favorite sayings.

"You don't know what you don't know" - Donny.

Once I got past my own ego about my lack of knowledge regarding sex, sexual energy and my own body things improved quickly. The primary challenge I had was letting go of my preprogrammed bullshit to allow me the opportunity to gain a better understanding of the mind/body connection when it comes to sex and self-gratification.

I would like to start this out with the introduction of a single rule. I'm not a big fan of rules myself as they typically create unnecessary limitations in potential growth. With that in mind

STICK TO THE FUCKING RULE!!

It's a rule that some of you will balk at but it's a very important rule.

120

I am free, I am free, I AM FREE

Rule 1: Stop getting your sexual gratification via outside stimulus that is not your direct partner. That's a nice way of saying put away the porn dude!

Your imagination is infinitely more powerful compared to tossing it to a screen of people going at it. Aside from the potential psychological damage you may be causing yourself and your sexual relationship with your partner once you embrace the power of your imagination you can utilize all your senses as opposed to vision/audio only.

Alas, that is not the primary reason why you should not be watching porn during this training. You will need to fully embrace the concept of the mind/body connection to gain full control of breath, heart rate and energy manipulation. External stimulus will have a negative impact and greatly reduce your ability to lock in and be fully committed and focused on these techniques.

The first portion of this information will be a focus on self-gratification practices. This reason is twofold.

First, to utilize these techniques later in your meditation and connectivity to your higher consciousness you will likely be doing this by yourself not for the pleasuring and strengthening of your relationship with your partner.

Second, you need to practice before you suit up (or in this case strip down) for game time. Game time will either be utilizing these techniques for connectivity to higher self or for sexual pleasure with your partner.

WHAT'S THIS ALL ABOUT

Before we get too far into this there are a couple of things for us to review.

I first started the journey to becoming MO many years ago and at that time I had three primary sources for gaining knowledge on the topic. Two of the sources were very well written books on the topic that took the time to teach specific portions of becoming and being a Multi-Orgasmic Man that are important. Many popular books that I research today on this topic can teach you some proper techniques that can be helpful, but they neglect to teach you the important portion of controlling your energy and moving it properly throughout your body. It's difficult to put into words how important this is and how dangerous it can be to re-channel your root energy and not properly circulate and either store it or release it. This probably sounds hippie, yogi, meditation-esque but it is an important portion of these teachings.

Although these writings are only loosely tantra base you should be aware that within Tantra there exist Black Tantra, Grey Tantra and White Tantra. My intentions are to give you the knowledge you need to move in the direction that suites you however, if you are a womanizer, a control freak or feel the need to hold power over others than you probably need to seek some other persons writings that will lean more towards Black Tantra. My voice does not lean in that direction and leans more in the direction of being gentle and kind to yourself and your partner(s).

The third source was self-discovery and practice. I spent months with self-discovery before I started bringing these techniques into the bedroom with my partner. I partially explained to her what I was doing and we both quickly became Multi-Orgasmic. After you learn some of these techniques it will be up to you to self-journey and utilize them as you see fit.

I could throw out some techniques that would help you, but I first must delve into some of the important aspects of energy flow and breath control. Without the proper channeling of your energy you can do real damage to yourself.

I am free, I am free, I AM FREE

Initially I wanted this to be a very short chapter that would act as a quick review of exercises and techniques you could incorporate to help improve your mental and physical health, but we will first need to dedicate several pages to review chakra, chi and the microcosmic orbit. Don't skip it, it's critical to learning the proper techniques for assisted spiritual growth.

SPECIAL NOTE REGARDING SCHEDULES

Various chapters within this section will present schedules for particular exercises. These schedules are merely suggestions and later after you have become proficient you will no longer need to adhere to any type of strict schedules and practice routines. You will be able to easily slip into MO mode while practicing safe sex with your partner(s) and will likely rarely need to continue a regular exercise regimen for these techniques.

Male body

Okay time for biology class guys. You probably believe you know how your cock works, I mean you've been using it your entire life. Let's give a brief overview just to be clear.

We all tend to think of our cock and balls first when we think of male sexuality. I could go into a deep dive into terminology making up the penis and our reproductive system but since we are not in med school we are going to keep this simple and in plain English.

Let's start with the big boy.

PENIS/COCK

As you are already aware your cock is mostly made of a spongy substance that has several arteries contained within to allow for a great deal of blood flow both in and out of that guy. You have your head also called the glans. Your entire cock is full of nerve endings making it sensitive to touch, heat/cold, etc. What you may not know is that on average about 2 inches of your cock is inside of your body and is inside of your pubococcygeus muscle (PC muscle). This is very, very important as we will be working a great deal to mentally connect to and strengthen our PC muscle. Like Kegels we can work our PC muscle to give it strength and control and just like Kegels we can do these exercises anywhere, anytime. We will be getting into the PC muscle and exercise routines in just a bit. Back to your cock. It's got great blood flow, it's sensitive particularly in the tip because of the amount of nerve endings.

TESTICLES

"All I've got in this world is my balls and my word and I don't break either of 'em for nobody!" - Scarface.

Balls. Their primary purpose is the production of sperm and the hormone testosterone. Sperm moves from your balls through the vas deferens to the prostate gland.

PROSTATE

I am free, I am free, I AM FREE

This guy is important in these writings for one primary reason. You need this strong and healthy to help ensure you will maintain a healthy and long-lasting sexual lifestyle. A big part of going through these exercises is to make the mind/body connection and strengthen our sexual body's and energy for better health as well as better sexual endeavors. We want to retain this sexual vitality into our 60's, 70's, 80's and beyond without the assistance of a stimulant in the form of a pill.

Secondly it is considered the male G spot due to its deep sexual connection in our bodies. You have probably already heard about male orgasms via prostrate massage. If your uncomfortable with a finger in your butt there is the option of massaging the prostrate externally. Not everyone will be into the prostrate because of its location in the center of your pelvis. Your fingers gotta get deep in that ass to reach the prostate which for some dudes just won't work. Keep in mind that you can massage the prostate externally and the sexual stimulation via the prostate is a different sensation altogether.

PC MUSCLE

This bad boy is located between your butthole and the base of your balls and it's important. It's often used as a sexual erogenous zone and is used during erotic massage. We will be using this spot as a kind of emergency brake if we are about to go over the edge with ejaculation and we want to create an immediate stop. The PC muscle will be getting a great deal of attention from us as it's going to be one of the keys to success for becoming Multi-Orgasmic.

BREATHING

The importance of knowing how to properly control your breathing while fucking or getting close to the edge can't be overstated. There are many breathing techniques that can be utilized, however we will be focusing on just a couple of simple ones that you will be able to easily remember and employ while you're in the heat of the moment.

ENERGY

One of the major points of this is to find and move your internal energy. There's a good chance that you maintain a lot of energy down

I am free, I am free, I AM FREE

in those balls. This can easily lead to very little control of ejaculation and of energy since this built up energy will go screaming for the tip of the dick to find the path of least resistance.

I am free I am free I AM FREE

CHAKRA

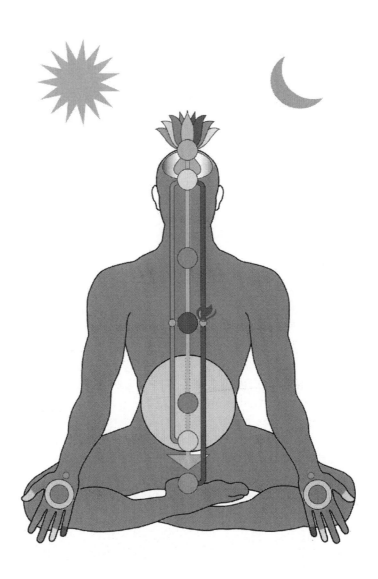

I am free, I am free, I AM FREE

To begin we must understand that we are going to do some exercises to build physical sexual strength and control. Another misunderstood and underrated portion of this is the mental connection you need to have to your sexual body and your energy. Most men at an early age are told to disconnect from the sexual experience by doing things like thinking of numbers or baseball stats while fucking. This is probably the worst advice you can listen to and choose to follow because in fact we want to do the exact opposite.

We want to be hyper focused on our cock, balls, breathing, and heart rate. We will quickly become very skilled at this and will start to be able to move our energy around our body to take that energy from the balls that is trying to push its way through your shaft and redirect and store this energy for later use. This allows you to utilize this energy throughout the day instead of wasting it by shooting it out of your cock. How often do you cum and then want to take a nap? Wouldn't it be nice to be able to control that energy and utilize it as you wish instead of losing it?

In many cultures and esoteric knowledge, it was known to move, control and cultivate this energy for healthy longevity of life. In ancient Egypt the orgasm was linked to eternal life and was strongly connected to the chakra system. In many cultures it was believed that allowing the discharge of your sexual energy on a regular basis was the culprit in bringing one closer to death as you are releasing your life energy in large spurts of uncontrolled lust.

In both the Hindu and Tibetan Tantra systems men are instructed to avoid busting that nut and instead they are taught to move the energy up the spine (the sacred 33) via the chakra points and store the energy in various higher energy centers.

The balls or rather the sacrum is the root chakra and is the lowest point in the chakra chain. This chakra point has to do with several things but self-preservation, and root support are two keys to the root chakra.

I will briefly cover chakra points and why they matter to us in our cultivation of our sexual energy.

Several years ago, my brother and I were working at the same company. My brother convinced the company to bring in a yoga instructor on a weekly basis for some company sponsored yoga classes. It was cool because I had wanted to try yoga for some time

I am free, I am free, I AM FREE

but just kind of never got around to it. I was very ego driven wanting to prove to myself that I could hit any pose and although I wasn't the best in the room I wasn't the worst either. The part that I never got into was proper breathing and chakra talk. To me at the time the chakra talk sounded like bullshit and was quickly dismissed by my ego. Years later when I first started researching being Multi-Orgasmic the first things I saw were related to breathing and chakra and I thought to myself…..Ok let go for a minute and just believe. I was still on the fence about it until after I started the exercises and started to feel and manipulate my energy throughout my body. If you're currently a skeptic regarding chakra like I was when I first started this practice, then it will likely take you longer to reach your goal of becoming Multi-Orgasmic. You will still learn a lot about control and you will strengthen your love making but if you truly want to take a leap forward in your connection to self you will need to believe and feel these chakra points to work with them to heal and grow mind body and spirit.

CHAKRA

Most cultures have a standard 7 chakra system.

Root Chakra:
Located at your sacrum this chakra color is Red and links the mind to the physical body.

Sacral Chakra:
Located in your lower abdomen this chakra roles with the color Orange or Red-Orange. This guy is associated with creative energies.

Solar Plexus Chakra:
Located in the gut it's easy to guess the color Yellow like Solar or Sun. The solar plexus has additional importance linked to additional lessons that will be presented in a later chapter of this book. Usually but not always I redirect my root energy to this chakra point. This point has much to do with ego and the term "gut-feeling" takes on greater meaning (to note the gut is another brain).

I am free, I am free, I AM FREE

Heart Chakra:
Located in the center of your chest near your heart this one is pink or green in color.

Throat Chakra:
Located at the throat this one is Blue or Sky Blue and is associated with truth.

Brow Chakra (Third Eye):
Middle of the forehead and linked to the color indigo. This is the center of wisdom and the ability to be taught and to learn. Many of the healing modalities in this book including things in this chapter will help to decalcify your pineal gland and create a much stronger connection to your third eye. It's important to note that much of your learning moving forward will come from inside and intuition not necessary from external 3rd party sources. The lessons in this book should act as a guide and a catalyst to get you started but you are the navigator of this journey.

Crown Chakra:
As the name implies this sits on the crown or top of your head. It's white and represents your higher consciousness and spiritual center.

For what we will be doing you don't need to memorize or even know very much about the chakra points. Know that they exist and that we will be pulling energy through them. In the lessons regarding moving your sexual energy it will end up in the Solar Plexus for safe storage.

Now that we have the basics of chakra covered let's move on to your microcosmic orbit. This concept may seem a bit dodgy to some but once you start practicing awareness of it you will quickly realize its power and how you are going to use it. After that we get into the breathing discussions and we are going to start some basic breathing exercises. Everything starts with breathing, so this will be the first set of exercises then we will move on to additional training from there. After that we will start to focus on the good stuff surrounding dick strength and control.

130

I am free, I am free, I AM FREE

MICROCOSMIC ORBIT

The concept and working machinations of the microcosmic orbit can get deep as it's rooted in old time China. I could get into the deep meanings and a lot of minutia but instead we're going to keep the concept simple and give you an exercise that will allow you to connect to your microcosmic orbit and feel its power.

Let's break the word down to decipher what Emperor Fu Xi was getting at.

Micro:
From the Greek this is a combining word meaning small.
Synonyms: little, small

Cosmic:
Of or related to the cosmos. Immeasurably extended in time and space; vast.
Synonyms: immense, enormous, stupendous

Orbit:
Latin root *orbita* meaning wheel track, course, circuit.
Synonyms: path, pattern, cycle, rotation, round

So, we're looking at a small, enormous, natural cycle.
Small/enormous? What the...?

Just as we have a microcosm inside of our bodies the Earth itself has a macrocosm and the various luminary bodies have their macrocosm. Your micro in microcosmic is referring to yours being small in comparison to the outside Universe. The cosmic is referring to the cosmos which resides inside of you.

With that little breakdown we can quickly see that we're talking about a tremendous power inside of you that is spinning and should be spinning in an orbit.

You have two primary channels for carrying energy (chi) throughout your body.

I am free, I am free, I AM FREE

BACK CHANNEL:

This starts at the tailbone and runs up the 33 vertebrae of the spine, over the top of your head down the front of your face and nose to the top of your lip.

FRONT CHANNEL:

This starts very near the same location of the lower pelvis and runs up the front of your body and completes at the lower lip.

For us to join the flow of these two energy channels we simply need to gently touch the tip of our tongues to the roof of our mouth. You then focus on brining energy up via the back channel and back down the front channel (more on that later). This creates the connection of your microcosm to allow this energy to flow in a circular pattern through the body creating the necessary orbit.

Our primary purpose in understanding and utilizing the microcosmic orbit is to use it as a pathway to move energy. We can conceptualize this as a road to carry your energy that has multiple hubs. Those hubs would be the 7 sacred chakra points. To open the flow of the road to allow the energy to move in a complete circle around the body you must lightly touch the tongue to the roof of the mouth to complete the circuit and allow the front and back channels to link.

BREATHING

For us bipedal humanoids without breath there is no life. You can fast with no food for long periods. No water, sure you can get by for a couple days. How long are you going to be around without breathing? Even after you read and practice the chapter on cold water therapy and learn to retain active breath for much stronger lung control you still aren't going to last long without beautiful prana baby.

Breathing is life but here's the rub. Nearly all of us do it wrong. Just totally wrong. Sure, the body is on autopilot and breathing for you, but you can take control of your breathing patterns and this is very important during sex or self-gratification for a couple of reasons.

1. The rate and control of your breathing is directly linked to the rhythm of your heart beat. What happens when you're getting ready to bust that nut? Your breathing rate increases like mad and your heart rate quickly follows. The pump down at your root chakra (the base of your balls) starts pumping like mad and before you know it….BOOM, energy dispersed through your dick. If you can control your breathing, you can slow down your heart rate and control your energy.
2. Your mind and the ability to be completely aware and in the moment, is crucial when attempting to stop ejaculation and move energy. When you control your breathing, you can become hyper focused and hyper aware which will allow for much better mental connectivity to your physical body as well as your energy and blood flow. This is beneficial while engaging in partner sex because instead of allowing your body to control you, you instead can be 100% visceral in the moment. In later sections once you have this control you will be able to feel your partners energy and start to connect to and manipulate their energy for a much deeper connection.

Laid out are two basic breathing techniques with an accompanying exercise. At first just practice these techniques a couple minutes a day and mentally focus while performing the breathing exercises. We will incorporate these techniques into

I am free, I am free, I AM FREE

self-gratification in the next chapter to create control. Proper breathing will always accompany you whether your practicing solo or with a partner as it is the first key to unlocking the concepts of being Multi-Orgasmic.

EXERCISES BREATHING

Belly Breathing

As mentioned earlier we are all breathing but most of us are breathing in a non-optimal fashion. We tend to be on auto pilot and take shallow breaths into the chest and upper back/shoulders. This keeps us alive but does not fully expand the necessary prana into our body as a whole. For belly breathing we will be focusing on breathing slowly and deeply into the belly. Concentrate not only on breathing into your belly but also filling the air from the bottom of your belly up towards your chest. Focus on getting the air in from the bottom of the belly up to about 90% capacity instead of a full breath.

Every inhale should be through the nostrils. This will help filter the air and warm it as it enters your body and fills your belly. I know most of us want flat 6 pack abs but for this exercise allow your belly to protrude outwards as the air fills your belly.

Breathing Exercise

How Often:
You should practice this at least once a day, every day.

Duration:
5-10 minutes.

Setting:
Unnatural lights extinguished and little to no distractions present.

Pro Tip:
If you have a busy household wake up early before everyone else. When possible, it is almost always better to practice breathing, meditation, yoga etc. outdoors for better air quality. The more you can be outdoors breathing that good ass prana the better.

1. Sit in a comfortable cross-legged position or in a chair with your back straight.
2. Inhale slowly and thoughtfully through your nose for 3-5 seconds. Feel and guide the air to fill your stomach cavity up from the bottom towards the top.
3. Once the air has filled your belly and you have allowed your belly to move outward slowly exhale through your mouth letting the air out from the top of the belly to the bottom. Let your belly slowly move back in towards your spine as it deflates and remain relaxed with as little tension in your overall body as possible. You may tense up at your shoulders and neck so ensure these areas are relaxed.
4. Repeat this breathing pattern for at least 15 breaths. As this becomes more natural and comfortable you can move this number up until you are reaching a point of being fully comfortable controlling your breathing pattern and being aware of your body and mind.

You can also practice this breathing exercise nearly anywhere, anytime. At work staring at your computer screen thinking about the horde of email vipers snapping at your energy. STOP! Take a couple minutes and practice this breathing routine and feel your energy return to you and return to your control. Let go of unnecessary negative energy.

This breathing technique will become a crucial element in slowing your heart rate and staying in control. You will then be able to start to focus on your energy and moving your energy to parts of your body away from your root chakra.

I am free I am free I AM FREE

Microcosmic Orbit

Now that you have a breathing exercise let's get into connecting with your microcosmic orbit, so you can learn to move energy.

Micro-Cosmic Orbit Exercise

How Often:
Initially you will want to practice daily, however as you become Multi-Orgasmic this will become natural for you, so you will later need to practice once a week or less.

Duration:
5 to 10 minutes.

Setting:
Unnatural lights extinguished and little to no distractions present.

Pro Tip:
If you're not familiar with meditation or forms of certain martial arts at first this may be a tricky concept to grasp. You can utilize an anus squeeze to get the energy that first initial push up the spine.

1. Sit in a comfortable position, close your eyes, relax and start to concentrate on any sensations you feel in your root chakra or down at the base of your balls.
2. Start concentrating on breathing slowly in and out. Breath into the belly filling from the bottom and when it's about two thirds of the way full slowly exhale and let the air out from the top down.
3. After several controlled breaths you should be feeling nice and relaxed and more in touch with your body. Now start to feel for any energy that might be sitting at the base of your balls (root chakra). If you don't feel much give several PC muscle squeezes to wake the energy up.

4. Once you feel some built up energy in the root chakra you can start to move some of that energy up your spine. To do this on an inhalation of a breath tighten your PC muscle to activate the energy in the root chakra. Lightly touch your tongue to the roof of your mouth and on the slow exhalation of breath let go of your PC muscle squeeze. This will release the energy and allow it to be sucked up the spine and into the head. Let it flow from the top of the head down the front of your face between your eyes down the bridge of your nose and feel it as it connects to the tongue bridge and then slides down into your belly.

This is a critical exercise to master. The primary purpose of this exercise is for you to understand and feel your sexual energy. Then feel and understand that you can move that energy up your spine and into your head. This is the portion where some people with knowledge will leave you. With this energy inside of your head. This isn't a good thing. It's important that you create that bridge with the tongue to create a true microcosmic orbit, so the flow of the orbit is circular. This allows you to safely draw the energy down the front and park it in your belly or solar plexus. You can also move this energy to another chakra point such as the heart chakra, so you can use your energy as you wish throughout the day.

I am free I am free I AM FREE

EXERCISES PC PULLUPS

Now we find ourselves creeping into the realms of focusing on exercises to both strengthen our cocks and our ability to stave off ejaculation.

With that in mind let's move our attention back to the PC muscle we discussed earlier. As a refresher the PC muscle is located directly behind your balls but not all the way back to the butthole. A very easy way to find this muscle is to go take a piss. When the stream is going good and strong stop pissing mid-stream. You will feel that your PC muscle flexes to stop the stream of urine. This muscle is very important in helping us not only stopping the flow of urine but also in stopping us from ejaculating when we've pushed just a little bit further than we wanted to. Let's get started.

How Often:
You should practice this at least once a day, every day. In the first couple of weeks your PC muscle may start to tire. Listen to your body and if you need to take a break for a day or two do it.

Duration:
There really isn't a set duration for this exercise since you can practice it anywhere anytime.

Setting:
When first starting out practice it at the end of your breathing exercises. Within the first week you can practice this anywhere. While driving, standing in line, whatever.

Exercise I

Pull Ups

1. While in a comfortable position whether sitting or standing focus on your PC muscle and give it a tight squeeze. Hold for 3 seconds then let it go. Do this for 5 rounds as a warm up and to connect to the PC muscle.
2. Now inhale slowly through the nose filling the belly from the bottom up, once the breath is full squeeze the PC muscle and hold for a 3 count. Let your breath slowly out while still holding the PC muscle tight. Once your breath has fully exhaled relax your PC muscle.

Perform the above exercise for as many rounds as you like keeping in mind that if you have not worked your PC muscle in the past it may become sore and be difficult to exercise within the first week. As you continue to exercise the PC muscle it will continue to grow in strength.

Pro Tip:
Now that you know you're flexing and strengthen a muscle while moving it to your controlled breathing pattern here are a couple of additional exercises to perform to strengthen the PC.

When you're driving in your car with the music on you can flex your PC muscle to the beat. I wouldn't recommend any techno or jungle beats until this bad boy has gained some strength and tenacity.

Flex and hold the PC muscle tight for longer durations. For example, if I'm watching TV maybe I will hold it tight for the duration of a commercial.

I am free I am free I AM FREE

EXERCISES MID-STREAM SUPPRESSION

Since we discussed using the PC to stop/start your urine flow let's put that into practice. Doing this on a regular at the beginning of your training will not only help strengthen the muscle it will allow you to feel and connect with it better and should build some confidence in being able to work and control it in a relaxed environment.

How Often:
2-3 times daily.

Reps:
I wouldn't recommend going too crazy with it. Just stop/start the flow 3-5 times while your handling your business.

Setting:
Don't worry about a breathing routine this is just to mentally connect to the PC and strengthen its ability to snap shut when you want it to.

Exercise II

Stop/Start

1. While standing taking a piss start your stream as normal. Part way through quickly squeeze the PC muscle to stop the stream. Your trying to stop it as quickly as possible. Hold for 1-2 seconds then let go and continue your stream.
2. Do the quick clench and hold several times during your urination session.

Pro Tip:
Digging in your feet and squeezing your eyes shut better emulates some of your natural body movements taking place directly before ejaculation. It's beneficial to simulate the body muscle spasm and the hard eyes closed clench while performing this exercise. Don't worry no one's looking at how goofy your face looks while doing this.

I am free I am free I AM FREE

Exercises Blood Flow

The following exercises are called Jelq. It is thought that jelqing originated in the Arabic culture as when a young man makes it to his thirteenth birthday he is taught the jelqing method as a rite of passage into manhood. The Arabic word jelq translates as milking and that's exactly what we're looking to do here.

The intended purpose for most men to use the jelq technique is to increase penis length and/or girth. For us we're only semi concerned about this, but we will use this tool for the primary purpose of strengthening our cocks, increasing oxygen and blood flow and forcing additional blood into the head of the penis so those tissues can expand in size. With this additional control and expansion, the tip of your dick will be able to allow more blood into it which will allow you to expand the overall size of the tip.

Another thing to keep in mind is that these exercises are not intended to stimulate you in a sexual way like the masturbation exercises. These exercises are mechanical and have the intended purpose of creating additional mechanical strength, stamina, blood and oxygen flow in your cock. While doing these exercises you should NOT be fully erect while performing said exercises.

Your erection level should be anywhere from 50% - 80% erect. If your dick is too soft, then you will not create the necessary blood pressure build up to squeeze through your shaft. Similarly, if your dick is too hard it will not allow for tissue expansion and for proper blood flow. For the first week of training I would suggest being in the 50%-60% range and then you can work your way up in the coming weeks if you like.

These exercises are incredibly beneficial if you currently have issues with gaining and maintaining an erection. In general, we are told that most erection issues are created in the mind which is probably accurate. Following these exercises will allow you to create actual physical strength in your shaft and will help to increase blood and oxygen flow to assist in getting and maintaining a strong erection. If you currently smoke cigarettes or drink copious amounts of alcohol I highly suggest you stop for at least a month. These two poisons can be a serious factor in limiting your ability to get that stiffy.

I am free, I am free, I AM FREE

Rounding out this thought and concept once you are gaining and maintaining a hard, erect cock your confidence will skyrocket and said mental limitation should fall by the wayside. If you are having a difficult time getting it up when being intimate with a specific person like your long-term partner than you must recognize that and figure out how you are going to work that out with your partner.

CAUTION:

These exercises work in a similar way to lifting weights. When you lift weights, you are creating micro tears in muscle tissue and they then repair themselves and the micro scarring creates stronger and larger muscles. Although you will want to make the jelqing technique part of a regular routine to maintain the high level of blood and oxygen flow you do NOT want to overdo these exercises especially when first starting off.

How Often:
Start off by performing the exercise routine 2-3 days a week for the first 2 weeks. As your cock starts to adjust and gain strength you can increase to 4-5 days a week, but this increase is not necessary. Consistency is the most important factor in ensuring you obtain strength gains. I wouldn't recommend more than 5 days a week. As you grow in strength these exercises will be limited to once a week or less.

Duration:
With all exercises that have you pushing blood into your cock and maintaining an erection you should keep it under 30 minutes. Although you will increase your stamina and can go longer than 30 minutes you run the risk of damaging the tissue of the penis when going too long during a single session.

Setting:
You're going to want some privacy for this one. Most guys probably do this during a morning warm shower routine, but I would suggest against this. It's preferable for you NOT to take long warm or hot showers so creating this routine based on the warm shower is not

146

I am free, I am free, I AM FREE

something we are looking to do. I would suggest making this part of your evening routine after you have come home from work before you have eaten dinner.

One of the benefits is that you can take your time without being rushed and it will ramp you up and prepare you mentally and physically for evening sex.

Another thing to consider about the setting is if you want to stand or sit. I highly recommend you stand unless you must sit. While standing it will be much easier and more effective to get your blood to flow properly to your cock. Also, you will be changing from pointing your cock up in the air sometimes and pointing it down towards the ground at other times. This is much easier to do whilst in a standing position. If sitting, you will need to find a way to get your legs raised above the height of your penis to ensure proper blood flow.

I am free I am free I AM FREE

Exercise I

Milking

1. Warm up. Although not necessary it is beneficial to first warm up the balls and cock for about 5 minutes. This will help prepare the shaft and penis head for the blood you're going to be pushing through.
2. To warm up run a wash cloth under very hot water and ensuring it is not going to burn then rub the towel all over your cock and hold it down on the balls to get them warm. If you are trying to get your lady pregnant this is not recommended as warming your balls on a continuous basis will significantly lower your sperm count.
3. Grab a lubricant such as organic coconut oil, or KY or Astroglide. Coconut oil has many uses and is cheap so it's a pretty good option. Don't use lotion and for sure don't use soap as they can contain chemical compounds you don't want to rub on your body but especially don't want to rub on your dick. Now lube up the entire cock ensuring you don't miss any spots.
4. While standing (preferred method) make the OK sign with your index finger and your thumb. It doesn't matter which hand you use as you will be using both hands with the OK sign during the duration of the exercise. You can go palm up or palm down. As you practice these exercises you will likely change it back and forth doing palm up sometimes and palm down at others.
5. With the OK fingers, grip the base of your partially erect cock and slide your hand forward forcing blood up the shaft towards the tip.
6. Once your hand reaches the top of your shaft immediately use the other hand in the same OK grip and with that hand starting at the base of the penis slide up towards the tip.

Keep doing this simple slide up technique alternating hands. You want to attempt to keep it going at a nice steady pace and don't allow yourself to become too erect.

Each stroke should last about 3-4 seconds from base to the top of your shaft.

148

I am free, I am free, I AM FREE

When first performing these exercises don't squeeze too much blood into the tip of your penis. As you continue to practice this exercise the tip of your dick will start to be able to retain more blood and will expand. As you get stronger you can start playing around with forcing blood all the way into the head of your penis by using the jelq technique. Be careful and don't force too much too soon.

To be clear you should be working this OK technique with your hands from the bottom of the shaft towards the top but stop just shy of the top of the glands (tip of your dick).

You should also change the direction of your penis. Sometimes pointing it up in the air sometimes pointing it down towards the floor.

UP

Pointing your dick up towards the ceiling generally is going to happen if the semi-erection is fairly hard. The upward angle stretches the tunica albuginea, which is directly involved in maintaining an erection.

The Buck's fascia constricts the deep dorsal vein which prevents blood from leaving which in turn ensures a strong erect cock.

DOWN

Alternatively, the downward angle will place greater strain directly on the ligaments of the penis. You have much more penis length maintained inside of your body and connected to your pubic bone via the suspensory ligament and the fundiform ligament.

When pulling down during the jelq technique you will feel these two ligaments at work as they help anchor your dick to your body. These ligaments create an arch in your penis and this pulling technique will allow for your cock to become slightly more straightened which will make your dick longer. Don't worry those ligaments are engineered with insane strength so if you're not trying to rip your dick off you shouldn't create any damage to your penis or surrounding tissues.

Start with 200 strokes per session for the first week.

In the second week move up to 300-400 strokes.

I am free, I am free, I AM FREE

Once your cock is conditioned and there is less risk of damaging cells get up to about 500 strokes or more per session. Your grip and strength will get stronger as your dick gets stronger.

Make sure to take rest days.

Pro Tip:

At times you may find that you get too aroused and too hard to perform the technique properly. If this occurs, you can wait and allow your dick to get a bit more flaccid or you can just move directly into one of the masturbation exercises as outlined next.

I am free I am free I AM FREE

HOW TO MASTURBATE

How to masturbate! What kind of chapter heading is that? I've been masturbating for many years my friend. I think I've got this one.

Calm down sir, this is no attack on your masturbatory prowess, but you could probably use some tips to make it more enjoyable and to better prep you for game time.

First and foremost, let it be known that historically men were predisposition to cum quickly. So, the theory goes that when our ancestors were living in much smaller tribes the options to procreate were not nearly as abundant as the world we live in today with its 7 plus billion and counting as well as the multitude of fuck me apps proliferating these "smart phones.

No doubt their dental hygiene wasn't on par either so getting digits, a date and eventual coitus likely was very different in the world of the human cave dweller.

If we believe scientism in this regard, then when men did have the option for sex they likely took it aggressively and quickly to ensure they had a better chance of offspring and continuing the lineage. Doesn't sound very romantic and if true, sounds downright horrible BUT if true it does lead one to a better understanding of why many men can be predisposition to ejaculate with the quickness. Aside from being overstimulated and allowing your body to be in control you may have traits passed down through the bloodline to push you towards a quick release.

Let's pile on shall we. Hop in the way back machine and travel with me to the mid 80's. Ah the land of big hairdos, parachute pants, acid wash jeans, and nonstop neon. This is my kinda town.

I was a nappy headed, light skinned, skinny boned goofball that hadn't quite discovered girls yet at the tender age of 13. To my credit I did have a pretty mean GI Joe action figure (don't you dare say dolls) and comic book collection going. Obviously, I wasn't what the "cool" kids would say was a lady's man. The talk around the pre-junior high locker rooms aside from arguing if you could truly die if you ate a whole bag of pop-rocks and then quickly drank a soda was the topic of girls. And Sex.

151

I am free, I am free, I AM FREE

Sex! Woah! Sex! When all my friends started talking excitedly about it I too joined in with my wealth of worldly knowledge on the subject. After all I had seen a couple Playboys and knew what a woman's breasts looked like, so I felt I was way ahead of the game. As the conversations proceeded, I quickly realized that many of my class mates had suddenly learned a new language. Was that Spanish? No. It didn't sound like Spanish. I had heard my friend Miguel's mom yelling in Spanish at him many times and this sounded nothing like that. Maybe Japanese or something because I had no fucking clue what these cats were talking about.

One day in my blissful ignorance of all things sex and girls off to gym class I go. At this time, I was well aware of the fact that my cock suddenly was doing things all on its own. I did have at least one experience of being called to the blackboard to solve a math equation while uncontrollably flying high. For those not in the know or those who have forgotten, the 80's was the land of bright colors and tight pants. Speaking of tight trousers (did I just use the word trousers) lets head back to gym class.

There we all are laced up in our Pro Wing kicks rocking our grey ring collar t-shirts and short, shorts. You guys remember those right? If not go watch an NBA game from the 80's. Knee high striped socks and short shorts were the style back then. It's one of many heart felt regrets that those of us that became products of the 80's hold onto with a knowing smile.

We're doing a rope climb at the beginning of class, so the teacher has us all circle up sitting cross legged in a circle under one rope which reached all the way to the big beam in the sky. I was lost in my thoughts of grandeur as I envisioned myself racing up the rope smacking the beam and with a big grin yelling out to my fellow classmates "YO, JOE!!"

Back to reality. As the gym teacher asks for a volunteer of course all us boys starting yelling for the glory of the rope to show the rest of the class our formidable greatness.

One girl also raises her hand. At the time I wasn't really attracted to girls yet, but something about her horned rimmed glasses and pigeon-toed stance just set me off. It could be that she was one of only two girls in our class that wore a bra which to my adolescent mind may as well have been the same as finding The Holy Grail or

I am free, I am free, I AM FREE
issue #1 of The Amazing Spiderman in a back bin of the local comic book shop.

Also, she was just the right amount of goofy, ignorant bliss that made me feel good inside. There was a kind of unspoken dork bond that we shared that perhaps she wasn't aware of, but I was keenly attuned to.

Already feeling a bit of a chubby coming on I quickly lowered my hand to ensure to save myself the potential embarrassment of a pitched tent in short shorts. It went from YO JOE to HELL NO with the quickness.

For the life of me I can't remember the girls name but as she starts climbing the rope and all of us of course looking up watching her climb my mind is suddenly blown and all of a sudden, I'm bursting at the seams with sexual energy. This is the first time I felt a surge of sexual energy and it was generated by an outside source. I look up at her climbing the rope and well.....I saw stuff I had never seen before because ol what's her face forgot to put on her undies when she changed out for gym class. Which in retrospect begs the question of why did she raise her hand to climb the rope if she knew she was bare assed under those tiny shorts?

I couldn't wait to get home after school that day. I had no idea what masturbation was or how to do it. Hell! I had never even heard of it, but I knew there was a devil seed inside of my cock pounding on the door demanding to be set free. I ran into the house, made a b-line for the bathroom, ripped down my pants and undies and started whipping it like mad. 5 seconds later as I ejaculated for the first time I though "WHAT THE FUCK WAS THAT"!!!

OH SHIT! I JUST LEARNED JAPANESE SON!!

No longer a stranger to the wilds of my own postpubescent manhood I stood poised for greater things like......sex. Yes SEX! OH HO!HO! Which unfortunately or maybe fortunately took much longer to come to fruition than my young adolescent mind dreamed of back then.

What's the point of that antidote? Aside from telling the embarrassing story of me first discovering masturbation and ejaculation it's important to take away from this story that from that

I am free, I am free, I AM FREE

day and many years moving forward I taught myself to cum as quickly as possible and taught myself that sexual pleasure was the act of ejaculating. Whenever I masturbated I wasn't doing it to be in touch with my body or sexual energy I was releasing pent up sexual energy as quickly as my right hand (sometimes my left) would allow.

I went through much of my sexual life not knowing what giving and receiving true sexual pleasure was/is. I understand now that for nearly all my life I had no idea what truly pleased me sexually because I never took the time to relax and enjoy my own moments of self-gratification. Instead I was chasing something. This my friends is what I have cleverly dub:

CHASING THE NUT

Most of us have done this our entire lives and often this has gotten us into trouble and helped to empty our bank accounts. Every time we masturbate or have sexual relations we are chasing that nut. Anything for that nut. Gotta have it! Eventually it controls you and you end up losing much of your power and basic wits to your programmed demands for sexual ejaculatory release.

Well I'm here to tell you that you will now be liberated from your ejaculatory prison. You are going to take your time and make it a special treat to find your sexual energy and to find out how to pleasure yourself with kindness and in a non-rushed atmosphere. After all, if you don't know what truly pleasures you how can you tell someone else like a partner what you prefer?

Perhaps even more important if you are not truly in touch with your own proper sexuality how can you have the attention and wisdom to be properly in tune with your partner while you're in the throes of passionate love making? Hhhmmm. Pretty good questions there.

For those of you who are currently more troubled with having a difficult time getting your manhood to perform, don't fret pet. We've got you covered like a jimmy hat. Sometimes this issue can be due to something physically happening within the body but the clear majority of the time it's psychological and/or something to do with your relationship with your partner. All kinds of things can cause

154

I am free, I am free, I AM FREE
these issues such as your toxic environment, stress, the foods you're eating, etc. Read on true believer, ecstasy awaits.

"EXCELSIOR!" – Stan Lee

I am free I am free I AM FREE

How To Masturbate Part Deux

Ok gentlemen let's get right down to brass tacks. I'm simply going to list out some steps to take to make this masturbation thing a bit more enjoyable and to assist you in becoming Multi-Orgasmic. Keep in mind that above all else we are taking our time and connecting to our bodies. From time to time you might need to just shoot some energy out for quick relief but for these practices we are focusing on taking our time and creating the mind/body connection. You don't have to apply everything written out here but don't be afraid to move in directions you've never gone before. With that said this section does not include cockrings, dildos, male vibrators, fleshlights or any other 3rd party objects. This is your body and mind working together. Don't forget to focus on your breathing, heartrate and energy location.

Rule:
Again, not a fan of rules but this is a save your cock rule so stick to it. There can be such a thing as too much of a good thing. I recommend you never go over 35 minutes in one session without taking a long break.

Step 1
Schedule:
Set time aside in your busy schedule to have between 15-45 minutes for this practice. I would recommend practicing at least 3 days a week. Remember as your skills increase you will stop spilling over and you will be conserving your energy not losing it. This is a reminder because you will not be sapping your energy, instead you will be building your energy up. I would recommend early morning hours while the rest of the house is asleep. This hopefully will give you privacy and will ensure that the energy build will be ready for a full day's use. If done in the late evening you may find that you will have a difficultly falling asleep.

Step 2
Location:

I am free, I am free, I AM FREE

You can of course have multiple locations to practice but typically you're going to go with a room in your domicile. I recommend taking the time to make it comfortable. It's not a bad thing to keep the lights low and create an ambiance that is relaxing for you. Whatever makes you feel comfortable and connected to yourself. Some soft non-distracting background music can be helpful.

Step 3
Required items:
Yourself. You can opt for oils (lotions are not recommended) and maybe a catch rag in the event you have a difficult time from stopping the burst of energy from spilling over but in theory you shouldn't need any equipment except for your hand and powerful imagination. Maybe a comfortable pillow or something of that nature can be helpful.

Step 4
Slow down:
Before you begin take just a moment to reflect on why you are masturbating. It's not to ejaculate it's to fully pleasure yourself with the specific purpose of not ejaculating. You're not chasing the nut. Here in the beginning your just taking time to truly discover your body sexually.

Step 5
Explore:
Don't just rush off to the cock and start stroking, take your time to explore your body. Your balls, abs, chest, nipples, the entire scrotum. Rub around a bit and explore to find out what parts of your body outside of your cock stimulates you. As you get more wound up you may find certain parts of your body become more sensitive to stimulus so don't forget to un-focus from the cock occasionally and let your hands travel.

Step 6
Awareness:
As you get going your likely going to start focusing more and more on your cock and the tip of your dick. Nothing wrong with that

I am free, I am free, I AM FREE

it feels good. When this starts to happen remember to stay aware of your breathing, heart rate and the buildup of energy in your root chakra. Typically, you would just let your breathing rapidly increase which would also speed up your heart rate, then the prostate pump would get going and you would explode. Not this time mister! If your masturbation hand is speeding up to get you that nut relax a bit and take some calming breaths. You may need to slow down your stroke as well to ensure you don't spill over.

Step 7:
Control:
Control started in the last step but here is where you start to really feel what you normally feel and that is your prostate pumping like crazy ready to shoot that seed out of your dick. You have a couple of options here.

Option 1:
Hands off and slow down your breathing. Feel the energy in your balls and with relaxed breathing let the energy calm down. The blood should start to empty a bit or a lot out of your cock. Let it empty just a bit then restart the session making sure to take your time and not to rush.

Option 2:
After you have practiced this at least a couple of times you will want to try out your PC muscle. As stated earlier I consider this more of the emergency break but it's nice to test it to make sure it's working and once you move to the bedroom where stimulus becomes more intense the PC close may end up being a good friend. If you've been doing your PC exercises, then you should be fully connected to it and able to snap it hard whenever you want. There are two things early on that will make it difficult to use the PC stop method effectively but as you continue to practice these will become easier.

Since you have been doing PC exercises and your body is new to these exercises your PC muscle could be a bit sore and tired making it difficult to use at the beginning of cultivating these practices. Like working muscles at the gym in a short amount of time your PC muscle will be strong and will not be as weak and sore making this

I am free, I am free, I AM FREE

technique easier to pull off. In the beginning even when using the PC close method, you may find that you did everything correctly, but the PC muscle was just a bit too tired for all that energy ready to release. The other difficult part of this technique at the beginning is the timing. You can for sure snap the PC muscle hard earlier than expected and ensure that you don't ejaculate. Once you start getting better at this you will start to get a bit cocky and will start snapping it closer and closer to the point of ejaculation and you may have some sessions where you snap it closed just a bit too late and boom your shooting semen.

Now repeat this as many times as you wish. If you go several rounds of nearly ejaculating and being able to stave it off congratulations you're getting there. If you need to release at the end of the session don't feel bad and go ahead and release. Moving forward we are going to be learning how to move the non-released energy.

I am free I am free I AM FREE

How To Masturbate Part Tres

Now that you have spent a couple of weeks practicing the masturbation tips from earlier let's shift focus to the more esoteric form of total dick control and move on to energy movements.

This can be the most difficult portion to wrap your head around but once you get it things really take off. The items we focused on earlier were primarily related to staving off ejaculation via physical means. A bit later when we get into moving this to the bedroom I will be adding a couple more tips and tricks for staving off ejaculation via physical means but for right now let's focus on your energy, where it is stored, how to move it around, when to move it around, and how to focus it into the correct chakra areas. I cannot overstate enough how important it is to refocus and redistribute your energy properly.

Separating Ejaculation from Orgasm

We're starting with the same steps as earlier. Get comfortable and start your regular masturbation session making certain to concentrate on your entire body not just your cock and shaft.
Masturbate and get close to ejaculation a couple times and perform the stop and restart method. After you have done this 4-5 times or more you're going to have a lot of energy sitting in your root chakra ready to go.
The next time you start to get close to spilling over and you stop instead of just waiting for the energy to calm down, close your eyes and focus on incorporating the steps below.

1. Inhale deeply and slowly and while inhaling concentrate on that built up energy at the rear of your balls. As your inhaling flex your PC muscle and tighten your anus. On each exhale you will relax your PC and anus muscles.
2. As you are performing the slow inhale of breaths on the 2nd or 3rd breath start focusing on moving that energy up the back of your spine to rise up your tailbone.

160

I am free, I am free, I AM FREE

3. After you have moved large portions of this energy up to your tailbone relax and focus on bringing that energy to the rear of your spine. This time as you slowly inhale you will let the energy build and as you slowly exhale bring the energy up the back of the spine all the way into the top of your head. You may feel a bit of a tingly sensation as the energy rises the 33 vertebrae of the spine.

4. Do the energy pull to the base of the skull for anywhere between 2-5 minutes depending on how much energy needs to be pulled up. You should start to feel a bit of pressure inside of your head as the energy is loaded. You will now need to focus on swirling that energy around inside of your head. Swirl the energy in a circle from the front of the head to the rear. Swirl the energy inside of your head around at least 40-50 times.

5. For the final step you need to move the energy from your head down to the Solar Plexus chakra point (the gut). To move this energy, you will move it down the front (when pulling energy up it goes up the rear of the spine to pull energy down it goes down the front channel). To start the flow of energy down the front channel first tilt your head up just a bit and touch the tip of your tongue lightly to the roof of your mouth. Now let the energy flow down the front of your head down the throat and let it fill your belly. To get this energy moving you can use your finger tips and gently slide them down your nose and down your throat. The built-up energy in your head should be able to follow the trail of your fingers and help get the energy movement started.

You can do this multiple times in a single session. You can masturbate using the stop method several times to build the energy in your root chakra. Once you have built that energy then you can move the energy up the back of the spine to the tailbone or skip the tailbone and move that energy directly up to the base of the skull. Cycle the energy several times inside the head then move the energy down the front into the gut chakra. You can do that as many times as you want and as it builds the energy will condense and bring strength to the entire physical body.

Pro Tip:

If you are already incorporating some meditation and breathing techniques on a daily or near daily basis it will be easier to connect to your energy stores and move them along your back and front channels. If you have not incorporated these practices, you may find it difficult to move the energy and the entire practice may seem like a bunch of hokum.

Everyone should be able to feel the energy. It's that same energy that builds up right before you ejaculate so it should be familiar. We are simply grabbing this energy tiger by the tail and redirecting its energetic flow. What can help to move it up the 33 vertebrae of the spine is to give your anus a quick tight squeeze as you imagine the energy being pushed up the spine via the anus squeeze. The anus squeeze can act as a pump to help push the energy up towards the skull.

Although this concept of staving off ejaculation and moving the energy may seem foreign and elusive with practice it will become natural. Once you start to master this practice you will gain great power in moving and storing your sexual energy.

After some weeks of practice and once more efficient you will be able to introduce and apply this energy manipulation to partner sex which is what we will visit in the next chapter.

I am free I am free I AM FREE

PARTNER SEX

All right time to put some of this training and self-cultivation practices to work with your partner.

This portion is written from the perspective of a Multi-Orgasmic man having consensual sex with a woman. It wouldn't make sense for me to write for homosexual sex because of my lack of experience and knowledge I wouldn't want to pass along information that could be misguided or damaging.

The primary focus of this section is on cultivating sexual energy and connecting the energy with your partner.

Now you've been practicing for a couple of weeks and are starting to feel the flow of your energy and you've built up some solid strength and control with the PC pull ups. The more you have practiced and the more in touch you are with your body, breathing and ability to move energy the more prepared you will be to start putting this to use once connecting with another person.

When you self-gratify you should now be operating on another level with your sexual pleasures. For those of you that chose you will find that energy manipulation allows you to utilize this energy in many ways outside of the pleasures of the flesh.

"With great power comes great responsibility". - Ben Parker

When you start to become proficient using MO with a partner you will find that you will be able to connect to and manipulate their energy as well as your own. Being completely aware in the moment and having the ability to be in complete control is an amazing thing but can also be dangerous. It's important that you understand you can assist in creating great ecstasy or you can assist in creating dark energies. That may sound a bit odd but if you consider for a moment that the practices of manipulating sexual energies have been around for thousands of years that comment should seem less odd. It's only because we live inside of a construct that highly manipulates our perceptions of sexuality and sexual gratification that saying something like light energy or dark energy when applied to sexual encounters seems at odds with our current knowledge and

163

I am free, I am free, I AM FREE

experiences. All writings here lean into gentle, light sexual energy movements and does not incorporate any dark or religious based energies.

There will be times you will find that you can keep going and you want to continue to build your energy and move it. When you are Multi-Orgasmic as the orgasms stack they become more powerful. You may also find that your partner isn't up to the task of marathon sex bouts on a regular basis. You may find yourself in the position where you want to continue but your partner will have spent all their energy. When these moments arise, you need to back down. You don't need to ejaculate so continuing to fuck while your partner is riding a wave of energetic ecstasy is not good for your partner or you. When these things happen simply relax into your breathing and move your energy through the orbit and down into your belly.

You also need to flex that PC muscle much earlier in the process when you are with your partner compared to when you are self-gratifying. Since you have been practicing this solo you can push right to the edge and flex the PC, take a breath and relax. This isn't nearly as easy to achieve when you're embraced in the throes of passion with your partner. It's best to stop earlier and tell your partner to wait so she too can stop the gyrations and the friction.

I am free I am free I AM FREE

PARTNER SEX WHERE TO START

Seems obvious. Start in the bedroom you fool!

Nope. Wrong answer.

A tremendous part of creating a deep loving sexual connection is to create the magic outside of the bedroom first. When you become Multi-Orgasmic sex becomes something much deeper as you start to feel and manipulate your energy and your partner's energy. The type of connection you gain from this movement towards energy connectivity is incredibly powerful, but it should not be based solely on genitalia and bodies.

I'm betting that we have all heard that the brain is the most powerful sexual organ in the body. Let's dive a little deeper into that because that is not necessarily true in my estimation.

We know we have electric bodies and brains, but many people forget that our hearts are an electrical system as well. If you research information regarding your electric heart via mainstream cardiology you will have a lot of excellent clinical information regarding the tiny cells of your heart being regulated via your hearts electrical system. You have conducting cells to carry the electrical signal and you have muscle cells to enable the heart chambers to contract. That's all well and good but what they tend to lose sight of is the fact that both your brain and your heart produce electromagnetic fields. In clinical settings these are measurable via a Magnetocardiography.

It's called a SQUID which is a Superconducting Quantum Interference Device.

Knowing and understanding that your brain and heart are electromagnetic is important. It's equally important to understand the measurable levels of electromagnetic activity in the brain and in the heart. In research (https://www.heartmath.org/assets/uploads/2016/10/biofield-nov2015-hammerschlag.pdf) conducted by Rollin McCraty and several others it was determined that the heart's electromagnetic field is about 60 times greater in amplitude when compared to the brain. Further the magnetic component is roughly 5000 times stronger than that of the brain's field.

I am free, I am free, I AM FREE

The point is that the heart is much more loving and powerful when compared to the brain. When people say that the most powerful sex organ is the brain I believe they really mean it is the heart.

Simply turning off outside influences such as the TV and spending time together will go a long way towards creating a deeper connection. I recall many years ago watching an episode of a show and they were interviewing a young lady that was dating a guy that had a life sentence in prison. I thought to myself "what an IDIOT! Why doesn't she date someone she can actually spend real time with"? She then went on to explain that a large part of why she was dating him was because of the deep connection they had created when she visited him. In the past when she dated men they were always too distracted and never had time to make a true connection. She further stated that in this relationship they spent hours just sitting and talking with each other and that she felt more connected to him than anyone she had ever known in her life.

In a way we all live inside of a social prison with so many distractions that keep us from connecting to ourselves and with the people we love. The example above should teach us all about the perception of shackles we allow to be applied to our psyche and how we can easily recognize and overcome these threads of invisible mental and spiritual bondage that hold us back from truly loving ourselves and others as we are meant to.

Work on building a foundation of love and trust in a relationship to open the heart connection. This doesn't have to be serious or a deep process. You just need to forget about the fake social construct occasionally and be yourself and have fun with your partner. To get started I am going to provide a simple list of things you can do with your partner before you get to the bedroom. These things should help stimulate the true love muscle.

Cook one of her favorite meals and get her talking about something she is passionate about. When conversing don't judge or give her a solution to something that she feels is broken. Just enjoy the meal with her and give her the space and comfort to discharge some of the negative energy that may be built up from her day.

Challenge her to a contest of who can find the best love song of all time on a music streaming app. As you are going back and forth pick something completely NOT a love song or pick a loud punk song

I am free, I am free, I AM FREE

that is about love. On your next pick choose a great love song and start slow dancing with her.

For the love of all that is Holy keep the TV and cellphones turned OFF!!

Go for a walk around your neighborhood or a nice location. Go for a walk around the neighborhood or drive a couple miles away and take a nice walk around a running river within a beautiful setting.

Don't underestimate the power of board games. It might sound a bit cheesy but keeping that TV turned off and playing fun games will help to create an intimate connection with each other.

Read a book out loud together. In the summertime make it an adventure to find new parks or other locations you have never been and make sure that at some point you bust out the current book your reading and continue reading from it. Pass the book back and forth and read it out loud to each other.

Go check out a sunset and wake up early one morning and check out a sunrise.

Drive around looking at houses in various neighborhoods and rank which ones you like.

Teach her how to play something that you like such as basketball, racquetball, rock climbing, thumb wars, etc.

Cook something together (maybe a desert you can use later in the bedroom).

Go to a nice museum and act as though you are the richest, snootiest people alive (it's super fun).

Dress up super fancy and go to the Opera or go to dinner. Let her know how beautiful she looks tonight.

Make her breakfast in bed.

Go swimming in the ocean or a river (stay safe).

We can keep going on this list, but I think you get the gist. Be spontaneous and have some fun just being you.

I am free I am free I AM FREE

SAFER SEX

When we address the topic of safe sex our initial instinct is to go through a list of various objects utilized to ensure we protect our physical bodies from STD's. While we will briefly review some of those options because they are important another key concept to address is being safe and in control of our intent.

As a young man I often had the intent to fuck a girl to boost my ever-expanding ego. It's rather comical considering how bad I was at the act, but the interworking's of a young man's mind often finds him pounding his chest and admiring his own greatness. The young ladies I was with were either vey kind or just as inexperienced. It's a funny thing when you believe your own greatness with something as natural and fundamental as sex.

When I was 20 I was in the Air Force and I had a dorm room of sorts. Very tiny room and I had a bathroom that joined to another service members room and we termed this as having a "sweep mate" or "piss mate". One Saturday evening I had a few drinks and went wandering around the dorms knocking on doors attempting to find some trouble to get into. Everyone seemed to be gone and I decided to make my way to a young female's dorm room because she often cooked delicious Mexican fare for me and one of my friends.

As I enter her room she is there with a girl that is not in the military. Her dad was some kind of high ranking official on base and everyone agreed she was the hottest girl in the area. She would come around and hang out with us occasionally, because she was 19 and it was an easy party spot for her.

As the three of us sit around talking shit and I unsuccessfully attempt to get Ms. A to cook me some food I notice that they seem to be flirting with each other a bit. My mind immediately snapped into action informing me that if I give a little nudge in just the right spot the dream of the ménage a trios is going to come to fruition this very evening. And for a couple of brief minutes the impossible was taking place. As I was guiding and coercing them into a threesome,
KNOCK! KNOCK!
NOOOOO!!!!

I am free, I am free, I AM FREE

Say it aint so! I try to convince Ms. A to ignore it but the soul sucking spawn of Hell on the other side of the door just keeps pounding on that son of a bitch and he breaks the spell.

At this point I'm feeling dejected. After all I had almost secured what to the peoples in my circle called the Holy Grail of sexcapades and I had allowed it to slip through my grasps. I wanted that damn Penthouse Playmate story but alas it was foiled.

Since Cat seemed already riled up a bit I told her to come back to my room, so I could show her.....well I don't remember some lame excuse to coerce her into my room. To my surprise the hottest girl in the area was down and we headed off to my room.

It didn't take long for us to get going and MAN was this the best sex I had ever had up until that point of my young and largely inexperienced sex life. She was scratching and screaming she even smacked me around a bit which was weird and exciting all at the same time.

The next morning, I made my way down to the common area to shoot pool and shoot the shit. My sweep mate approaches me, and we start talking about nothing of importance. He asked me if I had sex with Cat last night and my answer is what my answer always was when I was fortunate enough to get sex back then.

"HELL NO! I wish dude!"

I had a rule for myself to never talk about the sex I had with other people because that would be the first way to ensure that girl will not return, especially in small communities.

He then starts telling me that he heard me last night and knew that I was having sex with Cat. Eventually I started telling the great tale of my sexual heroism the night previous (even after being trained to only give name, rank and serial number while under interrogation) and felt pretty good because I could tell someone what an amazing lover I was.

After all she had been screaming my name and seemed to be losing her mind a bit while we were in the throes of passion and although I didn't want to betray my personal integrity I REALLY wanted someone to know. Then my sweep mate did something I

169

I am free, I am free, I AM FREE
completely did not see coming. He informed me that Cat was his
girlfriend to which I responded something to the effect of
    Oh....uh....ooops.

    But he didn't seem to care at all. He mentioned that he had just
broken up with her anyway and that's when it hit me.
    I wasn't an amazing lover that had gotten this girl to go crazy
with my amazing sexual prowess. She knew I was her ex-boyfriends
sweep mate and purposely and loudly oversold my performance as a
sex partner. In that moment I went from king of the jungle to the king
of shame.
    So, what's the point of that story? Both Cat and I had bad
intentions when having sex that night and as it turned out these bad
intentions had a negative impact on both of us.
    My intent was to prove how manly I was and to use Cat in a
sexual way to boost my super ego. Cat's intention is self-explanatory.
    Practicing this type of "unsafe" sex can and will happen to
young people the world over but as we learn and maturate we need to
move away from these unsafe sexual practices and ensure that our
intent is in line with keeping ourselves and our partner safe on a
physical, emotional and spiritual level.
    Check your ego at the door and learn to understand what your
intent is when making love with your partner. There may be times
when you both need a quick release of pent up sexual energy and in
these situations, you both should instinctively understand your intent.
There will be other times (hopefully most of the time) when your
intent will be to create a deeper connection to your partner and to help
them safely achieve greater levels of sexual consciousness.   To put it
a bit more succinctly.

    DON'T BE DICK!

I am free I am free I AM FREE

SAFER SEX PART DEUX

Let's make sure we overview protecting ourselves and our partners from those nasty STD's.

First get checked on a regular basis. If you have one sexual partner that you trust has only you as their sexual partner than statistically you're in a damn good place. You should still get checked as STD's can go for very long periods without showing any symptoms. It's best to know what you have if you do have something, so you can get the proper treatment.

Using physical barriers is typically the best resource for protecting yourself from potential infection of various STD's. This includes items such as condoms, female condoms or dental dams. The tried and true latex condom used by men is great for blocking most viruses, bacteria and other material that can be infectious.

Tips on condoms:
- Only use latex condoms unless you have allergic reaction to latex.
- Every condom only gets one use.
- Keep your condoms in a location away from direct sunlight.
- Don't use old condoms.
- During oral you can use a thin condom or a piece of plastic wrap.
- Put the condom on as soon as your hard.
- Leave some room at the tip to catch your cum and to lower risk of condom breakage.
- When pulling out hold the condom at the base to ensure it doesn't come off until you pull it off.
- Never double-wrap condoms. This increases the likelihood of breakage.

I am free I am free I AM FREE

GIVE AND YE SHALL RECEIVE

Short section here guys but one of my favorites.

The concept of give and receive should be self-explanatory in the context of sexual relations with your partner, so here are some simple ways to put it into practice.

She gets 20 minutes to do whatever she wants to you (within reason).
You get 20 minutes to do whatever you want to her (within reason).

She gets 20 minutes to tell you everything she wants you to do to/with her.
You get 20 minutes to tell her everything you want her to do to/with you.

That's it. Very straight forward. The 20 minutes can of course be adjusted lower or higher and you can expand on this simple concept.

I am free I am free I AM FREE

Let's Do It Right

Being a product of the 80's I didn't have access to porn like the youth of today. Back then getting your hands on a Playboy Magazine was a big deal. I was first exposed to sex on film when I was in the neighborhood of 12 or 13 which of course is much too young. I saw a couple minutes of one porn movie and felt confident that I had no idea what was happening on the screen.

When I was in Jr. High at about the age of 14 I had a friend, who had an uncle that ran a small video store. Yeah man VHS son! (please be kind rewind). Said uncle was closing his store for whatever reason and told us that we can take any movies and any number of movies we could carry with us in one trip before he sold his videos.

Of course, my friend and I made a b-line for the adult section which had its own separate room with black curtains drawn across the entrance for privacy.

I don't recall how many movies I got my hands on, but it was more than one and less than ten. When I got home I found a good stash spot and when my pops was gone on Saturdays and Sundays I would pop one in to educate myself on how to have sex. That was a HUGE mistake, but I think way too many American men have decided to educate themselves in this same fashion.

Let's look at people who are paid to fuck and take notes on how to have great sex. Bad idea guys. This rapid, deep thrusting doesn't make you more Alpha and in fact is going to get you closer to ejaculation much faster which at the end of the day is going to lead to a dissatisfied partner.

If you have derived your education on how to enter and move once inside of a woman from porn, then you need to let that knowledge go.

Guiding Principles
- Be fully in the moment
- Control your breathing and heartrate
- When getting close to the edge back off and take a short break or modify sexual positions.

173

I am free, I am free, I AM FREE

- Feel your energy mixing with your partners energy and be aware of the power of these two energies comingling.
- Be hyperaware of your partners levels of comfort and adjust accordingly both physically and emotionally.
- It's okay to talk dirty.

Well that's the end of the line for this fun filled chapter. There is a ton of stuff I left out but since this is a single chapter in a larger book, I must wrap this guy up (as should you).

Keep in mind that it's likely that your partner wants to reach the ideal heights of sexual pleasure and deep-seated passion. If you can master and control your physical body, you can then become fully aware and embrace the moment which can help to increase her levels of comfort as she has not been able to in the past. Even when we are with someone we have known and loved for many years it can be difficult and complicated to truly let go of fear when laying naked with your legs tossed open. A little graphic but the point is that even if you have been with someone for years and have had lots of sex there's a good chance they still feel vulnerable when it comes to their sexuality. With a renewed outlook which allows you to gain strength and confidence you can help to gently guide your lover towards a stronger connection in a safe fun-loving way.

Cultivate the solo practices, become proficient then share your new knowledge and strength with your partner.

I truly believe that you will create a deeper more meaningful sexual and overall healthy relationship with your partner when you practice this type of sexual healing. As this book is about self-healing keep in mind that in many circles sexual energy when cultivated properly is considered one of the highest forms of self-healing.

Please don't forget to be kind to yourself and your partner and don't put any unnecessary pressure on yourself.

With love,
Anan

Chapter 8. Electric Religion and Spirit

I've always had what I believe is a rather strange relationship with religion. Before I go on some diatribe that offends and derides organized religion, I would like to point out that today there are many small churches across the world helping to heal and empower their communities. From their perspective they are working to save souls and aside from the mega churches these community temples of worship are working hard one soul at a time to do what they believe is virtuous and righteous. And hey man I can dig that! Much of the writings and ponderings of this book are centered around sharing knowledge that I believe can help save people physically, emotionally and hopefully spiritually.

My first memories of the church were being dragged there against my will by our evil step mother. By evil step mother I don't mean the typical Cinderella story I mean the crazy bitch that body slams you into a wall for your dusting duties not meeting the proper criteria. What was the criteria? Who knows the bitch was crazy yo! Suffice to say for a 6-year-old to be forced into dress clothes that if he made the slightest mistake and got dirt on meant a beating getting dressed and making our way to church on Sunday was a nightmare. It often felt like dancing on a thin sheet of ice. It was bad enough to say something out of line in the house and get a smack but to say or do something potentially embarrassing or that anyway called attention to the family while at church would mean a deep plunge into the icy waters of despair.

Another downside to church in my adolescent mind was the indignity of having to be stuck inside instead of being outside playing in the park, laying in the tall grass staring up at the sky making shapes out of clouds. I would have to sit my bony buns on a hard bench, attempt to sit at attention, don't speak and listen to some old dude

I am free, I am free, I AM FREE

speak about......well I don't know I was a kid it was all gibberish to me. The bloodied, half-naked guy on the giant letter T seemed odd and out of place to my adolescent mind as well.

There were some good things about church though. For one I got a free donut which was a real treat. It was the primary reason I liked going to church as a kid so when there weren't donuts it was felt like a real drag. The other good thing about going to church as a kid is the fact that there were other kids there and sometimes they would toss us kids into a room and let us do what kids did in the 80's. Mostly played without fear of retribution for invading someone's safe space.

As time passed things in my young life got better and worse just as life tends to do to us humans. I think that's part of the deal with having this human experience and what better way to make sense of it then to go to church and try to figure out what the hell this is all about? At the age of 14ish I decided to do just that. I was now living with my sister and her husband and around 14 or 15 I decide I was going to figure this whole church, religion, soul, God, Devil thing out once and for all. I had always had a sense that God and the Devil were real but had no real teachings and no interest up until that point.

One hot summer I was visiting family in Boston. I had an amazing father in law Manny who was a hoot. He had a colorful past and wasn't shy to call anyone and everyone out on their bullshit.

The first night that were at Manny's house he cooks us all this amazing dinner. If I recall we had Seafood bisque and some other tasty vitals. That was an amazing treat for me since I had never experienced such fine dining and having it prepared within this house of joy and brutal honesty was exciting. This wasn't store bought preservative filled food this was pulled out of the waters and prepped in house.

At this time, I always said a silent prayer over my meals before I ate. For me it was a way to give thanks to God for the food upon my plate. Something I had been trained to do at an early age that had always stuck with me.

The foods on the table and Manny at the head of the table proclaims in his Bostonian accent.

"C'mon guys dig in. I slaved over this food what are you waiting for"?

176

I am free, I am free, I AM FREE

I steeple my hands in prayer over my plate, bow my head and start my silent prayer to give thanks.

"Son, what are doing over there"?

"I'm saying grace."

"What for?"

"To give thanks to God for my food."

"Well shit son you should be giving thanks to me. I pulled that food from the water and prepared it and put it on your plate."

I didn't say anything at that point. I went back to my silent prayer and after gorged my belly on amazing Manny prepped fresh seafood.

After I left Boston that summer a funny thing happened. That first meal with the family in Boston stuck in my head and heart. After getting back to Cali from Mattapan I started to think back to why I started blessing my food in the first place. I realized that it was drilled into my head when I was a young child by my step-mother. It wasn't drilled into me in a way that was loving and showed that taking a small moment to give blessings before consumption was a way to show respect and gratitude. It was more along the lines of do it or get a smack. That got me thinking deeper into God and religion and my brain started questioning everything.

Is God real?

How come none of my friends say grace?

If I can't hear or see God have I ever felt the presence of God?

The questions kept coming and I started to understand that these questions were too big for someone of my age with my limited life experiences to be able to step through.

So, I did what I often did in those moments of confusion. I put my head down, strapped on my metaphorical hard hat and decided it was time to go to work to sort this whole business out. That way the next time I saw Manny and was challenged I would have a better answer aside from a blank stare followed by silence.

177

I am free, I am free, I AM FREE

I visited several churches of varying denominations and spent time in bible study and community service. At 14-15 years of age Bible study felt like a real drag. All they talked about was DON'T HAVE SEX! God hates sex! I wasn't exactly a lady's man at the time, but I knew I wanted to have sex, so after several rounds of Christian Bible Study I told them "Good day" and never came back. It also didn't help that the hot 16-year-old girl running Bible study spoke at nauseum about waiting until marriage to have sex. When she started ramping up the no sex until your married talk my love affair with bible study quickly diminished.

I looked at the Catholic church but me and the Catholic church didn't get a long at all. I felt like I was being programmed like a robot and it struck fear in my young heart. Every syllable and body movement seemed to be a set of programmed commands followed by the exact necessary sequenced response from the human flesh occupying the pews. It was so insanely unnatural and bizarre to me that my Catholic adventure plunge into attempted soul searching was very short lived.

Next stop the Baptist church. I really enjoyed the Baptist church. Man, those Baptist churches know how to throw down and celebrate the word of The Lord. I started going regularly with a friend of mine from school. His dad was the pastor at the local church, and Chris and I had a group of about 10-15 teenagers that hung out regularly. Back in those days everyone just met up at the local food court. Chris was by far the most naïve of all of us but was a good person. He had a big heart but was incredibly easy to take advantage of because he seemed to instinctively trust everyone and didn't seem to have the ability to do anything out of spite or animosity. He genuinely cared about people and often went out of his way to help people. But he was also quite mischievous much like myself. Often Chris would have to leave the usual meetup spot early to help his dad at church and he would hear no end of the shit talking for it. Church boy, choir boy, etc. One day I decided I would venture to church with Chris.

We would go over on Sundays and Wednesdays and ran the sound board for his dads' sermons. It was fun mostly because I was hanging with my friend, watching people have a great time celebrating life and I was helping instead of sitting around attempting

178

I am free, I am free, I AM FREE

to ingest information I mostly wasn't ready for and mostly didn't understand.

I was already disillusioned with religion in general but one Sunday at this Baptist church I was instantly enlightened as to why I had this nagging feeling about church and religion in general.

I didn't know why it didn't fit for me, it was always just kind of an itch I couldn't scratch because I couldn't figure out where the damned thing was coming from.

On this Sunday in question Chris' dad and mother were standing on the bottom steps of the Church and warmly giving good wishes to his flock as they were existing. Chris and I were standing near goofing around talking smack as per usual. Chris' dad looks at me and says.

"Son, you shouldn't wear earrings in the house of The Lord".

We are now in the early 90's and most dudes didn't have earrings. Only the coolest of the cool wore earrings (and the gay's).

"Really? Why not?"

"It's disrespectful son."

"I don't understand. How are earrings disrespectful?"

"Well son, God gave you that body. By poking holes in it and then stepping into the house of God you show great disrespect for Gods work."

"But your wife is wearing earrings. Isn't that being disrespectful too?"

I didn't say it to be a dick it was just that his wife was right there and to me it was an obvious observation.

Chris punched me in the shoulder. Chris' dad glared at me then turned back to his flock and kept up his well-wishing duties. In that moment I understood what the religious itch was for me. I understood that these were men that were wielding the powers of mind control to interpret to others how they should live based primarily on the social construct and what society agreed or disagreed was right vs what was wrong.

Ok, so it wasn't the most profound of epiphanies but for a 15-year-old it was gold and I ran with it for most of my life from that point on. To be fair the television evangelical crooks of the 80's did nothing to help promote the word of God or the sanctitude of religion in general. Even as a little kid when I saw one of those crooks pop up

179

I am free, I am free, I AM FREE

on the tele it was obvious that they were thieves and they did a whole lot to disparage the name of God and organized religion.

I then started to delve into what it meant to be agnostic and atheist. I started to believe that there was some force that all of us were a part of, but that religion was simply man-made BS instituted to control the mindless masses. That felt like some deep thoughts on the subject to me at 16. I unfortunately fell deeply into the new religion of the day....scientism. Everything could simply be explained by beakers, tubes, 1's and 0's, and of course by one of the greatest unfortunate theories to hit modern man, Evilution. Not to worry evolution is easily proven just wait several thousand years and VOILA! Man is insignificant nothingness surrounded by infinite nothingness that came from.....uh....hey science where did we come from again?

The theologians say Genesis but that can't be correct because that is esoteric nonsense that is completely unprovable and without any merit whatsoever according to scientism. So, science what say you my good man? How did this whole shibangabang whirrlygig known as reality get going? Oh, that's right a singularity of nothing exploded into everything and we call that the Cosmic Egg/Big Bang theory. Wait!? Huh? That sounds strangely familiar. Where have I heard that before? Oh yeah "Let there be light"! Now who said that again? Could the Big Bang theory simply be Genesis with math?

Let's ponder a question. When you were going to school they taught you the Big Bang theory no? They did in fact provide these teachings to myself and my fellow classmates in our 80's and 90's American public schools.

Now as an a-dult without looking it up can you tell me who came up with the Big Bang theory (Cosmic Egg)? Yeah, I didn't think so. Don't feel bad I couldn't either.

Georges Lemaitre that's who. Who the fuk is that guy?! We should all know his name. He came up with the theory that governs all of physics and life as we know it. If you're reading a book right now it's all due to this here Big Bang theory that Georges has provided to us so why don't we know who this guy is? Every educated child in the so-called civilized world is taught it and our entire reality is governed by it. You should be asking yourself right

I am free, I am free, I AM FREE
about now. Who the fuk is that guy?!? Your Spidey-sense should be
tingling as you also ask yourself WHY you were never introduced to
who this guy is.

Regarding Evolution

Evolution is science, right? It's unobservable but does have
enough consensus from the scientific community to make it science.
Since it is not observable the scientific community must turn to the
fossil record to support their science of evolution. This is also
necessary because you cannot conduct science with Darwinism.

For humans the search for the "missing link" has been going on
for many years and we the collective consciousness of humanity have
been bamboozled many times over.

There was Ramapithecus in 1976. A small fragment of jawbone
somehow became an entire skeleton and the missing link. It also
turned out to belong to an orangutan.

Javaman was a Biggon monkey skull and a human leg bone
which later Eugene Dubois admitted he faked upon laying in his death
bed.

For 40 years evolutionist drank the Piltdown Man Kool-Aid.
This was a human skull combined with the jaw of once again an
orangutan. This hoax was pulled off in 1912 and it took 40 years to
figure out that the teeth had simply been filed down to appear more
human. Now that's just good science right there!

Neanderthal Man for many years was billed to the public as the
missing link due solely to the fact that some were found hunched
over. Turns out they were just good ol' fashioned humans who had
the misfortune of suffering from various types of bone diseases such
as rickets which caused them to stoop.

I am free, I am free, I AM FREE

In 1922 Nebraska Man was hailed as a great evolutionary find. What did they find? A tooth. Yeah, you find a tooth you can't identify and of course it's the missing link. Turns out the tooth belonged to an ancient pig. Not only did the "greatest" scientific minds of the time create an entire prehistoric race from a pig tooth they also famously denigrated William Jennings Bryan at the 1925 Scope evolution trials.

The one that really gets me is Lucy, primarily because I totally bought into this craptastic headline.

Do you guys remember Lucy? She was paraded around the world and had endless shows on popular television networks praising the finding of the oldest human skeleton. They sold us a bill of goods based upon a reconstruction that looked oddly human ape like and was displayed in many locations including the National Museum of Natural History in Washington D.C.

It's important to note that these findings allow the scientific community to further take humanity down the road of acceptance of evolution to prove that humans are powerless and beholden to random chemical changes. By this discovery they are now able to prove out their theory that human skulls and consequently human brains use to be smaller and via evolution our skulls and brains grew to allow us to evolve into the humans we are today.

Let's breakdown what they found and how they put this here fossil of proof together (mostly with plaster).

In the 1970's a French dude named Maurice Taieb discovered the Hadar Formation for paleoanthropology in Ethiopia. He thought to himself; this seems like a great spot to discover fossils and artifacts from ancient human cultures.

Frenchy invited a couple of friends to get in on the shenanigans. One American and a Brit to round out the crew.

November 1973 the American Johanson finds a fossil of a piece of a shinbone. He also finds a small portion of a femur near the piece of shinbone. He fits these scraps of fossils together and VOILA! The angle of knee joint shows that this is clearly an upright bipedal hominin.

182

I am free, I am free, I AM FREE

Sweet! We've got two tiny scraps of something that is potentially a human leg, let's find out how old it is.

Pretty old. Over 3 million years old according to their relative dating guessing, I mean "scientific" techniques. As incredibly flawed as radiocarbon dating is it can't be used for these types of fossils because the level of C14 in the atmosphere is even more incredibly inaccurate going this far back in time. Instead they rely on absolute and relative dating. Absolute meaning, they find a specific object with the fossils that they say they know for certain is from a specific date range such as a piece of volcanic ash. Relative dating involves comparing one object to others and to make up.....uh I mean scientifically outline a chronology. The date range is mostly made up because they can only account for the decay rate of the fossil.

In November 1974, a full year removed from the leg discovery Johanson is at it again. This time in a completely different location. A whopping 1.5 miles geographically detached from the location of the scraps of leg fossils found.

Not only is the location nearly 2 miles removed, but the depth of the location of the finds are completely different. 200 feet in depth difference yet somehow, amazingly still belong to the same single creature according to Johanson.

Mr. J and a grad student decide to check out a small gully. Wowza! Dowza! What's this!?!

BONES!

In the gully they discover 34 adults and 10 infants, and the prize of all prizes the impossible skeleton of Lucy which is 40% complete a feat before this discovery which was considered statistically near impossible.

Not only is the skeleton 40% complete but it is now humanities oldest ancestor and to complete the impossible trifecta is also believed to be an animal that walked upright.

How did Johanson and company know that this animal walked upright, after all they didn't recover any feet or hands which would have been a telltale sign. Let's read some comments from Dr. Johanson himself when questioned about this very topic.

I am free, I am free, I AM FREE

"In November 1973, during my first major expedition to Hadar, I found a perfectly preserved knee joint (minus the kneecap) at a locality numbered A.L. 128/129. All detailed anatomical analyses and biomechanical considerations of this joint indicate that the hominid possessing it, *Australopithecus afarensis*, was fully capable of upright bipedal posture and gait.

In 1974, "Lucy" was found in locality A.L. 288, situated some 2-1/2 km northeast of the knee joint locality. "Lucy" preserves a proximal tibia, as well as enough of distal femur, to indicate that the anatomy of this skeleton in the knee joint region was identical to that of the 1973 discovery. Hence, "Lucy" was also capable of fully upright bipedal posture and gait, as her hip and ankle joints also indicate. Stratigraphically, these two discoveries are separated by nearly 70 meters."

The LSD must have been flowing pretty heavy that evening during the celebration as they listened to Lucy In The Sky With Diamonds and so named this find.

With a handful of animal bones, a small fraction of pieces that appear to be a portion of a knee they pieced together an entire skeleton, a face with all too human eyes and paraded it around TV and the world selling it as proof of evolution and the "missing link".

Lucy's stats
Height: 3 feet, 7 inches
Weight: 64 pounds

Average female chimpanzee stats
Height: 3 feet, 9 inches
Weight: Range between 59 pounds up to 110 pounds

Every single major skeletal find during the Pliocene era (5.3 –
2.58 Million years old) is found in Africa. Specifically, in the
following regions:
Kenya
Ethiopia (a lot)
Tanzania
Chad

How many chimps are in South Africa?
No one knows because there are too many to even attempt to
count.
They did not find any feet or hands with the Lucy skeleton but
did find fossilized footprints in Tanzania that look exactly like human
footprints which is further proof for their cause.
What doesn't pan out as well is the fact that in later years they
find fossils from the Lucy species (Australopithecus afarensis) with
their hands and feet.
All of them have toes that curve like tree dwelling apes and
wrists that appear exactly as modern-day knuckle-walking apes. As
they find additional anatomic evidences that show Australopithecus
afarensis was a tree dwelling ape they seem to completely ignore it.
Which would lead one to believe that the fossilized footprints
they found in Tanzania that look exactly like human footprints were
probably human footprints as they clearly do not belong to
Australopithecus afarensis.
Another interesting tidbit regarding the Lucy find is the skull,
specifically the size of the skull. Evolutionist had assumed that these
in-between species would have developed large skulls to
accommodate a larger brain necessary for bipedal locomotion and
climbing down out of the trees. The thought was once they came

185

I am free, I am free, I AM FREE

down from the trees they would hunt and gather, creating tools and a bipedal gait all of which would require a larger brain and thusly a larger skull.

Unfortunately, the Lucy skull flies in the face of their own evolutionary concepts. Lucy's skull was roughly the same size of an average chimpanzee which brings the entire theory of how evolution supposedly evolved from ape to man into question by the very fossil claimed to be the link.

But alas there is a telling sign within Johansons own writings as to why the skull was put together to form such a small cranium.

When piecing together the pelvis they ran into some issues. The main issue being that when piecing together the fragments to form the pelvis they determined it must have been female due to the small size of the pelvis. So small in fact that it could only pass a very small skull through it. The skull size that could fit would be no larger than that of an infant chimpanzee which should make us all scratch our heads and wonder why this fossil wasn't simply determined to in fact be that of a chimpanzee.

There is much more damning evidence against Lucy being a link between ape and man which you can research yourself. Here are a couple of things to research and take note of:

Incorrect pelvic size for giving birth to larger brains/skulls.
Appendages for swinging from trees not bipedal movements.
Rib cage shaped like apes not humans.
Hausler and Schmid's reconstruction of Lucy (Lucifer)

Fun quotes from leading evolutionist around the Earth

"The evidence given above makes it overwhelmingly likely that Lucy was no more than a variety of pygmy chimpanzee and walked the same way (awkwardly upright on occasions, but mostly quadrupedal). The 'evidence' for the alleged transformation from ape to man is extremely unconvincing."

Albert W. Mehlert, former Evolutionist and paleoanthropology researcher. "Lucy - Evolution's Solitary Claim for Ape/Man." CRS Quarterly, Volume 22, No. 3, p. 145

I am free, I am free, I AM FREE
"Echoing the criticism made of his father's habilis skulls, he added that Lucy's skull was so incomplete that most of it was 'imagination made of plaster of Paris', thus making it impossible to draw any firm conclusion about what species she belonged to."

Referring to comments made by Richard Leakey (Director of National Museums of Kenya) in The Weekend Australian, 7-8 May 1983, Magazine, p. 3

"The absence of fossil evidence for intermediary stages between major transitions in organic design, indeed our inability, even in our imagination, to construct functional intermediates in many cases, has been a persistent and nagging problem for gradualistic accounts of evolution."

Stephen Jay Gould (Professor of Geology and Paleontology, Harvard University), "Is a new and general theory of evolution emerging?" Paleobiology, vol. 6(1), January 1980, p. 127

"We add that it would be all too easy to object that mutations have no evolutionary effect because they are eliminated by natural selection. Lethal mutations (the worst kind) are effectively eliminated, but others persist as alleles. ...Mutants are present within every population, from bacteria to man. There can be no doubt about it. But for the evolutionist, the essential lies elsewhere: in the fact that mutations do not coincide with evolution."

Pierre-Paul Grassé (University of Paris and past-President, French Academie des Sciences) in Evolution of Living Organisms, Academic Press, New York, 1977, p. 88

"Contrary to what most scientists write, the fossil record does not support the Darwinian theory of evolution because it is this theory (there are several) which we use to interpret the fossil record. By doing so we are guilty of circular reasoning if we then say the fossil record supports this theory."

I am free, I am free, I AM FREE

Ronald R. West, PhD (paleoecology and geology) (Assistant Professor of Paleobiology at Kansas State University), "Paleoecology and uniformitarianism". Compass, vol. 45, May 1968, p. 216

"The chance that higher life forms might have emerged in this way is comparable with the chance that 'a tornado sweeping through a junk yard might assemble a Boeing 747 from the materials therein'."

Sir Fred Hoyle (English astronomer, Professor of Astronomy at Cambridge University), as quoted in "Hoyle on Evolution". Nature, vol. 294, 12 Nov. 1981, p. 105

"Scientists who go about teaching that evolution is a fact of life are great con-men, and the story they are telling may be the greatest hoax ever. In explaining evolution, we do not have one iota of fact."

Dr. T. N. Tahmisian (Atomic Energy Commission, USA) in "The Fresno Bee", August 20, 1959. As quoted by N. J. Mitchell, Evolution and the Emperor's New Clothes, Roydon Publications, UK, 1983, title page.

"The entire hominid collection known today would barely cover a billiard table, ... the collection is so tantalizingly incomplete, and the specimens themselves often so fragmented and inconclusive, that more can be said about what is missing than about what is present. ...but ever since Darwin's work inspired the notion that fossils linking modern man and extinct ancestor would provide the most convincing proof of human evolution, preconceptions have led evidence by the nose in the study of fossil man."

John Reader (photo-journalist and author of "Missing Links"), "Whatever happened to Zinjanthropus?" New Scientist, 26 March 1981, p. 802

"The essence of Darwinism lies in a single phrase: natural selection is the creative force of evolutionary change. No one denies that natural selection will play a negative role in eliminating the unfit. Darwinian theories require that it create the fit as well."

I am free, I am free, I AM FREE

Stephen Jay Gould (Professor of Geology and Paleontology, Harvard University), "The return of hopeful monsters". Natural History, vol. LXXXVI(6), June-July 1977, p. 28

"And in man is a three-pound brain which, as far as we know, is the most complex and orderly arrangement of matter in the Universe."

Dr. Isaac Asimov (biochemist; was a Professor at Boston University School of Medicine; internationally known author), "In the game of energy and thermodynamics you can't even break even.". Smithsonian Institute Journal, June 1970, p. 10

"Why do geologists and archeologists still spend their scarce money on costly radiocarbon determinations? They do so because occasional dates appear to be useful. While the method cannot be counted on to give good, unequivocal results, the number do impress people, and save them the trouble of thinking excessively. Expressed in what look like precise calendar years, figures seem somehow better ... 'Absolute' dates determined by a laboratory carry a lot of weight and are extremely helpful in bolstering weak arguments.

"No matter how 'useful' it is, though, the radiocarbon method is still not capable of yielding accurate and reliable results. There are gross discrepancies, the chronology is uneven and relative, and the accepted dates are selected dates. This whole bless thing is nothing but 13th-century alchemy, and it all depends upon which funny paper you read."

Robert E. Lee, "Radiocarbon: ages in error." Anthropological Journal of Canada, vol.19(3), 1981, pp.9-29. Reprinted in the Creation Research Society Quarterly, vol. 19(2), September 1982, pp. 117-127 (quotes from pp. 123 and 125)

"The intelligent layman has long suspected circular reasoning in the use of rocks to date fossils and fossils to date rocks. The geologist has never bothered to think of a good reply, feeling that explanations

I am free, I am free, I AM FREE

are not worth the trouble as long as the work brings results. This is supposed to be hard-headed pragmatism."

J. E. O'Rourks, "Pragmatism versus materialism in stratigraphy". American Journal of Science, vol. 276, January 1976, p. 47

"A five million-year-old piece of bone that was thought to be a collarbone of a humanlike creature is actually part of a dolphin rib ... He [Dr. T. White] puts the incident on par with two other embarrassing [sic] faux pas by fossil hunters: Hesperopithecus, the fossil pig's tooth that was cited as evidence of very early man in North America, and Eoanthropus or 'Piltdown Man,' the jaw of an orangutan and the skull of a modern human that were claimed to be the 'earliest Englishman'.

"The problem with a lot of anthropologists is that they want so much to find a hominid that any scrap of bone becomes a hominid bone.'"

Dr. Tim White (anthropologist, University of California, Berkeley). As quoted by Ian Anderson "Hominoid collarbone exposed as dolphin's rib", in New Scientist, 28 April 1983, p. 199

Keep in mind that the evolutionary diagram that you have seen hundreds of times was first created in the early 1850's and was based on what they EXPECTED to find by digging for bones. In other words, it's completely made up symbolism.

Why is this a big deal anyway?

When digging for fossils evolutionist run into a glaring problem. The Cambrian.

As one digs into the Earth, they will go through various layers which have been named and categorized. When one digs deep enough, they get to the Cambrian layer. The Cambrian is the last stratum which contains fossils. Everything below this layer contains only single-celled fossils such as bacteria. The Cambrian layer is full

I am free, I am free, I AM FREE
of animal fossils from animals that are still roaming the Earth today.
All except vertebrates. That's a real problem for evolutionary theorist
considering there are no ancestral fossils below the Cambrian layer to
prove out the theory of evolution. The Precambrian strata should be
full of lower evolved fossils which lead up the higher evolved fossils,
but this simply does not exist.

Darwin quote from, Origin of the Species:
"To the question why we do not find rich fossiliferous deposits
belonging to these assumed earliest periods prior to the Cambrian
system I can give no satisfactory answer ... the case at present must
remain inexplicable; and may be truly urged as a valid argument
against the views here entertained" (p 309).

Richard Dawkins
"It is as though they [fossils] were just planted there, without any
evolutionary history. Needless to say, this appearance of sudden
planting has delighted creationists. Both schools of thought
(Punctuationists and Gradualists) despise so-called scientific
creationists equally, and both agree that the major gaps are real, that
they are true imperfections in the fossil record. The only alternative
explanation of the sudden appearance of so many complex animal
types in the Cambrian era is divine creation and both reject this
alternative."

Stephen J. Gould (evolutionist, Harvard University)
"Every paleontologist knows that most species don't change.
That's bothersome....brings terrible distress. ....They may get a little
bigger or bumpier but they remain the same species and that's not due
to imperfection and gaps but stasis. And yet this remarkable stasis has
generally been ignored as no data. If they don't change, its not
evolution so you don't talk about it."
Lecture at Hobart & William Smith College, 14/2/1980

Stephen J. Gould (evolutionist, Harvard University)
"We can tell tales of improvement for some groups, but in honest
moments we must admit that the history of complex life is more a
story of multifarious variation about a set of basic designs than a saga

191

I am free, I am free, I AM FREE
of accumulating excellence. ...I regard the failure to find a clear 'vector of progress' in life's history as the most puzzling fact of the fossil record. ...we have sought to impose a pattern that we hoped to find on a world that does not really display it."

Why does this matter?

The theory of evolution has lead scientist in modern history down dark and evil paths. Human zoos created in the name of Darwinian evolution were still around in America as recent as 1958. It also led to the American Eugenic Movement as American "intellects" rushed to embrace the theory of Darwinian Evolution and use it to remove historical American human rights. Darwinism in the mind of these high society scientist removed any sense of racial equality. From their point of view Darwinism proved out that some human races were more evolved than others and that man does not have free will.

The base concept for Eugenics was for man to take control of his own evolution by deciding who could procreate and who should not.

Why and how does that apply to you today?

Margaret Sanger was the founder of Planned Parenthood and by many is viewed as a champion of women reproductive rights. She also based most of the pillars of Planned Parenthood on the Eugenics model.

Let's look at an excerpt from her autobiography.

"I accepted an invitation to talk to the women's branch of the Ku Klux Klan...I saw through the door dim figures parading with banners and illuminated crosses...I was escorted to the platform, was introduced, and began to speak...In the end, through simple illustrations I believed I had accomplished my purpose. A dozen invitations to speak to similar groups were proffered". (Margaret Sanger: An Autobiography, P.366)

I am free, I am free, I AM FREE

Many will write this off as Margaret simply being a product of her generation and that this does not truly equate eugenics with Planned Parenthood. But she wasn't alone.

Vice President of Planned Parenthood Henry P. Fairchild was formerly the president of the American Eugenics Society.

Samuel Anderson sat on the board of directors for Planned Parenthood and was a member of the American Eugenic Society.

Edward (Hilda) Cornish was the Arkansas Planned Parenthood executive director. She was also part of the Arkansas Eugenics Society which later morphed into the Arkansas State Affiliate of Planned Parenthood.

Dr. Charles Dight was president of the Minnesota Eugenics Society and penned a letter to that most glorious gentleman Adolf Hitler. He wished Hitler great success in "your plan to stamp out mental inferiority among the German people."

For a real kick in the head let's look at Margaret Sangers work with "The Negro Project" then scratch our heads and ponder why there are so many Planned Parenthood abortion clinics within black and Latino neighborhoods. To note when they kicked off this plan in 1939, they enlisted the help of the clergy to deliver the message to their congregations.

"We should hire three or four colored ministers, preferably with social-service backgrounds, and with engaging personalities. The most successful educational approach to the Negro is through a religious appeal. We don't want the word to go out that we want to exterminate the Negro population. And the minister is the man who can straighten out that idea if it ever occurs to any of their more rebellious members." - Letter from Sanger addressed to Dr. Clarence Gamble

She wasn't saying they wanted to exterminate the black populace but instead was concerned that blacks in the south would view birth

I am free, I am free, I AM FREE
control as the white man's way of exterminating the black community.
Sanger for her part mostly despised the poor and feeble minded
regardless of their skin color. Black, White, Yellow, Puerto Rican or
Haitian if you didn't have money you should not be allowed to
procreate.

The new march forward in human evolution will be
transhumanism which is already rearing its ugly head. Buyer beware.

Wow that was a serious side note even by my standards. Let's
get back on track. Time to move on to the next chapter to find out
about our boy Georges Lemaitre

I am free I am free I AM FREE

GEORGES LEMAITRE

Good old Georgie boy was born in the year 1894. He spent his early years being groomed as a Jesuit at the school College du Sacre-Coeur.

For those not in the know it's of interest that Jesuits are an offspring of the Catholic church. It goes like this. There was this cat named Ignatius of Loyola who was a nobleman hailing from northern Spain. He obtained a leg injury during the Battle of Pamplona (or Siege of Pamplona if you wish) and while recovering from his wounds he came up with a "new" kind of formula for worship. He decided to write it down and teach it to others of faith. The primary principles being MEDITATIONS, CONTEMPLATIONS and PRAYERS. The meditation part makes more sense a bit later in these musings.

Anyhow, Ignatius along with six others took it to the next level by professing vows of poverty, chastity, and obedience. Obedience to who? Why the guy that sports a fish hat and walks with a stick with a pinecone embedded in it. Oops there I go getting ahead of myself again. More on that later. We're talking about the head honcho, the big cheese, El Hefe known throughout the World as none other than the pope. In this instance it was Pope Paul III in the year 1540 who probably said something to the effect of.

"Wait. What? You guys want to create a special vow of obedience to the Pope in all matters of your mission and you want to become my own personal soldiers? Sounds swellariffic to me! We should call you something like "Gods Army" because if there is one thing God wants of man it's to have an Army with his name attached to it. Ok, approved fellas."

The pope didn't approve this, but it was put to committee and they all said. "Hell yeah! Let's do this damn thing"! (or something to that affect).

This was great for the Pope on many levels but one of the keys being that one of the primary missions of the Jesuits cantered around education. These guy's love setting up schools, colleges, and

I am free, I am free, I AM FREE
universities and what better way to program....uh I mean "teach" than to get your own centres of scholastic learning in place?

Ok, all caught up on the bases of what it means to be a Jesuit? Good, let's move on.

It was only about a year that Georgie boy was hanging out with the Jesuits as he left to serve as an artillery officer in the Belgium Army during World War I.

After the war Georgie decided to further remove himself from the Jesuits as he decided to prepare for the diocesan priesthood. The diocesan's differed from the Jesuits in several ways but the primary difference was that Jesuits often were assigned to geographic locations that were terrible and were surrounded by people who were in desperate need of assistance. The diocesans on the other hand hang out in one spot and since they don't take vows per se they also don't have to fuss with the whole vow of poverty thing, so they can make it rain at the club without guilt.

While studying for priesthood he was also studying physics and mathematics. By 1920 he had his doctorate and by 1923 he was ordained as a priest. In 1923 he was introduced to cosmology and astrology.

In 1927 after a whopping 4 years of studying cosmology he published a paper which moved away from viewing the Universe as a constant and instead viewing it as an expanding Universe. Pretty wild stuff back then but nobody knew who the fuk this guy was so no one in the circle of astronomy groupthink gave a rat's ass about it. If you have spent nearly your entire life studying (and let's be honest creating) theoretical physics, it sure would be a kick in the nuts to give up a flat stationary Universe for an expanding Universe from the theory of a priest who does this as a hobby and is loyal directly to the Pope.

This does become very advantageous to the Pope by the way. Here he has this loyal priest with a doctorate who has now created the first "Cosmic Egg" for science to worship. How big of a grin would you have on your face knowing you may now have the ability to create the "let there be light" moment within the spectrum of scientism? And if you're really lucky this will be taught in public schools throughout most of the World. Good day to be Pope.

196

I am free, I am free, I AM FREE

One problem though. Most people thought the theory was garbage. After having a rap session with Einstein in Brussels in 1927, Einstein said.

"Your calculations are correct, but your grasp of physics is abominable"

Which leads me to another point. How do you spot a shill? Someone that is bought and paid for.

In January 1933, Georgie gave a seminar detailing his theory and Einstein stood up, applauded and said.

"This is the most beautiful and satisfactory explanation of creation to which I have ever listened".

At the same time, I imagine Nikola Tesla (not a shill) was probably saying something along the lines of.

"Oh, look Rockefellers dog is at it again. First they remove the aether now they went and made a "Cosmic Egg" to be worshiped".

Real Tesla quote:
"Today's scientists have substituted mathematics for experiments, and they wander off through equation after equation, and eventually build a structure which has no relation to reality."

Also, of note is the fact that Einstein informed President Franklin D. Roosevelt that Germany MIGHT be developing some sort of atomic weapon. This led to the U.S. creating the Manhattan Project which lead to "Fat Man" being dropped on a civilian population in Nagasaki, Japan which killed an estimated 60–80 thousand people. Also, of note Tesla was working on a "death ray" so maybe all these guys are nuts.

And there you have it. Einstein and several others backed the theory of the Cosmic Egg and here we blindly believe today. Science got their "Let there be light" moment to explain away their unworkable theories and Catholicism gets to usurp the energy of a bunch of suckers worshiping a Cosmic Egg.

One such backer of the theory at this time was Pope Pius XII who declared the Big Bang theory and the Catholic concept of creationism to be totally in line with each other. The Pope embraced Georgies Cosmic Egg theory as scientific validation for the very existence of God and the Catholic Church.

What's wrong with the theory that nothing exploded and became everything anyway?

Well,
Conservation of Angular Momentum for one.

If a spinning object breaks apart in a frictionless environment the fragments will all spin the same direction.

If the entire Universe began as a swirling dot, why do we have 2 planets and several moons spinning the opposite direction of everything else?

Both Venus and Uranus (too easy) being within our own galaxy have been observed and recorded as spinning the opposite direction as Earth and all other observable planets. If everything is supposed to be spinning from west to east, why do we have 2 planets spinning from east to west within our own local galaxy?

Oh, there's an explanation and it's fantastic and totally makes sense.

The French research institute Astronomie et Systemes Dynamiques has a beautiful theory about this. It's not that the Big Bang theory is a giant steaming pile of excrement. No, no, no!

You see Venus initially spun in the same direction as most other planets and it still does. It just uh you see it simply flipped its axis 180 degrees at some point. Yeah that's it! So, see this makes sense it's actually spinning in the same direction it's just that it's upside down now so when we look at it from Earth or anywhere else it just appears to be spinning backwards. Well either that or it just you know slowed down then reversed itself.
https://www.scientificamerican.com/article/why-venus-spins-the-wrong/

I am free, I am free, I AM FREE

There are also 6 observable moons spinning the wrong direction. Neptune, Saturn and Jupiter all have moons orbiting in both directions and all of these stellar bodies are found within our own galaxy. Which really makes one consider how you can have a theory that doesn't work within your own local galaxy but still boldly proclaim it does work and extrapolate it out to the entire Universe.

We're going to dive just a bit deeper into this line of information. Next stop, Dark Matter!

Why? Partially because Dark Matter is a pretty kick ass topic and because it's yet another craptastic theory and it will help lead us a bit further into another topic of interest. So, let's keep the flow going.

I am free I am free I AM FREE

WHATZZAMATTA WITH THE DARK MATTER

Georgy boy and gang put us in a great spot today if you're playing in the field of theoretics. You already have the truth, now you just need to build a computer model making up whatever variables you wish to ensure your theory fits within the model of this so-called truth.

If for example you theorize that gravity works as a constant and then when viewing the various stars in the Universe you find that Ooops that doesn't work, and you just broke the entire gravity model well there is a very simple solution.

Make up a new theory.

Let me set the scene for you trusty reader.

The year is 1975. Vera Rubin and a fellow staffer Kent Ford are two astronomers and they have the hefty tasks of figuring out how to view and measure the workings of gravity and gravitational pull within galaxies. Fortunately, Kent has an advanced spectrometer which allows them to work as a team to view Dark Matter (which isn't possible) allowing them to analyze the spectrums of light given off by a given galaxy (Andromeda in this instance, Vera's favorite).
The idea is that stars situated further away from the center of the various galaxies will spin around said galaxy at a different rate of speed compared to the stars closer to the center of the galaxy.
Once this can be viewed and measured it will help further prove gravity is the leading actor of movement throughout the Universe. This is a big deal because everything and I mean EVERYTHING is currently based on the gravity model.
One problem. As they find a way to view these movements they realize that everything is spinning at a relative constant, consistent speed. Regardless where stars are situated within the galaxy they are moving at the same rate of speed as all the other stars around the core of the galaxy. Like a spoke and wheel configuration (well get to that next).

200

I am free, I am free, I AM FREE

Basically, these guys broke the entire gravity model which makes for a really bad day of work. But hey this is all theoretical and we already know our answer is correct so all we must do is figure out how to prove our answer is correct. After all there is no way that gravity is not king.

So, they sat down talked it out and came up with a new/old theory to fix the mistake of inadvertently viewing something they shouldn't have. I imagine the conversation went something like this.

"Oh my Mr. Ford it looks as though we just broke the entire model governing the movements of all things within any observable galaxy"!

"On the bright side at least, my kick ass image-tube spectrograph can detect and track light better. Red shift rocks!"

"Look here Mr. Ford I'm a champion of the power of women within the scientific community. I can't be associated with breaking the entire model of gravity within the known Universe".

"Well it's not that bad. Look, we know that it must be gravity because we are correct, maybe there's just, I don't know more gravity everywhere that we can't see? You know Fritz Z already lobbed us up a softball back in 1933. Maybe we can just expand on that idea?"

"Hey that's pretty good. So, if we can't see it and everything moves in a completely different manner than we supposed, it must be there because gravity is king. It's just invisible on the limited spectrums of light we are able to measure."

"YEAH! Invisible gravity! That's fucking awesome"!

"It's a great theory but we need a better name. You know something that can be marketed and sold to the masses. Maybe something a bit more sinister, darker."

"That's it! We will call it…….DARK MATTER!" (insert maniacal laugh).

I am free, I am free, I AM FREE

"Yes. Yes! It can't be that our theory that gravity a relatively weak force within the Universe is somehow magically able to do the impossible is a dog shit theory. I mean after all by using our own tools for observation we can clearly see that the Universe would fly apart based upon our own observations but who cares this is all theory which means we can make up any BS we want. No. It makes WAY more sense that 98% of the known Universe is made up of an invisible substance, cleverly labeled "Dark Matter" (copyright, trademark all rights reserved)."

"Yeah that's perfect! Now when we can't explain things with the gravity model we will just use invisible gravity but name it "Dark Matter"

"Oooohhhh say it again!

"DARK MATTER"!!

"Sweet brosef. I see at least 40 more years of grants to study our friend "Dark Matter" God I love theoretical BS, I mean astronomy."

Ok, maybe those weren't their exact words, but you have to be drinking a whole lot of the Kool-Aid if when using your own theories your observations don't jive but you still decide to lean on yet additional older theories to support your other theories that do not align with what you are clearly observing.

They even have a name for this which they call the "galaxy rotation problem". The problem being that what they observe does not align with Newtonian Dynamics which is the underlying base driving all their theories. Dark Matter is ONE theory they must explain away this gaping hole and just so happens to be the most popular theory today, but of course this theory is sold to the public as an absolute truth. Not only that but nearly all other models and theories now need to account for Dark Matter.

Dark Matter is a form of matter that CANNOT BE
Directly observed

I am free, I am free, I AM FREE
Measured in anyway
Detected in anyway

It can't be seen, detected or captured in anyway and it's supposedly measurable because its existence is ***inferred*** through baryonic light matter.

The best theoretical model that today's astrophysicist present accounts for a whopping 5% of the known Universe. The other 95% is made up of Dark Matter and Dark Energy. By the way they need Dark Energy to help explain an expanding Universe, the root of support for that Genesis generated Cosmic Egg. Dark Matter is considered a repulsive force that allows the Universe to expand at an accelerated rate.

Numerically the current theoretical model of the Universe pans out like this:

Normal matter: 4.9%
Dark matter: 26.8%
Dark energy: 68.3%
For a grand total of 95.1% bullshit.

All of this collected data that tells you what the Universe is and how it functions is collected via radio telescopes. They collect radio frequency emissions from space and with this they then can tell you what reality is outside of the planet Earth.

At this point you may be scratching your head and wondering.

If Dark Matter is made up BS and gravity isn't nearly powerful enough to do the things claimed by scientism what in the heck can it be that allows for the formation of round like planets and something that even more fantastical is able to set these round balls spinning?

If you can't get behind the idea that space and the Universe don't truly exist. That we are unique and that we live on a motionless, infinite flat plane than please continue to the next chapter for some insights.

If on the other hand you do believe in the flat Earth model, I still encourage you to read on into the next chapter.

I am free I am free I AM FREE

EU or the Electric Universe. I know that sounds kind of crazy right?

What is this Electric Universe you speak of you might ask? I know I did.

For me the journey began with flat Earth. Perusing the online video outlets of fame, I kept seeing flat Earth pop up. At first, I just assumed it was a small collection of people trolling trying to get a rise out of the populace, but they just seemed to keep popping up.

Finally, out of frustration I decided to listen to the flat Earth theory/model, so I could point and laugh and shake my head in sympathy for all the silly flat Earthers out there.

How in the heck can anyone believe that the Earth is flat and motionless in today's day and age?

There are many reasons but before we get too far down that rabbit hole, I would like to point out something to all of those that believe that flat Earthers are somehow stupid or have addled brains.

Part of the beauty of the flat Earth movement is the willingness to ask questions. To stop blindly believing that the folks that are the keepers of the keys have your best interest in mind and are always telling the truth.

To me it comes down to some simple things here.

In one corner you have people that are looking at the world around them using physical science to view and measure the 3D reality around them. Within the confines of this view the Earth truly is both flat and motionless.

In the other corner you have large, collective bodies such as NASA and various colleges and schools of thought. Because of the amount of money getting thrown around they have high end equipment which allows for an expanded view of things outside of Earth. People working within these walls are programmed or indoctrinated to believe/worship specific "facts".

I am free, I am free, I AM FREE

Side note (I know again right): Even the Catholic Church has a very large telescope pointed out at the Universe looking around. This telescope is housed on a mountaintop (Mount Graham) in Southeast Arizona and is very impressive.

According to an article in Popular Science (April 23, 2010). Well it's not a telescope in and of itself but it is attached to a large telescope on Mount Graham which is 100% financed by the Vatican state.

This chilled instrument is supposed to help scientist at the University of Arizona to better see how stars are born. And this instrument has a pretty amazing name.

"Large Binocular Telescope Near-infrared Utility with Camera and Integral Field Unit for Extragalactic Research".

Wow! That's a mouth full. I wonder how or why they came up with such a long-winded name. Fortunately, they simply use a simple acronym for the device.

LUCIFER

Hhmmm. Curious. So, the Vatican has a large telescope pointed out at space which they have for some reason named Lucifer? Sounds legit, keep the money rolling into the coffers.

I got a little side tracked. What were we talking about?

Oh yes, flat Earth.

Flat Earthers are typically limited to their physical senses and some low-grade measuring tools. This certainly creates an environment of limiting the scale to which you can observe and record anything outside of Earth especially compared to the big boys.

On the big boy side, they have many more problems.

First and foremost, as mentioned above if you are in this camp you MUST believe certain truths regardless of the fact that many and most of these are theories, piled on top of mountains of computer models, on top of yet more theories. It's all become a ludicrous stack

I am free, I am free, I AM FREE

of cards, balancing vicariously between a lack of common sense and a lack of honesty.

Additionally, they have a MASSIVE issue of what lies at the base of the stack of cards. The guy holding all of this up is gravity.

Flat Earthers incorrectly believe that gravity is non-existent and believe that everything gravity related can simply be explained away by density.

This is only partially true, but gravity does exist and is measurable. The fact that it is in fact measurable should be something that every self-identified flat Earther embraces. Using scientisms own measurements for gravity disproves gravities omnipotent powers. Using their own measurements, you can see that gravity cannot do nearly anything that they claim it does and yet they base ALL their models and theories on it. Even if you think a flat, motionless Earth model is crap you should still be feeling a tingling sensation creeping up the back of your neck at the realization that the entire model of your perceived reality is potentially a complete and total fallacy.

In other words, if you use their own measuring variables for gravity it is FAR too weak of a force to do nearly anything, they claim it is currently doing. Every time they gain additional insight or observations into the various regions of the Universe, they discover that gravity is NOT the champion they claim.

So where did the theory of gravity come from? I think we all know what "truth" we have been indoctrinated into. An apple fell on some dudes head then he went "Oh hey look the local galaxy (he never meant for the theory to be extrapolated out to the entire Universe by the way) is put together and runs on this here thing called gravity. Yeah see there's this force that is like invisible ropes that hold the moon to the Earth and the Earth to the Sun and it's called gravity".

Sir Isaac Newton certainly was a very brilliant man and his works Principia which was published in 1687 eventually changed humanities outlook on universal gravitation, planetary motion and classical mechanics. As amazing as these accomplishments were Newton was at a great disadvantage when he wrote his great works which helped usher in a new era of man's place in the cosmos.

I am free, I am free, I AM FREE

Although he had access to many and all things necessary for a man of scientism of his time there was one thing absent for his century.

Electricity!

In the world we live today we are born into a reality in which we have always had the ability to cultivate flowing electrons and put them to task for us. We were born into this world that has streetlights, TV's, computers, transformers and all number of electrically powered devices that both work to ease the pains of living inside of perceived harsh natural environments and allows for 24/7 unnatural light to be available.

Newton and company did not have a true concept of electricity and certainly did not have the means to work with and test electrical currents, which really put him at a great disadvantage compared to today's scientific oligarchs.

The problem today is that they have built their tumultuous house of cards on a theory from yester year that isn't really panning out very well.

Now you have flat Earthers that understand that these theories are mostly garbage and as such use what they've got to make sense of the reality around them. Instead of using crazy theories they use physical sciences which mostly present a flat motionless potentially infinite plane.

The charge for the flat Earth model is increasingly ramped up by some people within various religions looking towards these physical sciences as proof of a creator. This I imagine can have a profound emotional impact on someone that is researching the flat Earth model. Once they realize that many in the scientific community have been indoctrinated into a specific model of reality and although they often are very intelligent people, they are putting their energy behind a false reality based on theories.

Losing faith in the scientific community one might go to greater lengths and start looking towards NASA for answers. Unfortunately, NASA has been producing cartoons for too many years to be taken seriously.

Another side diatribe here dear reader.

I am free, I am free, I AM FREE

It makes sense to look towards NASA and say, "Hey they've got all these pretty pictures of space, nebulas, galaxy's, etc. That is 100% proof that NASA is correct, and any doubters are just haters."

So, let's dig into let's say a pretty picture of a nebula.

These images are breath taking to look at and really puts into contrast just how little and insignificant I am and heck the entire hue-man race for that matter.

So how do they get these pictures anyhow? I doubt they bought the latest, greatest DSLR on the market and hitched a ride on a rocket and started snapping away, so what kind of camera took this picture (actually they kinda do)?

No camera took these picture because they are not pictures. It is in fact complete and udder rubbish!

Here's how they sold you bullshit and told you it was cow chips.

A satellite is outfitted with a "camera" that detects photons. They point this "camera" into the far reaches of space and take a "picture". What that really means is they capture the information regarding the photons then NASA's Deep Space Network beams this information to Earth in the form of a collection of 1's and 0's.

They then toss this photon captured information into a piece of software that convert the columns and rows of information into a black and white visualization.

A simple black and white won't do so they need to spice things up with a nice color scheme to ensure we are hooked.

Hhmm. But how to choose the colors for this black and white image? Usually they just assign colors to specific chemical elements. They then in essence play the coloring game by filling in the assigned color to the detected chemical elements and voila! BS beautiful picture complete. If it's not fancy enough just change some of the color pallets based on specific bands of light.

To fully understand how silly this is here are some steps I took today to find some of the beautiful images presented to us the public by NASA.

1. Went to the NASA website that displays an "Astronomy Picture of the Day" every day. (https://apod.nasa.gov/apod/archivepix.html

208

I am free, I am free, I AM FREE

2. Today is May 23rd and the image I clicked was "Spiral Galaxy NGC 4038 in Collision". The image is very beautiful in fact.
3. At the bottom of the page with the image I read who processed and had the copyright to the image.
4. I followed the link to the copyright owner who had credit for processing the image.
5. It belongs to a random dude with a flickr account that has 32 followers. Well that's odd now isn't it? Shouldn't these images being placed on the NASA website being marketed as "images" they captured actually be processed and have a copyright ownership to NASA instead of a random flickr user?

Quotes from NASA officials regarding how various telescopes such as Hubble capture images.

"We often use color as a tool, whether it is to enhance an object's detail or to visualize what ordinarily could never be seen by the human eye,"

"Creating color images out of the original black-and-white exposures is equal parts art and science"

In short, the human eye can't even detect the ultraviolet and infrared light utilized when capturing this data, so they run it through a computer to create made-up color images based largely on the chemical elements within the region of where the data was gathered.

Example
Hubble captured some data in 1995 of the Cat's Eye Nebula (gorgeous picture).
Oxygen Atoms
Hydrogen Atoms
Nitrogen Ions

A team at NASA then assigned each one of these captured data sets a color.
Oxygen: Blue
Hydrogen: Red

209

I am free, I am free, I AM FREE
Nitrogen: Green

Each color is applied to each chemical to create well BS.

Now you've got this beautiful image that is really nonsense.

Why does this matter?

It's another way in which you are being deceived for sure, but it
goes just a bit deeper than that.
  Philosophers have debated for many centuries as to whether
objects carry colors and we huemans merely detect these colors of
refracted light or if colors do not truly exist. They exist within each
hueman mind and thus perceived and experienced differently in each
hueman mind based upon many subtle factors. If you blindly believe
in these images it's a very subtle way to ensure you buy into the
reality that your mind does not create your reality but instead reality,
simply is and you are merely here experiencing it. It's a subtle way to
make you subservient to the 3D reality you currently find yourself
surrounded in. It may be a small thing but enough of these small
things proving to you that you are not special or in control of your
reality works to slowly chip away at the reality of your true nature and
power.

Side mission complete back to the thick of the plot.

Gravity does exist and is measurable and nearly every flat Earth
model removes gravity completely which puts us into a position of
some serious head scratching.
  Now we know that there is something else out there that we can
measure that might lead us down a slightly different path.
  Keep in mind that with the weak force of gravity it is believed
that this weak force is SO incredibly powerful (which it isn't) that it
sucked all the land mass of Earth towards it's center and is keeping
everything tightly stuck to it. And it spins. Hhmm. So why does it
spin? Did you ever stop to ask yourself why does everything in the
Universe spin including the Earth? I know I did. Let me give you the

I am free, I am free, I AM FREE

current official theory of why the Earth and all other planetary bodies are spinning.

13.7 billon years ago there was a spinning dot of singularity.
BANG!
(but not really rather space appears in the Universe)
Now everything expands rapidly at a hundredth of a billionth of a trillionth of a trillionth of a second (sounds legit).
Things start to cool down and get less dense and as expansion slows matter is formed.
It's dark for a really long time until the age of "reionization" which is a fancy way of saying hydrogen showed up to the party.
Now suddenly there are incredibly massive "clouds" of various cosmic material.
For some reason the clouds start to get heavy (hey it's not my theory).
So, what's causing the massive clouds to get heavy? Why gravity of course (when in doubt gravity is the answer).
Our own galaxy the Milky Way is formed 9 billion years after the Big Bang. Gravity causes a nebula to collapse and for some reason it starts spinning until it's spinning so fast it flattens into a disk to become the Milky Way galaxy.
Seriously that's it guys. It's all spinning due to angular momentum.

So, the Earth you are on right now is spinning because gravity, angular momentum and inertia.
This theory came from the mind of a philosophy professor by the name of Immanuel Kant somewhat borrowed from the astronomer William Herschel in 1785. Huh? You mean that the basis that forms NASA's current model on how everything in the entire Universe was formed and currently exist is based on a theory thought up by a philosophy professor in the 1700's?

YEP!

This Big Bang/Gravity model has no reasonable explanation for how all the cosmic dust just suddenly started spinning. It has no

211

explanation for how or why massive gassy clouds started forming into separate clumps and distinct bodies.

The base for the view of an expanding Universe is primarily based on the RedShift Light Theory which mostly doesn't work.

Another issue with gravity is of all thing's dinosaurs. That is the ones often depicted in Hollyweird movies. You know the ones that are 60 stories tall and easily roam about the Earth. The issue is that with our current measure of gravity vs. what paleontologist dig up and put together as dinosaurs are at great odds with each other. Our current measurements of gravity do not allow for these dinosaurs to have been able to take a single breath or heartbeat to push blood from their chest up to their sky-high heads. A heart strong enough to force blood that high would burst all surrounding vessels along the path. The mass of their heads would have been much too heavy to stay aloft in today's measurements of gravity. At 50-60 tons and over 100 feet tall these behemoths never could have existed in today's measurements of gravity on Earth. So, what's the deal? Are all the dino bones fakes? Was gravity acting in a different way during that period on Earth? Has gravity changed overtime on our planet and if so why and will it do so again? Either way I have a bone to pick with Dino.

How weak is gravity?
It is so weak that at the distance squared
4 times the distance it falls by 1/16 strength
8 times the distance it falls by 1/64th strength
16 times the distance it falls by 1/256th strength

That is not enough strength to hold stars lightyears away towards the center of the galaxy for which the star resides. Therefore, they had to invent Dark Matter which is just more gravity because measurable gravity is far too weak to account for what they themselves observe.

As we discussed earlier when observed by Vera and Kent it was found that stars spin very rapidly, nearly in sync like a bicycle wheel.

Imagine a bicycle wheel with the center of the wheel being the galactic core. The stars are like spokes on the wheel and regardless

I am free, I am free, I AM FREE

how close or far the star on the spoke is from the center it still moves at relatively the same rate of speed.

These are called Catherin Wheels. Gravity is nowhere near strong enough to hold a wheel of stars together, whereas it has been observed by plasma physicist that plasma particles can travel down a column to form Catherin Wheels. The exact same thing that is observed in space.

Since gravity alone cannot account for these observations we then move into black holes and Dark Matter to explain away the gaping holes in the gravity models.

Is there something that we can measure that does have the proper amount of strength and would allow for stars to rotate around the galactic center at the same rate of speed?

Back to our friend electricity and electromagnetism.

How much more powerful than gravity is electro magnetism?

Hold on to your hat's boys and girls because these numbers are mind boggling.

A thousand, trillion, trillion, trillion times stronger! That's a whopping 39 zeros following that 10.

BUT WAIT THERES MORE!

You know all that empty stuff that scientism has now labelled as Dark Matter to help explain why weak ass gravity is not able to prove out what their observations show them? Well it's much more likely this is plasma and is present in 99.99% of the known Universe.

Plasma is the fourth state of matter.

It fills the in between and is full of charged particles which carry electrical currents.

Why is this important?

As above, so below.

I am free, I am free, I AM FREE

Scientism will have you believe that you are a small insignificant piece of nothingness. Made up of various chemicals and atoms most of the scientific ilk pass humans off as a chemical mistake completely bypassing the awe-inspiring reality of our very existence. Your time here is short and is meaningless and you are tiny within the great expanse of this Universe in which we reside.

They are SO wrong!

You have an entire Universe living within your own electromagnetic body. Your body is electromagnetic, just as the stars above your head.

Every cell in the living body contains a small electrical charge.

Your nerve impulses are electrical signals which create energy fields. These energy fields form around your body. Billions of nerve impulses are generated by electric energy in your nerve cells.

What do you suppose is happening in the sky's above your head? A bunch of nuclear explosions or flowing electrical impulses just as in your body and every other living thing on Earth?

If you skipped the chapter on Partner Sex let me include an excerpt from that chapter here which will help to show the link between the Electric Universe and your electric body.

We know we have electric bodies and brains, but many people forget that our hearts are an electrical system as well. If you research information regarding your electric heart via mainstream cardiology you will have a lot of excellent clinical information regarding the tiny cells of your heart being regulated via your hearts electrical system. You have conducting cells to carry the electrical signal and you have muscle cells to enable the heart chambers to contract. That's all well and good but what they tend to lose sight of is the fact that both your brain and your heart produce electromagnetic fields. In clinical settings these are measurable via a Magnetocardiography. They call it a SQUID which is a Superconducting Quantum Interference Device.

Knowing and understanding that your brain and heart are electromagnetic is important. You normally are not going to be privy to this information looking at clinical data. It's equally important to understand the measurable levels of electromagnetic activity in the brain and in the heart. In research

I am free, I am free, I AM FREE

(https://www.heartmath.org/assets/uploads/2016/10/biofield-nov2015-hammerschlag.pdf

) conducted by Rollin McCraty and several others it was determined that the heart's electromagnetic field is about 60 times greater in amplitude when compared to the brain. Further the magnetic component is roughly 5000 times stronger that the brain's field.

I am free I am free I AM FREE

Let's talk Birkeland.

Kristian Birkeland went on and on about the aurora borealis being due to an electrical phenomenon. Birkeland believed that the Sun was shooting down charged particles towards the Earth and that the Earth's atmosphere worked to show the explosions of the charged particles against the atmosphere.

This of course was hearsay and the talk of a lunatic. This could not be possible in the current model of the Suns configuration. Birkeland was ridiculed by his peers who thought him crazy.

It wasn't until 1967 long after Birkeland's mysterious death in Tokyo that a US Navy satellite equipped with a magnetometer above the ionosphere was able to detect and observe the same magnetic disturbances which are attributed to Birkelands original findings.

It revealed that it was not in fact hot gas the Sun was shooting towards Earth but rather ionized particles running in currents to the Earths poles. This insight further points to the possibility of the sky's above our heads being full of electrically charged particles as are nearly all regions of the hueman body.

Going by the observations leads one to surmise that the Sun is not a thermonuclear furnace shooting explosions all over our galaxy. The observations point more to a gigantic ball of electricity powered by Birkeland currents tying into all other electric stars throughout the Universe. The Sun does not necessary generate electricity but is a gathering point for electricity from throughout the galaxy. This is further proved out by the fact that the Sun when measured shows to be cooler on the inside and hotter on the outside. If this was thermonuclear it would be the exact opposite in that it would be much hotter towards the center and become cooler as it moved towards the surface.

Electric currents flow towards the Earth and are called "solar winds" although that title makes little sense. Earths magnetosphere is a covering of plasma that works as a protective barrier for the flow of electromagnetic energy hitting the Earth.

Telluric currents are electrical currents which run through the Earth's oceans. Don't believe me? These currents have been mapped by oil companies for many years in their attempts to find large oil deposits. I came across a wonderful book that had many stories

I am free, I am free, I AM FREE

regarding humanities work with electricity and in one story the author took a deep dive into the creation of the telegraph system in the United States and Europe. By his findings these same telluric currents were utilized to help power the telegraph system (amazing story actually).

There are 5 known states of matter that we are currently aware of. We are going to outline 4 because the fifth doesn't help us in these discussions. If you want to know what it is it's the Bose-Einstein condensates.

Matter:
The makeup of the Universe such as atoms, molecules and ions. Matter is anything that has mass and takes up some sort of space.

Solids:
Tightly packed particles of matter that have little room to move because they are so tightly packed together. Because they can't move much they generate low kinetic energy.

Liquid: Bit of an oddball. The particles are still packed tightly together but takes on an undefinable shape. Still generates low amounts of kinetic energy because they are still tightly packed.

Gas:
Gas particles are loosely packed. You can confine a gas but if you don't it will just keep spreading out. If you put it into a container it will spread until it fills the entire container. Gas has a much higher level of kinetic energy.

Plasma:
The guy we are less familiar with. Primarily because we don't see it here on Earth much, but plasma is considered the most common state of matter in the Universe. Plasma has highly charged particles with incredibly high kinetic energy.

The gravity model as outlined by Newton and carried on today by NASA and others is a complete failure when attempting to test. It fails every simulation, computer modelling and everything they observe through a telescope.

217

I am free, I am free, I AM FREE

The plasma model on the other hand has been tested and when tests are conducted in a lab they form the same Catherine Wheels just as what is observed through a telescope throughout the cosmos.

It's odd and disconcerting that astronomers know that 99.9% of the known Universe is in a state of highly charged raw electrical power called plasma yet completely ignore the possibility of a model of the Universe that is electric at its base and utilizes localized gravity instead.

There are several books written about the EU.

As above, so below.

Time to press on into something completely different (kind of I guess). To Egypt HO!!

Chapter 9. The Spirit

Egypt and The Ankh

Salvation is to be found by selflessly serving others, being in nature, with people and the Universe for the simple sake of loving fully without expectations.

You have been deceived by scientism to believe that you are a mud man descended from an offshoot of apes. Over billions of years you "evolved" from mud slime to the human you are now. Humans are thought and taught that we exist as a mistake.

Although you can experience and create love, you and your children are told that is just random happenstance. This was all random and although you can witness all the beauty of the creation you are and the creations you are surrounded by you are taught this is

I am free, I am free, I AM FREE

all random (or a computer sim, or whatever newfangled theory they supply tomorrow to cull the masses).

Prior to scientism, religion was the king of confusion. You can only get to God and Heaven through the church as we are the only ones deemed able to speak directly with the higher powers. Who appointed us this role? We did so suck it! For better or worse Martin Luther (not King) changed all that.

One thing that did not change was the fact that the church (the Vatican) is a secretive organization that continues to work to confuse you and prevent your true ability to find your higher self. If you are agnostic or atheistic in your world view your probably asking yourself why you should give a crap? I will give you what are a couple of reason why to care. Don't believe this is an open secret society, you should consider a couple of things.

The Vatican has over 50 MILES of shelves lined with documents dating back to at least the 8th Century. Why not share this knowledge of human history? Even if you are not catching the Holy Spirit this should be a cause for concern as it's likely hiding historical human events of significance.

Almost no one is permitted into these secret vaults. In fact, only "qualified" clergy and from time to time some academics.

If you are somehow permitted you have to write ahead of time requesting the exact material you wish to review, although this is impossible since you can't possibly know what materials actually exist within these secret vaults.

These vaults are guarded 24/7 by the Pontifical Swiss Guard. It's interesting to note that Vatican City has its own de facto military. Why? If this church state exists to hold your hand and take you to a place of higher consciousness why do they have their own military? Recruits must be unmarried Swiss Catholic males between 19 and 30 years of age who have completed Swiss Armed Forces training.

The courtyard located at Vatican City has a huge bronze pine cone statute representing the pineal gland. The largest pine cone statue in existence.

The Pope carries around a ceremonial staff which has a pine cone embedded towards the top or "crown" of the staff. The staff representing your spine and the pine cone representing your pineal

I am free, I am free, I AM FREE

gland at the "crown" of your head (they are not hiding this information and wear the symbolism outright).

The Pope along with Catholic Cardinals and Bishops all wear the open fish-mouth mitre (hat) which was also worn by the Babylonian priests as a representation for the worship of a fish God Cybele and Dagon.

Pope Francis Coat of Arms depicts a SUN, an eight-pointed star and of course a pine cone.

The Vatican represents one of if not thee greatest financial power on this Earth. They are shrouded in secrecy, and rituals which they force their followers to practice that are in place to worship hidden esoteric Gods.

There are many leaders in church's working hard to try to do what they believe is the right thing. To save souls and bring salvation to the masses.

Genesis 32:30 (King James Version) "And Jacob called the name of the place Peniel: for I have seen God face to face, and my life is preserved."

This is interesting. What is Jacob referencing here? One would assume he is speaking of a geographical location called Peniel during his worldly travels. If these writings are based in allegory however then we get a completely different reality of which Jacob speaks.

Pineal Gland:

The pineal gland physically exists within all humans. It's smack dab in the middle of your head right between your brows. It lacks the variable lens and other features of your other two physical eyes. Even so the pineal gland is sensitive to light as we are light beings which plays a significant role in your circadian rhythm. The pineal gland along with the suprachiasmatic nucleus play a key role in regulating your circadian cycle.

The pineal gland in esoteric and modern times is symbolized by the pine cone. The word itself comes from the Latin word 'pinea' meaning pine cone. As most of our language is backwards and determinantal to who and what we truly are symbols represent our true language of communication. Throughout human history we can

I am free, I am free, I AM FREE

see that many languages are represented with symbols as opposed to some form of letters.

Portions of ancient Egypt represent one such civilization. Nearly any time you reference ancient Egyptian culture you will see their hieroglyphs. One very popular symbol within the Egyptian culture is the Eye of Horus. The rod of Osiris was also topped with a pinecone further symbolizing the pineal gland.

One thing you may not realize is that the Eye of Horus is a symbol for the 3rd eye or pineal gland.

That guy is inside of your head right now. And doesn't that seem odd that these ancient people created a symbol that is a replica of the very eye that is located in the middle of your forehead right now? Isn't it yet more odd (probably just a coincidence) that in the medical world this is referred to as the pineal gland and that the Bible specifically references visiting the land of Pineal to come face to face with God?

A further deep dive into the Egyptian culture and we find much more information presenting itself. As outlined in the Multi-Orgasmic chapters (told ya it would come around again) I outlined the fact that the act of sexual intercourse can and should go much deeper than the physical pleasures of the genitalia. It's a bit fitting that we live in a world today that both glorifies and is horrified by sexuality. This is because sex has been perverted on both sides of the coin.

The church often will pontificate about the sins of the flesh whereas the television and social media outlets by contrast will attempt to overstimulate your frontal cortex with overtly sexual depictions that focus solely on the physical acts of sex. Both sides have manipulated and distorted sexuality to empower themselves. Hollyweird primarily for profit and the church to garner control.

The Egyptians used some of the techniques I touched upon in the MO chapter, however they took it several steps further which ties into sexual energy, vibrational resonance and religion to an extent. They had a deeply involved Egyptian Tantra which outlined the ability to use sexual energy to move energy through the various chakra points to reserve vitality and stave off disease. This is very much in line with what the ancient Taoist also practiced but one of the roots of the

I am free, I am free, I AM FREE

Egyptian sexual energy workings lie in that very famous Egyptian symbol the Ankh.

If you decide to listen to the popular theory (you know the crap you will hear on popular cable outlet channels and repeat it to others as truth) you will be told that the Ankh symbol you see on Egyptian staffs is a representation of their sandals. Yeah, seriously.

The famous Egyptologist Sir Alan H. Gardiner thought the Ankh developed from a sandal strap with the top loop going around the ankle and the vertical part that goes in between your big toe. To be fair not everyone is on board with this theory. Another popular theory is that the Ankh symbol derived from the belt buckle of the goddess Isis which might make more sense as this would represent the vagina and symbolize the fertility of life (in the afterlife).

Even scientism agrees that energy does not die it simply moves from one place to another. We also know that our bodies are coursing with energy that animates us and gives us life. If you have practiced some or all the items from the MO chapter your further aware that you can move this sexual energy up the spine and into various chakra points and can retain this energy for better health and vitality.

The Egyptians knew this as well but believed in a different practice for moving energy. They believed that the male sexual energy needed to be controlled in a deeply esoteric fashion unlike those found in other ancient cultures. They believed that they could control their sexual energy in a way to allow for infinite pranic energy and further worked to create their own Merkabah's (light bodies). They believed that the Ankh was the key to this success.

We're getting ahead of ourselves, first let's talk about the Ankh and believe it or not we will also touch on its relation to one of the most recognizable faith-based symbols in our reality today.

It is thought that the Ankh known by the Egyptians as "the key to life" (afterlife) started showing up around the Dynastic Period (3150 - 2600 BCE). It was also affectionally known as the "cross of life". The Ankh largely represented the breath of life for preparation for the journey into the afterlife. The early Coptic Christians understood this and took the Ankh symbolism as their own. These early Christians utilized this symbol to represent the promise of Christ to provide them everlasting life but it's almost as if they only partially

223

understood the meaning of the Ankh and did not fully grasp how it was utilized to move energy through the body.

In the MO chapter we learned various chakra points and reviewed the human Microcosmic Orbit. I provided only basic information to accomplish the ability for you to experience moving energy up your spine and into various chakra points. What I did not explain is that there are additional "meridians" within your microcosmic orbit. Imagine lines of energy (similar to Earths telluric currents) shaped like tubes going up and down your spine. Now imagine these same types of loops coming from the front of your body and looping over your head to your back.

Everything starts and comes back to the Heart chakra. If you can visually imagine that you are only aware of energy flow from the heart chakra straight up and down the spine and left to right, you have the symbol of the Christian cross. The same symbol that over time morphed from the full Ankh symbol that the early Coptic Christians were using.

If you further understood that there are additional meridian lines that loop from the heart chakra if you were to view these energy channels from the side instead of just straight ahead you would find that the symbol changes from a cross into an Ankh.

Christianity continued to grow in popularity (even though they are unfortunately a target it seems by every available media outlet) and by the 4th century CE most symbolism of various older religions ceased to be worshipped, but not that of the Christian cross which appears to have derived its symbolism from the Ankh.

The Coptic Christian church inherited the cross symbolism to represent the eternal life through Christ. The Egyptians however revered the Ankh in many ways including it being the key to eternal life as well as the union of two opposites such as male/female energies (sexual energies). It is here within the union of these two energies that we find an interesting use of the Ankh, sexual energy and the Egyptian rod.

These ideas are going to bounce around a bit, but they do all relate to each other. The Egyptian rod was a straight staff typically made of wood. If we recall Moses had a most famous wooden staff as well. The Staff of Moses was used as a key symbol in the Bible as it served many functions including transforming into a snake and then

I am free, I am free, I AM FREE

back again. This symbolism represents your spine as the wooden staff and the energy power of your Kundalini which is the coiled snake at the base of your spine that rises up your spine (wooden staff) to find its way to your crown chakra to find Christ consciousness.

The Egyptian rod was further equipped with a tuning fork at the base of the rod. The top of the rod had the ability to attach an Ankh to it. In this scenario the Egyptians were putting the Ankh on the top of the rod and using the rod like the human spine and would use the tuning fork to send vibrations up the rod and into the Ankh. The Ankh would serve the purpose of looping the vibrational energy back down the rod (spine) to allow this energy to flow and reverberate for long periods of time. This was used as a teaching tool and a symbol for moving sexual energy up the spine and into their Ankh conduit to allow their sexual energy to loop. All of this was to achieve adding energy to their Merkabas (light body's) to prepare for higher consciousness and the afterlife.

The Saqqara complex was utilized for teaching the healing arts of vibrational healing. These Egyptian temples were used as sound healing rooms and were surrounded in cone racks to resonate frequency for healing the cells of the body.

All this talk about sexual energy, Egyptian symbolism and religion specifically Christian religion all comes to a crescendo in the next chapter. Hold on tight it's going to be a bumpy ride.

CHRIST WITHIN

Yep Christ within, but first another rudimentary anatomy lesson that we will apply some esoteric knowledge on top of currently understood medical knowledge.

<u>Claustrum:</u>

It's common knowledge that your brain has a right and a left hemisphere. I'm sure you've heard people say they are either left brained or right brained.

Two Hemisphere Characteristics	
LEFT	RIGHT
Linear Thinking	Imagination
Math	Intuition
Logic	Holistic Thinking
Sequencing	Visualization

The claustrum is a thin layer of grey matter located in each cerebral hemisphere of your brain just above your ears. These two thin layers are your claustrum a term derived from "cloister" (German: kloster) which is a term that historically means a place where monks and nuns go to live a secluded life of studying scripture.

The claustrum is sagially located in the cerebrum. There is an oily fluid produced every month within the claustrum in men once they hit puberty. In esoteric terms this oily substance is referred to as Christos (Christ, Greek: Christos "oil", Manna from heaven). This Christos fluid flows down from the claustrum into the pineal gland. The pineal gland then uses this sacred secretion and secrets its own yellow substance (honey) to the Pingala (electric) and the Pituitary Gland (Mary, mother of Christ). It also secrets a white (milk) substance to the Ida, thus the term the land of milk of honey.

The pineal gland (male essence) gives the oily substance it's electrical properties whilst the pituitary gland (female essence) gives the oily substance it's magnetic properties.

This area is also the area that resembles the eye of Horus. When the brain is sliced in half this area is the exact shape of the eye of Horus which is depicted in so many Egyptian hieroglyphics.

These two different sections of the secreted oil then continue the journey and flow down then go through the semi-lunar ganglia and the solar plexus where they then produce a seed.

The solar plexus is also referred to as "Bethlehem" which is also the house of bread and biblically is the birth place of Jesus of Nazareth. Jesus also referred to himself as "the bread of life" and this is part of the reason that within some religions they ritualistically

I am free, I am free, I AM FREE

practice eating the bread of life. There is also the Lord's Prayer which
has the line "give us this day our daily bread". Even the word bread
in the context of the Lord's Prayer is derived from the word Epiousios
which is a hapax legomenon meaning a word that only occurs once in
the written record and the entire language. The term epiousios/bread
does not simply mean food nourishment and is so peculiar that it has
stumped scholars for centuries.

In the Bible it is said that Israel is promised to return to the land
of milk and honey. Understand that the land of milk and honey is not
a geographical location but resides within your brain where the oil is
initially split into the milk and honey as described above.

Returning to the land of milk and honey is referring to the seeds
necessity to journey back up the 33 vertebrae of the spine and back to
the pineal gland. It's important to note that the human spine has 33
vertebrae and that Jesus died at the age of 33 (or there a bouts) in the
year 33 AD.

The fishy, oily substance is said to be the Christos whilst the
seed is said to be Jesus. The fishy oil must migrate back up the spine
(swim up) The first internal biological process (miracle) the seed
(Jesus) performs is to transform water and oxygen into red blood cells
(wine) during the chemical fusion (wedding) in the lungs (Cana)
which are connected to the blood circular system (Galilee).

The seed must journey out of the lower levels of the body which
is represented as the physical world we live within. This lower region
is your root chakra where your primary energy is based in sexual
energy. The 3D reality that our two eyes (the two thieves crucified on
the left and right of Jesus) present to us is the fallen world of Saddam
and Gomorrah (sex, sex, sex). As the two thieves represent our two
eyes that pick-up photon light Jesus is crucified in the middle of these
two thieves and represents our third eye, our pineal gland and the eye
of Horus. In this depiction of the Bible Jesus represents the greatness
of the enlightenment that exist within all of us if we can migrate the
seed out of the sexually energized reality of the physical world.

During the Christ's mass the seed within the body, allows for the
son/sun to be reborn. Illumination works through the process of
putting down the ways of riotous behavior during the rebirth of the
seed (typically 3 days during your moon sign) and attempting to walk
the path of righteousness. In this way the seed will allow you to be

228

I am free, I am free, I AM FREE

reborn and spiritually transformed from the lower mind (physical 3D reality) and rise up to enlightenment. By rising this reborn oil back up the grey matter is activated and reborn "Thou anointest my head with oil".

If you've been following along through the journey of these pages and specifically were able to practice some of the items laid out regarding moving your energy up your spine then you will be familiar with the actual sensation of moving your energy up your spine and into your head. For any of the above to make any sense whatever having performed some of these exercises first and experiencing these sensations yourself allows for this information to make a bit more sense.

There are many groups out there that state that The New Testament is a book about meditation, yoga, and moving pranic energy through the body. They further believe that the teachings of Jesus were rooted more in internal enlightenment which at times make sense as much of our written historical records tell of people becoming secluded from society for a period then coming back enlightened (Jesus fasting alone in the wilderness for forty days and nights for example).

On the other hand, you have practicing Christians that I imagine are tired of people high-jacking their religion to fit their own narrative.

And now for something completely different before we move forward towards our healing modalities.

I am free I am free I AM FREE

NIKOLA TESLA

NIKOLA TESLA.

I am free, I am free, I AM FREE

The light of the body is the eye; if therefore thine eye be single, thy whole body shall be full of light ~Christ
Matthew 6:22

"If you want to find the secrets of the Universe, think in terms of energy, frequency and vibration." ~Nikola Tesla

"If you only knew the magnificence of the 3,6,9, then you have the key to the Universe." ~Nikola Tesla

According to the synoptic gospels Jesus was hung on the cross on the third hour.

According to the Bible he died on the 9th hour.
So, he hung on the cross for 6 hours.

What is so important about the numbers 3,6 and 9?

Let's start by reviewing one of our greatest minds of modern history. No not Einstein silly.

Nikola Tesla.

Strange that this man is responsible for allowing us to enjoy and often take for granted the incredible world of electricity surrounding us in this 3D reality. This articulating current (A/C) that surrounds us and brings great ease and too much comfort to our everyday lives exist because of Nikola Tesla.

Yet, I don't recall his name ever being mentioned through my stint of public indoctrination.

So, who is this cat? Why is he important to helping us achieve our higher selves and why is his quote about the numbers 3, 6 and 9 so important?

Let's give some background on Nikola Tesla.

Nikola Tesla was born in July 1856. He was of Serbian descent and spent most of his youth learning craft making from his mother who was considered exceptional with her ability of creativity.

I am free, I am free, I AM FREE

Nikola Tesla credits his mother with being a great inventor that allowed him to nurture and grow his own prowess in this field as well as develop his eidetic memory. His father was an Eastern Orthodox priest and he too was known for having an amazing memory. Tesla's father had a rather extensive book collection and was known to give sermons in which he would recite exceptionally long passages in several languages. Nikola had a special connection with his mother and loved her dearly. He also had a somewhat odd connection with his father who he referred to as his "earth father".

"Altho I must trace to my mother's influence whatever inventiveness I possess, the training he

gave me must have been helpful. It comprised all sorts of exercises—as, guessing one another's

thoughts, discovering the defects of some form or expression, repeating long sentences or

performing mental calculations. These daily lessons were intended to strengthen memory and

reason and specially to develop the critical sense and were undoubtedly very beneficial. "

Early on it was obvious that Nikola had a specially gifted mind. He studied advanced education in engineering and physics and Nikola had an affinity for the physical sciences. That is when testing he was not a fan of large equations to explain his theories. Instead he utilized real life testing inside of this 3D reality to show his inventions work.

That's not to say that he was bad at math. In fact, he was so gifted at being able to perform advanced integral calculus equations in his head....... WHEN HE WAS 14!

Some of his teachers thought that he must be a cheat because it simply should not have been possible for him to be able to perform these feats.

We should consider the fact that he was in Croatia/Serbia and in 1884 the schools in Europe and the US were much more demanding compared to what is shoveled into our brains in today's century. Back then high school children and younger were expected to take calculus, and either Greek or Latin. Even so Nikola Tesla clearly stood out from the rest as a particularly gifted mind even at a young age.

He was also rather precocious. In his own autobiography he writes about several incidents including almost drowning a dozen times, nearly being cremated and almost getting boiled alive and entombed lost and frozen. Tesla believed he survived these various incidents not by chance but by the fact that his ability to have visions flash in his head which often showed him visions that would inevitably lead to his escape from danger.

A major factor in Nikola Tesla developing a mind that could 100% see his creations in every detail was due to an infliction which caused him great pain and sorrow in his youth.

He would receive strong images inside of his head accompanied by flashes of light. These images were so powerful that Nikola could not see physical objects in our 3D reality clearly. The images were of objects and scenes in which Nikola had truly seen they were not made up from his imagination.

At times someone would speak the word of an object and Nikola's head would explode with an image of the object in vivid detail and Nikola could no longer differentiate if the objects were truly tangible or were simply a conjured vision from his mind.

These images were so clear and vivid that Nikola at times would reach out to touch them only to find that they were not truly there in 3D space. It was more like a 3D virtual reality in front of him.

Nikola came up with a clever way to rectify the pain of these images constantly presenting themselves. Whenever an object would appear he would then force it to be replaced by an object he was familiar with. This helped but he quickly realized that he had a limited supply of objects to conjure as he was primarily conjuring up images of objects from his limited surroundings within the cottage.

To move past this limitation, he started traveling deep inside of himself to travel to far away cities and towns. Initially he had difficulty and the foreign objects were blurry and indistinct. After a period of deep concentration (meditation) he was able to bring these things into deep focus and clarity. He states in his writings that he traveled to these cities and met people and made great friendships. He in fact felt that these friendships were greater friendships than the ones he made with fellow students in school.

He kept this up until he was 17 when he decided to become serious about inventions. It's kind of crazy to consider the fact that he had hundreds of patents and was able to create the concept of AC and the electric motor completely in his head before he built it but that's

I am free, I am free, I AM FREE

how the man worked, and this is why so many of his concepts could be flushed out successfully.

After escaping his predetermined fate to be a clergyman he became a full-time inventor and in 1844 traveled to the US seeking out Edison to show him his great AC invention. Tesla had no luck in attempting to sell his AC invention across most of Europe. Unfortunately, Edison too wanted nothing to do with AC and instead hired Tesla to work in his workshop to perfect DC.

Edison had just invented the light bulb (not really but that's what the masses believe). Edison needed something to power his light bulbs and electricity was a new and wonderous element.

Edison was a genius business man, and a great inventor. His first patented invention was the automatic vote recorder in 1868 but it was his invention of the quadruplex telegraph in 1874 that really helped him take off as a business man and inventor.

He sold the rights to the quadruplex telegraph to Western Union for $10,000.00 then a couple years later invented the sextuplet telegraph.

Being infused with money he was able to setup a workshop ("invention factory") and went on to hire several inventors to toil away the hours within the invention factory. He paid them to do much of the remedial tasks such as repetitive testing, so he could free up his time, but he would also patent their inventions in his name and then would aggressively market the inventions.

After working in Edison's lab for a year Tesla found himself in a difficult situation. He left Europe because he could not get anyone to invest in his AC invention. He came to the U.S. in the hopes of convincing Edison to fund his AC invention, but Edison wanted nothing to do with it. Tesla was working from 10:00am until 5:00am day in and day out for Edison so he could build his promised wealth and start working on his own inventions.

At the end of the year Edison did not pay Tesla and Tesla obviously wasn't very fond of this outcome. George Westinghouse then bought Tesla's patents on AC and Tesla now able to be properly funded was able to overtake DC with his AC invention along with his electric motor. It's a fun brilliant story of these going back and forth in the public in an all out brawl to attempt to make their electric invention the de-facto for society.

234

AC power was superior in several ways but one of the keys was its ability to push electricity over great distances. If society would have adopted Edison's DC we would have electrical power plants on just about every block.

Tesla also was not a big fan of Einstein's theories and works or the works of most scientist of the time.

"Today's scientists have substituted mathematics for experiments, and they wander off through equation after equation, and eventually build a structure which has no relation to reality."

And it is within this realm of mathematics that we find ourselves diving into one aspect of mathematics that may be unfamiliar to you. First note that humans did not invent math, instead we discovered the existence of math which may seem benign but is a rather important distinction when considering how we and the Earth on which we reside came about. Math is everywhere and is considered the universal language. Math resides within patterns. Some of these patterns are known as "The Golden Ratio" and "Sacred Geometry".

Since both The Golden Ratio and Sacred Geometry have been discussed at length by many let's look at another lesser known pattern of mathematics and see how this may play a role in our greater understanding of ourselves, the Universe and quantum physics.

I am free I am free I AM FREE

Vortex Math

Vortex math is found nearly everywhere not just numbers on a computer screen or calculator for the old folks. It's found in your DNA, in plants and animals as well as within galaxies.

Vortex math is base 9 math not base 10 as is the norm that most of us have been taught. As such only the digits 1-9 are utilized. In vortex math there is an important repeating pattern.

Most mathematics as utilized today are useful tools for utilizing numbers to obtain quantities. Vortex math on the other hand is utilized to define qualities of numbers which is a different concept when applied to number theory.

The discovery of vortex mathematics goes back at least to the ancient Babylonians, although their version was much more complex and beautiful compared to what we do with vortex math today.

At its base vortex math helps us see just a bit of how mathematics can show energy expressing itself. This concept further shows numbers being alive not simply being utilized as equations to derive quantities.

Let's begin with an important repeating sequence at the root of vortex mathematics.

1,2,4,8,7,5 1,2,4,8,7,5 1,2,4,8,7,5

This repeating pattern creates an "Infinity loop."

Notice the missing numbers 3,6 and 9.

The 1,2,4,8,7, and 5 represent the physical world while our 3,6 and 9 numbers represent polarity in energy, frequency and vibration.

One of the basic concepts of vortex math is doubling and the 2-binary system.

Cells and embryos follow this doubling pattern while developing.

I am free, I am free, I AM FREE

3,6 and 9 do not belong to this physical world. They work in the quantum and govern the physical realm in which our bodies reside.

The governance of energy, frequency and vibration is the key to free energy which is something that Nikola Tesla claimed that he could achieve. This may be part of the reason why his papers were taken by the United States government upon his death. Till this day there is much speculation regarding his papers since Nikola Tesla worked on many fantastical projects aside from free energy including a "death ray".

The primary tenant of working with vortex math is to double the number then add the remaining digits until you have come to a single digit.

Let's start the doubling and reduction to a single digit with the number 3.

$3+3=6$
$6+6=12 \ (1+2=3)$
$12+12=24 \ (2+4=6)$
$24+24=48 \ (4+8=12, \ 1+2=3)$
$48+48=96 \ (9+6=15, \ 1+5=6)$
$96+96=192 \ (1+9+2=12, \ 1+2=3)$
$192+192=384 \ (3+8+4=15, \ 1+5=6)$
$384+384=768 \ (7+6+8=21, \ 1+2=3)$

Here we can see that 3 bounces to 6, then back to 3 and back and forth they go for infinity. As you double the numbering sequence, then add the remainder down to a single digit you bounce back and forth between the numbers 3 and 6.

We know that 3,6 and 9 operate outside of the physical realm but as we start doubling starting with 3 we see that 9 is still further freed from this pattern. The pattern consistently continues to equate to 3 and 6 only. The 3 which governs the Southern Polarity of our physical reality bounces over to the 6 which governs the Northern Polarity then bounces back to itself. On and on it goes.

If we now move on to the number 6 we will see that it first bounces over to 3 in the Southern Polarity, then back to itself in the Northern Polarity and continues for infinity. So, 6 repeats the same pattern as 3.

6+6=12 (1+2=3)
12+12=24 (2+4=6)
24+24=48 (4+8=12, 1+2=3)
48+48=96 (9+6=15, 1+5=6)
96+96=192 (1+9+2=12, 1+2=3)
192+192=384 (3+8+4=15, 1+5=6)
384+384=768 (7+6+8=21, 1+2=3)

Next let's start doubling with 9 since it is being so elusive.

9+9=18 (1+8=9)
18+18=36 (3+6=9)
36+36=72 (7+2=9)
72+72=144 (1+4=5+4=9)
144+144=288 (2+8+8=18, 1+8=9)
288+288=576 (5+7+6=18 (1+8=9)
576+576=1152 (1+1+5+2=9)

Notice in this pattern that everything always comes back to 9. It's as though 9 operates within its own Universe in which it does not need to adhere to any patterns that all other numbers are bound to.
Imagine you have a Northern polarity and a Southern polarity.

The North side is governed by the number 6 and the number 6 is responsible for governing the numbers 8,7 and 5.

The South side is governed by the number 3 and the number 3 is responsible for governing numbers 1,2 and 4.

These are two opposites represented in many ways to man such as Yin and Yang, white and black, masculine and feminine and magnetic polarities.

A circle is 360 degrees

3+6+0=9

I am free, I am free, I AM FREE

We can see that 9 governs the entire circle for all perceived reality. That is all other numbers reside within the 360-degree circle.

Let's half that circle to 180 degrees.
1+8+0=9

Let's half that to 90 degrees.
9+0=9

And then to 45 degrees.
4+5=9

Then to 22.5
2+2+5=9

11.25 degrees.
1+1+2+5=9

5.625 degrees.
5+6+2+5=18, 1+8=9

2.8125 degrees.
2+8+1+2+5=18, 1+8=9

You can keep going and you will continue to see that the angle always reduces to the number 9.

We can see by connecting 3,6 and 9 within the circle we get a triangle.

The angles of the 3 sides of the pyramid is 60 degrees.

60 degrees multiplied by the 3 sides equals 180 degrees.
60x3=180 degrees
1+8+0=9

How about we toss a square in that circle since it has 4 sides instead of 3.

239

I am free, I am free, I AM FREE
Those four sides would be at a 90-degree angle from each other.
90x4=360 degrees
3+6+0=9

You can keep expanding the sides and multiply the angle by the total number of sides and you will continue to reduce to 9.

As we bisect the circle it continues to reduce to 9 until we reach a point of singularity.

When we bisect our polygons inside of the circle it continues to an outward vector of divergence.

Number 9 represents both the yin and the yang. It is both a singularity and a vacuum. The so called Cosmic Egg and the vacuum of space itself.

The sum of all digits excluding 9 equals to 9.
1+2+3+4+5+6+7+8=36
3+6=9

If we do the opposite and add 9 to any other digit it equates back to that number.
9+4=13
1+3=4

9+5=14
1+4=5

9+6=15
1+5=6

9+7=16
1+6=7

9 equates to all numbers and to 0 or nothingness.

1,2,4,8,7,5 is the repeating pattern of our 3D reality.

I am free, I am free, I AM FREE

The number 3 governs the Southern Polarity of the 3D reality, whereas the number 6 governs the Northern Polarity of the 3D reality. The numbers 3 and 6 can be equated to Quantum Physics from the human perspective.

The number 9 operates outside both the physical realm, quantum physics as well as operating within both realms. This could be equated to 4D or greater perceptions of reality without our limited 3D perceptions.

Quantum physics is now starting to catch portions of scientism up to some of the realities that have been written by peoples of past cultures for thousands of years with regard to polarity and electromagnetism and how these exist within humans, the planet Earth, throughout the Universe and into dimensions beyond our 3-dimensional reality.

Side note for the flat Earth community that also seems to have a love affair with Nikola Tesla. If you look at his works, they are based on a spherical Earth not a flat Earth model. Many of his patents contain his illustrations which clearly depict a spherical Earth.

In fact, one of his greatest ambitions of creating free energy is based specifically on the spherical Earth model.

Tesla performed calculations based on a spherical Earth with a crust made of heavy metals and silicates. His calculations showed that if he was able to create a very powerful EMF at the proper resonant frequency the entire planet would shift to a new electrical oscillation. The same thing we visited in the sound chapter regarding frequency's coming to resonance. This in theory would have made Earth a giant electrical capacitor.

The flat Earth model would never support the ability to create a new frequency resonance. The electric wave being created would need to bounce back towards the originating location in a symmetrical pattern to propagate and feed itself for amplification, which wouldn't work if the Earth was flat unless the originating location is dead center of a flat Earth. Colorado Springs is not anywhere close to center on any flat Earth maps/theories and Tesla's works were being conducted in Colorado Springs.

Tesla proved out his calculations via experimentation. An experiment in which he managed to short out a dynamo at the power

241

I am free, I am free, I AM FREE

plant. This experiment proved that his calculations which took into account a spherical Earth with a fixed diameter were successful.

Nikola Tesla further details Earths electrostatic charge within two specific patents.

Tesla received two patents for this radiant energy device; U.S. Patent No. 685,957 – Apparatus for the Utilization of Radiant Energy and U.S. Patent No. 685,958 – Method of Utilizing Radiant Energy.

Part of the reason this is important is with regard to the fact that what Tesla was attempting to do was to condense and harness the energy that lives between the Earth and its upper atmosphere. His goal was to transform this into an electrical current. Tesla the gentleman that brought us the AC power we still use today pictured the Sun as a giant ball of positively charged electricity. The Earth being negatively charged energy.

The positively charged Sun particles bombard the Earth but get trapped in the upper atmosphere (ionosphere). This leaves about 60 miles of space between the positively charged Sun particles in the ionosphere and the negatively charged Earth particles. This leaves a high level of voltage differential sitting inside of these 60 miles of airspace. The various gases living inside of this space act as an insulator between the negative and positive charged particles, meaning this in between area is full of massive quantities of energy making the spherical Earth electrical just like a capacitor, as it keeps the negative and positive charges separated using gases in the air as an insulator.

Now that your head hurts let's move along to additional healing modalities to wrap these writings up.

CHAPTER 10. BEAUTY SCHOOL DROP OUT (GO BACK TO HIGH SCHOOL)

We are merely a tiny voice in a world of 7 billion people. We are so small and cannot affect large scale changes within ourselves and throughout the Universe.

NO! NOT TRUE!

The world is small, and we are infinite consciousness living within a reality of infinite possibilities!

Most of us are not aware of how powerful our words and interactions with others are.

You have a HUGE footprint your leaving on the world. Your words and intentions are permeated throughout the world.

The great news is that your power already exists inside of you, you just need to look inside, find it and awaken your passions. Many and most of us are simply sleep walking through this reality being systematically manipulated via our unconscious conscious to move from one automated programming sequence to another 1,2,4,8,7,5.

You must first and foremost REALIZE your infinite power. You are infinite consciousness experiencing this 3D reality via your perceptions of having a limited body accompanied by limited senses. So, let's expand your senses. Let's reboot your body and reset it back to where it is supposed to be.

Your true purpose here in this reality is just to be you. You can lead with confidence just by recognizing your power then choosing to fully be you. You have been programmed to believe you have very little power and to listen to others especially those in make-believe states of authority that exist from Queens and Presidents to the inanimate traffic lights that dictates your movements. Inside of this social construct reality you have been programmed since birth to give

243

I am free, I am free, I AM FREE

up your freedom of self. Your true self. You have been programmed to believe your voice is tiny and insignificant in a world of 7 plus billion voices. You have been programmed to believe your small, however this is but a fallacy put in place to control you on multiple levels. One day soon you will come to the realization that it is the world which is small and you that are infinite consciousness. You leave a footprint in the sands of minds and spirits every waking moment with your words and intentions. This power has always existed within you, you must simply recognize it then journey inward into it, into you.

When an artist sculpts a statue from stone it is said that the statue already exists within the stone the artist is merely chipping away the barriers to the true soul of the stone. You are an artist and you will utilize healing modalities as your hammer and chisel as you chip away at limiting beliefs and years' worth of bad habits which have worked to poison your body, mind and spirit.

Your true purpose will become your passion. Your passion will make you an expert and people will feel your passion because it will radiate from within you and without to the rest of the world.

Facts and figures do not teach you to find the source of your passion these are simply in place to distract you and pull you away from your true self.

It is time to start eliminating outside distractions which pull you away from your true self and your true passion. If that burning passion is not properly attended to it will either burn out or burn too big for you to ignore any longer.

The most difficult and the easiest thing to do in this world is just being you.

I am free I am free I AM FREE

MIND BODY

Nocebo effect:

If you don't believe it, it won't work.

Just as the placebo effect has become part of our daily vernacular, we should also account for the nocebo effect.

If you do not believe that your body is purpose built for self-healing it will be difficult to near impossible to heal yourself while attempting to avoid the turnstile rotating door of allopathic medicine.

Everything begins in the mind. All illness and disease begin inside of your mind.

The mind creates a thought pattern.

The thought pattern turns into an emotion.

The emotions inside of the body are hormones and chemicals that are bouncing around your millions of cells.

You feel these hormones and chemicals as an emotion inside of your mind.

These various chemicals have different impacts on your physical body. Some "good" some "bad".

If you move through this reality in a chronic state of emotional distress your mind will continuously create negative chemicals and hormones for your body to then deal with. Even though your body is purpose built for perfect homeostasis this overabundance of negative chemicals will have a negative impact on your body and can lead to dis-ease of the body. This will then show itself with various symptoms. If you stick to the current method of treatment when you find some sort of symptom you will make an appointment to see an allopathic medical doctor. The doctor will nearly always prescribe a pharmaceutical which will simply mask the symptom but will not consider the underlying dis-ease that both the mind and body are currently suffering from.

The body is already dealing with an insane amount of outside negative impacts such as the foods you eat, the air you breath (can you imagine how the body has had to adjust since the industrial revolution), water you drink, etc. but also the body is heavily

I am free, I am free, I AM FREE

impacted by your emotional state. These extreme emotional states are in place for emergency situations to help protect us but in todays fucked up social construct the fight or flight type of emotional states are constantly being triggered which is causing harm to your mind and body. Even something as benign as watching a scary movie. Why do people watch? To trigger the fight or flight response which is a built in emergency response system.

You need to deal with your chronic states of emotional distress to properly heal both your mind and body. You can make many strides in body healing modalities but if you neglect your mind and spirit you will continue to find that your progress towards healing will be stifled.

It's important to note that many people report unexpected emotional healing occurring after undertaking various healing modalities. Many have reported long bouts of crying as an emotional state from their childhood is brought forth unexpectedly. If you have these occurrences you should look to embrace the child within knowing that you are here to now comfort that child as your adult self. Perhaps giving comfort and emotional closure to your younger self in a great and unexpected way.

But before we get too far into the actual healing modalities let's look at our current reality.

I am free I am free I AM FREE

TRUST ME I'M A DOCTOR

And with that beautiful intro let's dive head first into the tried and true, fully tested and vetted world of allopathic medicine.

In the last several years I have read text after text from individuals on the holistic healing side of things that balk and berate the allopathic medical practices and doctors in general.

I on the other hand prefer to attempt to view all things through a prism of attempted unbiased which of course can be difficult to damn near impossible due to the way that we have each been programmed as individuals as well as our propensity to always want to feel correct and justified with regard to our staunchly held beliefs.

Much like most things in our reality allopathic medicine has its pros and its cons. In today's landscape the cons are starting to stack up due to several factors but the most damaging one being environment. The medical establishment hitched a ride with good ol' Louis Pasteur and the theory of germ-disease and in doing so has greatly modified the environment of the human body. Add in a dash of gene splicing, GMO foods, pesticides, "beauty" products, hormone manipulation, massive amounts of vaccines, polluted airs and waters due to large industry production, micro-plastics being introduced into the food chain and the list goes on and on.

The point is that humans and animals of the Earth in general tend to adapt to their environments and in the last 200 years the various environments of the plane(t), the human body and the food chain has greatly and grotesquely been modified making it nearly impossible for the human body/mind/soul/spirit to properly adapt to the massive upheaval in such a small window of perceived time.

So, in my estimation the allopathic medical establishment is a part of the problem but not THEE problem. After all, in general people don't go visit a doctor's office for funsies they are usually already suffering from some sort of ailment or various physical, mental, emotional ailments.

It is my belief that in general those in the medical field are in that field because they tend to care deeply for saving human lives. After a couple of years working within this environment and seeing a

I am free, I am free, I AM FREE

rotating door of death, I imagine that many become numb to death and disease partially to protect their own internal emotional environment.

When allopathic medicine was first kicking off there was a lot more "bed side manner" and although some of the methods were very damaging, they were also saving lives. For example, if I was showing off to a group of friends and decided it was time to bust out my chainsaw juggling routine and ended up losing an arm, I would lean more into allopathic medicine routines to stop the quick decent towards physical death. If I got hit by a bus, break an arm and don't know how to properly set it myself, badly burn myself, get my tongue stuck in a blender, you name it. These traumatic physical injuries line up well with allopathic medical practices and although their knowledge in treatment for physical ailments has grown over time their attention to treating the entire person has not.

Bedside manner also meant actually spending time with the patient. It is estimated that the average doctor now spends anywhere between ten to twelve minutes and some estimations for newer doctors down to a paltry eight minutes per patient. The absurdity of attempting to heal someone by feeding them pills and charting their progress with twelve-minute appointments is complete insanity but that is the current reality with the majority of allopathic medical practices.

I do believe that despite the thuggish racket of the pharmaceutical industry there are still plenty of docs, nurse practitioners, midwives and many others working in allopathic medicine that truly wish to heal. And how frustrating must it be to see the rotating door of the same and new patients regardless what new-fangled gadget or pill is introduced to the hospital and the medical market at large. It seems they are always looking to chemistry and biology for that magic "cure all" bullet which if ever found they would gladly trade to you for let's say a lifetime of slavery and your first born.

To make matters worse the medical field is rife with unimaginable types of stresses. Just for funsies let's take a gander at the 10 professions with the highest suicide rate and let's rank them in order starting with 10 and working our way up to the number 1 spot.

I am free, I am free, I AM FREE

10. Scientist: Yikes! Who knew? As has been outlined in several writings within this book scientism is the newfangled religion of the last couple centuries. Oh, what pressure must be carried on the shoulders of a young scientist attempting to break into the field. Your scientific forefathers fought against the tyrannical rule of the church (Roman Catholic mostly) to bring humanity into the new age of human enlightenment. Talk about pressure! This is part of the reason why there is so much BS science garbage littering the airwaves of human consciousness. It's a cut-throat BUSINESS!! Want to hear something really bonkers? C'mon I know you do. For every 45 male scientist that take their own lives per year 5 female scientist do as well. With one distinct exception. Chemist. Yeah chemist are the most likely of the scientific ilk to take their own lives and they tend to commit suicide by swallowing cyanide when they are refused a research grant. That's some crazy shit right there!! Now if we reflect a bit on why there is so much fake science being inundated onto (and sometimes into) the masses (even the peer reviewed kind) you can conceive a better understanding of the kinds of pressures put upon this class of citizens.

9. Pharmacist: I know we should be shocked but, really are we? Aside from the emotional trauma that must at some point eat at you when your pushing pills to the sick and dying I would think that over a short period of time you would become disillusioned with the industry as a whole. You essentially become a salesperson for big pharma and end up stocking your shelves with the latest and greatest drug that does God knows what to the mental and physical health of your patients. And low and behold as you become disillusioned and start to spiral into depression you realize that your sitting on a mountain of readily available pills. In fact, the average pharmacist has a nearly 20% higher than population average of substance abuse, which is really saying something all things considered.

8. Farm Workers: It's considered one of the nation's deadliest jobs. It also doesn't pay much and is extremely labor intensive. We also learned that since we have greatly manipulated our topsoil we can unintentionally create catastrophic effects on crops

249

I am free, I am free, I AM FREE

leading to massive upheavals in the financial viability in this field of work.

7. Electricians: Ok, this one did surprise me but really it shouldn't have considering the various avenues of research I have conducted along the lines of cell towers and electromagnetic fields. Some studies have suggested there is a link between long-term exposure to high levels of electromagnetic fields and an electrician's brain chemistry. They believe that this long-term exposure could have a negative impact on melatonin (not so nice to see you again melatonin) production which could lead to depression which carries over to suicide. Don't live under high power lines boys and girls.

6. Real Estate Agents: Once again I was blown away a bit by this one. I suppose it goes into the ol' adage of feast and famine much like a used car's salesman. Another shocking stat with regards to this career field is that over one-third of job-related deaths are due to murder. WTF? Not sure why real estate agents are getting merc'd but I imagine this could also be a very stressful situation to live your life within.

5. Police Officers: BOOP! BOOP! THAT'S THE SOUND OF THE POLICE! BOOP! BOOP! THAT'S THE SOUND OF THE BEAST! Ok, I think number 5 brings us back into the yeah that makes sense realm. Regardless of what you think about the police I can't even begin to imagine the stresses and struggles one must go through on a daily when most of your day is spent dealing with some of the lowest levels of human consciousness (not including government). Not knowing if you're going home alive at the end of your shift. Most police officers get very little sleep and although I haven't done the homework I imagine that the rates of alcohol and other abuses are likely much higher than the public (not to put down the general public, after all with the opioid crisis in full swing nationwide many Americans and the pharmaceutical industry are doing their part to help ensure a drug crazed society). Well that was a rather depressing sentence.

4. Lawyers: Another gimme! What an incredibly stressful environment. Nearly 40% of all law students in the U.S. suffer from depression before they even graduate. Damn! One thing

250

I am free, I am free, I AM FREE

this study did not point out was the specific type of law. Criminal law is a damn site different compared to patent law or entertainment law. My amazing brother is an entertainment lawyer and his lifestyle is the thing of envy to many and most in this social construct. Although I'm sure it comes with its own brand of stressors an entertainment lawyer isn't nearly as vilified as a criminal lawyer can be. When someone is paid to manipulate the truth to exonerate a guilty party for a heinous crime not only does the majority of the public at large think very little of you (being polite here) but I can't imagine what you think about yourself if that little voice called your conscious has any voice at all. Couple this with long hours and a massive level of testosterone fueled competition and it's amazing these people live into their 40's.

3. Financial Workers: I was a bit taken aback by this one until I started contemplating the recent 2008 deep plunge the made-up stock market and housing markets took that created a global catastrophe with regards to value of the fiat petrodollar currency. Sure families were put on the streets because of the abusive nature of the subprime mortgage industry and the stock market which continued to falsely grow even when Fannie Mae and Freddie Mac had extended more than $3 Trillion worth of mortgage credit, but hey these aren't people their just account numbers (well, not all of them after all we had our good friends over at Wells Fargo creating up to 3.5 Million fake accounts to pat their states. That's just good business sense). Being part of this system as a financial worker while looking at the irrational growth of the subprime mortgage market along with the (how shall we put it) *interesting* investment vehicles created from these practices must in some way claw at your guts. As a financial advisor you have a fiduciary responsibility to help improve the financial security of your clients, however the climate so recently created did the exact opposite and with great vigor.

2. Dentist: Let's face it people mostly don't like dentist. After all, if I don't take proper care of my health and teeth it's probably nothing to do with me but the fault of my dentist. That feels sound and reasonable. Dentist much like doctors have a

251

I am free, I am free, I AM FREE

reputation to protect while simultaneously living a life of high stress and having day to day dealings with most people that likely aren't feeling too gitty or chipper while on their visit to the office. Much like doctors, to keep their upstanding rep in place they can't really seek help when they know they are having a difficult time mentally and emotionally.

1. Doctors: No surprise here and the reason why I started this list in the first place. Unfortunately, the person you turn to tell you how to take care of yourself has the highest risk of suicide amongst all professions. Not to mention their insane high rates of alcoholism and drug abuse. Doctors are damn near 2 times more likely to commit suicide when compared to the average American (the actual number is 1.87). If that doesn't make you question your own sanity of seeking out the help of allopathic doctors for every ailment, then I don't know what will.

That's not to say that at times it makes sense and is downright necessary to see an allopathic doctor. Let's say I inadvertently poison myself and do not have the tools or knowledge of how to properly purge my system of the poison. It's likely that any hospital within the region of a somewhat densely populated area is going to have expertise in this area. What they aren't going to do is treat you holistically for full recovery so upon release it would be in your best interest to be able to selfheal as much as reasonable without incurring further injury. Also, I'm just going to come out and say it they are hot garbage on a sunny day when it comes to treating chronic conditions. Because they have been programmed into a reality of germ-disease therapy they will always have difficulty realizing the nature of the human body.

Now for some truly sobering news with regard to allopathic medicine. I know right, isn't this chapter supposed to be about healing?

Medical errors are currently the THIRD leading cause of death in America taking a back seat only to heart disease and cancer which not so ironically are both conditions being treated by allopathic medicine by default for most Americans.

The numbers are rather staggering with the current estimate being between 210,000 and 440,000 patient deaths each year who received care from a hospital end up suffering death as a result of some type of *preventable* harm that was sustained due to the hospital visit.

But as alarming as those numbers are I believe those numbers do not do true justice to what the numbers actually look like. Those numbers are estimates based on direct harm created by the hospital, however it does not consider all the various patients that are released from care with a thumbs up only to end up with life altering/shorting ailments from the myriad of drugs and other highly intrusive procedures which greatly disrupt and lead to the ultimate destruction of the human lifeform. It's odd that we are in an unprecedented era of tech/medical symbiosis to help mitigate intrusive harm to the human body, yet we still see these staggering statistics.

The current estimate for serious injury caused by medical error is 40 times the number of deaths. That means that more than 10 million Americans are seriously injured each and every year by medical errors, never mind the negative impacts caused by the very treatments and drugs administered.

The author of the report that estimated these numbers is one John T. James who is/was employed at NASA's space center as a toxicologist. His young 19-year-old son unfortunately passed away from what James believes was negligence on the part of the hospital.

That set off conflict of interest alarms for me but when other leading patient safety researchers were asked to peer review James' study, they all agreed his methods were sound and the findings credible.

The numbers were derived from an estimate that just over 1 percent of patients die each year due to medical errors. Apply that percentage to the 35 million people hospitalized each year and it translates into just over 400K deaths annually.

Here's another troubling fact.

According to U.S. government statistics, FDA approved prescription drugs kill 290 Americans per day. Every day on average 290 Americans dead from FDA prescription drugs. WTF!

This is considered a success!

I am free, I am free, I AM FREE

More fun facts to persuade you to eat that apple a day (see the later chapter on Apple Cider Vinegar).

Surgical procedures do not require to be proven <u>safe</u> and <u>effective</u> before being tried on patients (seems as though it's called medical <u>practice</u> for a reason).

It's been proven that psychiatric drugs can and do promote violent shootings which are occurring repeatedly across America.

Only in America can you have your bank account emptied, put into deep debt all while being healed to death.

The insane amounts of fiat currency they charge for this type of care is largely based on living in an era of attempts to create a safe, high quality and high valued medical healing environment. I think instead we are largely paying for high end tech toys for people good intentions or no are playing with them like drunken teenagers behind the wheel of a sports car.

In 2015 healthcare cost sat roughly at $3.2 TRILLION dollars according to the federal Centers for Medicare and Medicaid Services. That's nearly $10K per American which makes up just about 17.5% of the gross national product.

This is partially because the healthcare system is not run on a free market system as the media outlets will have you believe. It's a monopoly. We lucky Americans are now mandated (at gunpoint if necessary) to pay into the allopathic medical system twice. Your money is extorted from your pay check to pay into Medicare and with the recent push for the Affordable Care Act (Obamacare) we are also forced to purchase private insurance. BLAKA! BLAKA! (double-tap)

At one-time hospitals were run by doctors and nurses but in today's age they are ran by C-Suite executives and investors who make decisions that ultimately can lead to a patient's death. Many nurses and physicians are doing their best to deliver both safe and quality care but working within a monopolized hyper capitalist environment largely disrupts the ability to deliver proper care to patients. This toppled with the fact that treating the entire body/mind/spirit is not taught or even considered has led allopathic medicine down some dark roads.

I am free, I am free, I AM FREE
Sobering numbers regarding annual leading causes of death

Heart disease: 614K
Cancer: 592K
Medical error: 251K (the low estimate)
Respiratory disease: 147K
Accidents: 136K
Stroke: 133K
Alzheimer's: 93K
Diabetes: 76K
Flu: 55K (better get that vac)
Kidney disease: 48K
Suicide: 42K
Numbers based on National Center for Health Statistics

One might ask oneself what is the solution? Federal government oversight? Additional Federal/National rules and regulations? Although a federal money grab to implement additional laws, rules and regulations is the norm it seems to me that within the realm of our current broken healthscare (not a typo) system that adding money hungry, ineffectual bureaucrats to the equation will only add additional trauma to the hospital staff and patients.

A start would be to properly staff hospitals with qualified individuals. Hospitals already deal with greed, golden parachutes, insurance fraud, big pharma and big egos but likely one of the leading causes of mistakes is not being properly staffed when and where necessary. Also, with so many people going to the ER the odds of having a mistake made rises significantly. How are ER personnel realistically able to be trained to know about all trauma and have the time and expertise to immediately treat during a life or death situation?

In my opinion the focus should be on changing the systems incentives. Currently it's a for profit system and each individual hospital set's its own prices for procedures, medications, room stays and so much more. There is no universal cost's associated with medicine. You could have your blood drawn at one hospital and at the next have the same procedures with the same results but end up paying wildly different amounts. This is partially due to the work of

I am free, I am free, I AM FREE
the hospitals charge master whose job it is to set pricing for each
procedure. Heaped on top of this messy business is of course co-
pays, medical insurance, 3rd party vendors the list goes on and on.

BUT WAIT THERES MORE!

To pile yet more dog dew on this financial mess we should
consider the fact that many hospitals simply don't get paid after
performing various procedures. In 2004 U.S. hospitals were paid
about 38 percent of their charges by patients and/or the patient's
insurer. That certainly leaves the chargemaster and hospital chief of
staff in a bit of a pickle. To further pile on (I know this load is getting
heavy) hospitals now need to vehemently compete against one
another for the latest and greatest technology from fancy beds, water
warmed sheets all the way up to A.I. enabled laser guided procedures
and nano-tech. It's the hospitals responsibility to update the
chargemaster regarding patient charges and billing but there is no
uniform structure in place for this procedure. One hospital may just
increase pricing on all procedures by 1 percent across the board
annually, while another may update pricing based on type and number
of procedures done within said hospital. In most states the
chargemaster has zero obligation (or incentive) to publicly publish
their price lists.
    As much as reasonable you should dedicate time to reading and
understanding healing and preventative body maintenance you can
safely perform at home on yourself and those family members that
depend on you for safety and longevity.
    As a secondary tier of attempting to keep your body/mind/spirit
in tip top condition you should make it part of your conscious
thought. We are what we think. The more you dive into internal
healing the more your mind forces your body to heal. I know that
might sound like bullshit so let me give you an example that damn
near all of us have experienced at some point in our lives usually
during our capricious youth.
    Remember that time you were dating that person and then some
sort of silly emotional thing happened and against your will the
relationship was abruptly dismembered and torn asunder? You were
left pondering why oh why did the love of your life (as short as your

I am free, I am free, I AM FREE

life experience was at the time) suddenly disappear just as suddenly as they arrived to flip your world upside down.

Then a strange thing happened. Your brain and heart started to stiffen up a bit. Foods that you use to love had no more taste, flavor or pop to them. Blue skies turned grey. Feel free to fill in another metaphor of your own that applies here. They even have a name for this. It's called being LOVESICK!

Think about that for just a moment. Your physical body becomes physically ill from emotional loss of your relationship. This simple example is to point out the power of mind over body. It stands to reason that the more your consciously thinking happy, healthy thoughts the more the trillions of electric cells within your body are soaking up these happy, healthy thoughts and the more they want to respond to said positivity. If you can make your physical body lovesick how can you then not make your body/mind/spirit LOVE!?!

Okay ladies and gents it's time to move on to one more topic before we migrate towards step by step instruction's for healing modalities.

So, take just a little more reading time and journey with me into the wonderful world of comic book/movie lore and the strange mixing of contaminants. Yeah that's right. Somehow, I managed to work in my prepubescent penchant for comic books into a book about healing. What can I say when your good your good.

https://www.healthaffairs.org/doi/full/10.1377/hlthaff.25.1.57

257

MIXING CONTAMINANTS

You guys ever see that 80's Batman movie directed by a young Tim Burton? You know the one with Michael Keaton as Batman and Jack Nicholson as The Joker? If you did then maybe you remember this plot point and if you didn't then let me explain.

The Joker being the campy psychopath he was in the late 80's decided to fuck with the residence of Gotham City by poisoning......well just about everything. But The Joker is a special kind of crazy. The kind of crazy that appreciates his own twisted maniacal ways and is willing to go the extra mile to put in the time and resources necessary to show that he truly cares about HOW he is going to poison and kill you. Sure, he could just poison the water supply, but any run of the mill supervillain could pull that off (or a local government such as in Michigan who inadvertently poisoned the residents to save a buck).

The Joker decides he is going to put different ingredients in various items such as perfume, cologne, deodorant, shampoo, etc. If you put on just the cologne you're probably going to be just fine. But if you combine let's say your cologne with your shampoo BOOMSHACKALACKALA!! Your ass has been poisoned and Smile X is taking you to your grave with a wide smile plastered wide across the landscape of your face.

This somewhat campy but fun romp of an early super hero movie couldn't be more spot on with what we are paying into and what these large corporations have created in terms of mixing contaminants that destroy the living organism that is our human body. The fact that we consume these items often with big smiles on our faces further speaks to the reflection of our reality to this fantastical movie world.

Our exposure to physical contaminants comes from many and varying sources. Food, water, dust particles, air, the cancer-causing chemicals sprayed on your couches, chairs, loveseats and curtains. Great they won't catch on fire, but they will give you cancer. Sounds reasonable.

I am free, I am free, I AM FREE

You can research for yourself and find hundreds if not thousands of studies about the potential health hazards with any single one of these chemical compounds, but I dare you. Nay, I triple dog dare you (yeah that's right I skipped the double dog dare) to find research which delves into the potential negative impact of these chemical compounds when combined. I was able to track down a very small amount of published research documents from 2017 in this regard, but they are few and far between.

One more stop off at the vaccine station then we are off to healing modalities.

WE NEED THE NEEDLES

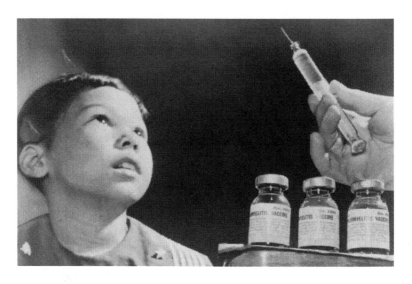

Vaccines. Uh oh here we go! This topic is rather frustrating to me on several levels. The number one thing that bothers me about vaccines is the debate around it. I like and appreciate the fact that there is debate and it should exist. But from where I'm standing the debate either goes one of two ways.

"YOU ASSHOLE!! HOW DARE YOU NOT VACCINATE YOUR KID! YOUR GONNA KILL US ALL AND YOU SUCK AS A PARENT! GO KILL YOURSELF!"

Or

"ARE YOU INSANE, HOW CAN YOU INJECT POISON DIRECTLY INTO YOUR KIDS MUSCLES/BLOODSTREAM? HAVENT YOU WATCHED THAT VIDEO ON YOUTUBE THAT CLEARLY SAYS YOUR KID IS GONNA GET AUTISM IF HE/SHE GETS THESE SHOTS!! YOU'RE A BRAINWASHED SHEEPLE AND A DICK!"

I am free, I am free, I AM FREE

If any of you reading these words have spent any time looking at this issue than I feel confident you have seen many posts like the hyperbole of both sides of this argument.

For me I have kids, so obviously I have a concern but also understand that you shouldn't look at only one side of a situation and take it as truth. After all, "truth" is popular belief as well as your interpretations of our shared reality based on your programmed mind.

I decided to conduct my own research and attempt to figure this out, at least for myself and my own family. What I have put together is some information based on history, some on intuition and some on scientism. I believe what will now be presented will at least attempt to be fair and balanced from both extreme sides of this issue to attempt to find some middle ground to allow you to be greater informed and make your own decision. Please note that you will still need to perform much of your own research regarding vaccines, but I hope to give you some solid information to reference as a starting point.

Of important note is the fact that the biology surrounding vaccines is rather broad but can also get insanely detailed regarding the inner workings of how the various protocols are supposed to work. Although I have done a deep dive into the functions we can easily lose focus of the forest through the trees. Much of these writings is to give a broad view of the landscape starting from a grounded root of how we started and got to this point in our vaccine world.

Please turn the page read on and attempt to leave behind your current prejudices regarding vaccines whether pro or con.

I am free I am free I AM FREE

In The Beginning

To get started. Yes, that's a great idea. But where to start? We could start with Louis Pasteur considering the current vaccination protocol as well as most of the allopathic disease treatment is based on his work. But he was a fake, a fraud, a charlatan. Hailed as the great discoverer of germ theory amongst other accomplishments (most of them stolen) Pasteur is a name you should recognize at least from the term pasteurization.

He didn't so much discover the theory of germ therapy and partially therein lies our problems when researching the beginnings of vaccines and the vaccine protocol. Many of his works appear to be falsified, he was constantly riding the coattails of his contemporary BeChamp and he was drunk with power making the official story line of Pasteur the hero and germ therapy altogether questionable.

When we discuss Pasteur, we must also bring one Mr. Antione BeChamp into the discussion.

To learn some of the intricate details tied into the tale of BeChamp and Pasteur is a pleasure ride and I eagerly await the made for TV movie. It's a deep dive into a convoluted relationship between these two French Academy Scientist. We don't want to spend too much time on this but it's important to note that Pasteur essentially stole or rather claimed the discovery of germ therapy which was a theory that had already made its rounds amongst the medical establishment several years prior.

Although Pasteur and BeChamp were contemporaries it appears Pasteur was always one step behind BeChamp and Pasteur's processes and all-around findings were incompetent when held against the light of BeChamp's works.

The larger issue was that Pasteur had the power and weight of the aristocrats and crown of the time whereas BeChamp was a bit more steadfast and dedicated to his works and the process.

Why do we care about Pasteur and BeChamp? Western medicine in its current state is wholly based on the germ therapy THEORY pushed by Pasteur. There is a reason why physicians are not taught to treat the entire body/mind/spirit holistically and one of

262

I am free, I am free, I AM FREE

the primary reasons is due to our current understanding (misunderstanding really) of germ therapy.

Twentieth century main stream medicine/science followed Pasteur down the road of madness based on his lies, manipulation, stolen and bastardised medical science.

17 years prior to Pasteur's ground-breaking work that helped to establish him as the de-facto authority, individuals of the established medical/scientific community were already debating the topic of germ therapy.

Here are some musings from that most famous English nurse Florence Nightengale which she published in 1860:

"Diseases are not individuals arranged in classes, like cats and dogs, but conditions growing out of one another.

Is it not living in a continual mistake to look upon diseases as we do now, as separate entities, which must exist, like cats and dogs, instead of looking upon them as conditions, like a dirty and a clean condition, and just as much under our control; or rather as the reactions of kindly nature, against the conditions in which we have placed ourselves?

I was brought up to believe that smallpox, for instance, was a thing of which there was once a first specimen in the world, which went on propagating itself, in a perpetual chain of descent, just as there was a first dog, (or a first pair of dogs) and that smallpox would not begin itself, any more than a new dog would begin without there having been a parent dog.

Since then I have seen with my own eyes and smelled with my own nose smallpox growing up in first specimens, either in closed rooms or in overcrowded wards, where it could not by any possibility have been 'caught' but must have begun.

I have seen diseases begin, grow up, and pass into one another. Now, dogs do not pass into cats.

I have seen, for instance, with a little overcrowding, continued fever grow up; and with a little more, typhoid fever; and with a little more, typhus, and all in the same ward or hut.

263

I am free, I am free, I AM FREE

Would it not be far better, truer, and more practical, if we looked upon disease in this light (for diseases, as all experience shows, are adjectives, not noun-substantives):

- True nursing ignores infection, except to prevent it. Cleanliness and fresh air from open windows, with unremitting attention to the patient, are the only defense a true nurse either asks or needs.

- Wise and humane management of the patient is the best safeguard against infection. The greater part of nursing consists of preserving cleanliness.

- The specific disease doctrine is the grand refuge of weak, uncultured, unstable minds, such as now rule in the medical profession. There are no specific diseases; there are specific disease conditions."

So, you mean to tell me one of the most famous nurses in history thought that the germ therapy theory was horse shit? Why yes indeed she did. How did she have the credentials to call bullshit on such a theory? She had spent nearly her entire life working within environments of infections, epidemics and contagions, that's how.

It should catch your attention that last bit Florence shared with us way back in 1860. Not just that germ theory is shit but that disease can grow in shit.

It's rather easy to understand that if you remove the feces and fecal matter from the living space and bring in fresh water you tend to have a clean environment that does not easily allow for the growth of disease. On the other hand, if you root and frolic in your own feces you're going to get sick and it has nothing to do with germ therapy.

The body works the same way via the Lymphatic System which for some reason doesn't seem to be taught very well within the confines of the current medical establishment. Rarely if ever do I hear those of the medical establishment speaking about the importance of the lymphatic system in cleaning the human body.

Speaking of feces here's a not so happy example. As I write this the city of San Francisco just had a large outbreak of Hepatitis. Was this a germ just sitting idly by waiting to pass from person to person?

Certainly not in this example. The counties of both San Diego and Los Angeles were hit with the largest Hepatitis A outbreak in the US in decades. Although splendid with all it's great wealth and Ivory

I am free, I am free, I AM FREE

Towers these counties also are dealing with a horrendous homelessness problem that seems to have had grown out of control by 2017. So bad in fact that many are living in squalor and filth.

Because the city is not able (or willing) to clean these areas of high concentrated feces and other shit like by-products people start getting sick. We then label this as this germ equates to this disease and Bodda Boom! Badda Bing! Germ therapy at work once again.

The city, after getting far too much bad national and international press to keep their seats of office started cleaning the streets, sidewalks, etc. and then guess what happened? The germs magically disappeared. Nothing to do with the fact that the human bodies already beaten down by drugs and alcohol were living in their own filth. No, it was just germ therapy at work.

The two key things they did was clean the streets of the fetid shit and drug paraphernalia and distribute vaccines to the homeless population. Today they are still dealing with an unprecedented homelessness issue and have far too many living inside of a world of feces and filth. This tends to bring rats and rats tend to have these tiny little rat fleas which then migrate around the entire populace creating a health crisis for all humans in the vicinity.

The hepatitis A vaccine was introduced to the US in 1996 and has largely not been an issue with regard to large outbreaks. These recent outbreaks aggressively hit the homeless populations in San Diego and Los Angeles.

Back to our history lessons.

Okay so Pasteur passed off other people's works from the past as his own. That's no smoking gun for me because damn it Pasteur was the leading scientific mind of his time who brought us vaccinations that have saved so many! Now maybe if you had some serious proof of him being a fraud.....what's that? You do, do you?

Why yes! We do.

For you see it appears Pasteur was a bit of a magician or at least had pretty good scientific sleight of hand.

265

I am free, I am free, I AM FREE

Unlike BeChamp, good ol' Louis loved adulation and applause. So much so that he would often take to the streets to show the wonders of his works and would bask in the glory of the applause from his adoring audience.

Keep in mind they didn't have the horrendous onslaught of "entertainment" we are bombarded with today so a self-proclaimed science nerd performing on the streets I imagine would have been a pretty good form of entertainment for the period.

Turns out good ol' Loius was faking it the whole time. But, how can we make such a claim?

For decades Pasteur's research papers were kept in the family as they were/are highly prized works, mostly because our current basis for medical treatment is largely based on his work. Louis had told his family to never release his lab notes which offhand seems downright curious.

Pasteur's manuscript material was held in Paris at the Bibliotheque Nationale starting in 1964. Louis' grandson Louis Pasteur Vallery-Radot the editor of these works had this material held here and informed that it could be released to the public upon his death.

In 1971 he died, and the veil was lifted on Pasteurs papers. For the first time Pasteurs papers were available and open for public consumption. Care to hazard a guess at what happened next?

It was discovered that Pasteur faked his demonstrations for applause.

It took time due to the necessity for someone to translate the content from French to English but once done the cat was out of the bag.

BeChamp was a biologist from France and gained popularity in the late 1800's. History did not make him popular. Instead they gave that popularity to Pasteur who essentially stole BeChamps information and passed it off as his own in later years.

BeChamp for his part was considered a prominent research biologist of his time and did teach at University and medical schools.

I am free I am free I AM FREE

Considering there is so much history and information surrounding BeChamp and Pasteur let's oversimplify the two schools of thought keeping in mind that the current medical establishment is based on the Pasteur model.

PASTEUR (Germ Theory)	BeChamp (Microzymian Theory)
Diseases derive from outside of the body and are attributed to micro-organisms.	Diseases are organisms that reside within the cell of the body.
Each disease can be associated with specific micro-organisms	Each disease can be associated with a specific condition.
Disease can attack anyone.	Disease grows within unhealthy conditions within the host/body.
Outside organisms are to be protected against.	Disease arises from within damaged cells of the body.

Even by this over simplified table we can see that allopathic medicine lines up directly with the Pasteur model and has greatly failed humanity in this new era of cell bombardment. Looking at the BeChamp table we can see that this largely makes sense when dealing with healing the body holistically and ensuring that the cells of the body are well oxygenated and full of a healthy blood medium to help stave off disease and premature death.

Enough about those guys. Let's fast forward a bit in this vaccine timeline.

One thing that always comes up when speaking about vaccines is the polio vaccine. I know for my part the first thing that popped into my head was "Hold on a tick. The polio vaccine saved the children. How can a vaccine possibly be considered bad if the polio vaccine saved so many"?

Then I did some homework only to discover some very unfortunate information regarding the polio vaccine. Just this past weekend some friends and I were having a spirited debate regarding vaccines. I did not prompt the conversation and in fact did not chime in with any information and just watched as the conversation unfolded in front of me. My assumption was that most of the room would be all for vaccines but to my surprise there was a bit of heat to the conversation and everyone at the table was livid that they were forced (California) to vax their children regardless of how they felt about the current vaccine protocol.

Then out of nowhere a wild card joined the party. She loudly exclaimed. "What about polio huh?" And I watched as everyone's shoulders slumped just a bit and they quickly moved the conversation along to steer clear of polio. That was a bit frustrating to me as I had already done so much research into the polio vaccine as this was my first knee jerk reaction as well.

With that in mind I decided these writings can use the information regarding the polio vaccine, so we can help paint a more robust picture that can show you more pieces of the puzzle besides....But polio bro!

So, let's push along turn the page and dig a bit deeper than you are probably accustomed to and let's see what was really going on in the days of the polio epidemic.

I am free I am free I AM FREE

Polio DDT

DDT (Dichloro-Diphenyl-Trichloroethane)

The killer insecticide being marketed heavily in the 1940's for everyday use. Spray it on your kids' cloths, spray in airplane cabins, in your house. Hey, look it just might kill fleas and flies that might be carrying the polio disease. This was great for industry. Who might industry be? Why our good friends at Monsanto of course. After all they were losing money not being able to mass produce arsenic and lead and placing those poisons in everything, so DDT was basically spiking the football after getting in the end zone. Even the US Government promoted the use of DDT for American households. Then a funny thing began to happen. Kids started getting sick.

Really incredibly sick!

This sickness was largely labeled as Polio and everyone living in areas of the new industrial revolution started losing their shit as their kids were being diagnosed with polio. What to do? Blame it on an invisible germ and create a vaccine (that didn't actually work by the way. Do some research into Jonas Stalk and his 17,000 monkeys). Stalks vaccine was released to the general public in 1955 and what happened next?
The rates of polio exploded. It had the opposite effect it was supposed to have on the populace. In some areas the rates of polio quadrupled! At this time U.S. soldiers in the Philippines had a polio rate 10 times higher than that of the mainland. The difference being that the areas the U.S. soldiers were in was being sprayed with........DDT of course (probably just a coincidence).
DDT is a neurotoxin that works to paralyze and kill humans. When DDT is sprayed on animals on people or on people's food they tend to get polio. When DDT was used in this way the rates of polio skyrocketed. What do you suppose happened once DDT was banned from use? Do a little research on Jim West. This guy ran the numbers in the 1940's to show the correlation with the increase of

269

I am free, I am free, I AM FREE

DDT in areas that line up with the increase in polio cases in those areas shortly after DDT arrives.

West also asked questions like; when cows eat DDT sprayed grass and that cow's milk is delivered to a school and the school suddenly has a mass polio outbreak is that due to a microscopic germ or perhaps to the DDT? This was bad for the polio vaccine since it not only failed miserably but also increased the rates of polio. What to do? Destroy all batches to ensure you don't injure or kill more members of your community?

Anyone with any sense of a moral compass may have chosen this course but when the hyper-capitalist money machine of big industry is at stake all's fair in death and war.

The CDC instead decided to simply change the definition of what polio is. Once they were able to redefine what polio was BANG! POW! ZAP!

VICTORY!

The vaccine is a smash success!

We're saving all those poor children. Come bring your child in to get shot full of monkey balls and kidney cells, no worries it's healthy for them. I think I know what you're thinking. If the vaccine was such a failure, why is polio pretty much eradicated?

Firstly, remember they simply redefined polio. In 1954 they changed it to define it as "severe paralysis". This was a significant change which allowed the number of polio cases to drop significantly over night. To further create a swift kick in the populaces nuts they also introduced a new rule and boy was it a brilliant victory.

The 15-day rule.

If they gave you the polio vaccine and if within 15 days, you suddenly get polio well then you always had polio. Nothing to do with the SHOT they just gave you! All those other cases that in the past were labeled as polio simply vanished like a magician's assistant. Polio symptoms were simply given different names such as "aseptic

I am free, I am free, I AM FREE

meningitis (which is polio), West Nile virus and more. In today's environment you may see headlines like "12 children contract polio like symptoms". Huh? So, it's not polio anymore it's simply polio like symptoms? It's been given the name acute flaccid myelitis and currently the CDC is reporting that it has spread to 24 US states with 72 confirmed cases (as of October 2018). Officials began tracking AFM in 2014 because they received reports of 120 new cases nationwide. Since 2014 there have been a total of 386 confirmed cases of AFM which is a low number unless one of those numbers belong to someone you love.

An oddity regarding AFM is that it peeks in late summer and fall. Currently this is considered a mystery disease, but they also say that it can occur as a result of a variety of viral illnesses including POLIO virus, enteroviruses, West Nile and adenoviruses. They also state that none of the children in the US tested positive for polio. So, it's a polio "like" disease that can occur as a result of polio, but no one has tested positive for polio? Maybe we should look at how they test for polio and how they define polio because this sure sounds an awful lot like polio to anyone paying attention.

In 1960 they simply modified the numbers required to state polio as an epidemic. They nearly doubled the number required to define it as an epidemic which also allowed for further cooking of the books and charting the plot points on the growth in a downward trajectory.

Before the polio vaccine the numbers were 20 or more cases per 100,000 of the populace.

After the polio vaccine the numbers were 35 or more cases per 100,000 of the populace.

That nearly doubles the number required to report it as an epidemic which is fantastic when charting your graphs because you can now show that the polio epidemic has rapidly dropped (without informing the public that you cooked the books to make that fancy chart reflect what you want).

Hold on there's more.

After the release of the Salk polio vaccine another change was implemented. Post Salk polio vaccine only the CDC was permitted to officially diagnose polio. Prior to the release of the vaccine a

271

I am free, I am free, I AM FREE

standard set of objective criteria was used by physicians to determine
whether a patient had a form of poliomyelitis. This further allows
your polio numbers to drop dramatically as now only entities you
control (the CDC) are permitted to even diagnose polio.

Aside from DDT another interesting thing happened during the
massive polio vaccine rollout.

Between 1954 and 1955 some 1.8 million children were injected
with the Salk polio vaccine/virus. In the Western and mid-Western
US states approximately 200,00 children received the Salk polio
vaccine which was distributed by Cutter Laboratories. Within days
reports of paralysis started pouring in and within a month the first
mass vaccination program against polio proved a failure as it had to
be abandoned. After further investigation it was determined that the
Cutter Laboratories polio vaccine had caused 40,000 cases of polio
leaving 200 children's lives forever altered with varying degrees of
paralysis and 10 confirmed deaths.

One of the most abhorrent things about this event is the fact that
this was easily avoidable. In the 1950's regulations around vaccines
were much different compared to today's landscape but even so all 5
polio vaccine manufacturers at that time including Cutter Laboratories
had their polio vaccine tested prior to injecting them into the
populace.

Let's introduce ourselves to Bernice Eddy and Elizabeth
Steward. Bernice was an American virologist and epidemiologist
working for the National Institute of Health.

In 1954 Bernice Eddy's job at the National Institute of Health
was to test polio vaccines from five different companies. Eddy and
her team performed their testing on 18 monkeys and discovered that a
vaccine manufactured by Cutter Laboratories contained live
poliovirus which passed along to the monkeys. She reported her
findings to the head of Laboratory and the NIH director William
Sebrell was notified but her findings never made their way to the
vaccine licensing advisory committee as Sebrell chose to ignore the
findings and license the Cutter vaccine anyway.

Not only did this lead to both crippling and killing American
children it also led to an incredible discovery that even today is rarely
spoken about when talking about vaccines. What Bernice and
Elizabeth had discovered is now termed the SV40 virus.

272

I am free, I am free, I AM FREE

Bernice Eddy and Elizabeth Steward warned that if the polio vaccine kept being distributed that within 20 years there would be an explosion of cancer related illness and death unlike the world had ever seen. The reason being that in the 1950's and 1960's vaccines needed to be grown in a medium (as they still do today) and at that time they were grown mostly in monkey parts. Monkey balls and monkey kidneys to be exact. Bernice and Elizabeth discovered that monkey kidney cells were able to pass along viruses to other species namely humans which may have led to an explosion of cancer in humans. SV40 literally means the 40th virus found in rhesus monkey kidney cells, yet they continued to utilize rhesus kidneys as the medium in which to "grow" their polio virus. In 1961 Bernice and company took the material used to grow the polio virus and injected it into baby hamsters. Guess what happened next? The hamsters grew tumors. Guess what happened next? Bernice and company were discredited and had their reputations run through the mud. But somehow this odd tale gets a bit worse and a bit more sinister.

For their part in 1961 the federal government passed a law which forbad the use of any vaccine with SV40. What they failed to do was require that all vaccines still on the shelves be destroyed and even more of an oversight they did not require that the contaminated seed material used to make these vaccines be destroyed. This meant that up until 1963 children across America were still being injected with polio vaccines that contained both the live virus and monkey kidney cells and consequently a much higher potential for cancer cells forming in those individuals injected with this vaccine. The seed was still being used up into the 1980's.

Also, of important note is the fact that Salk came up with the polio vaccine protocol and as such stood to make massive amounts of money. Instead Salk did not patent the vaccine and when asked by Edward R. Murrow who the patent belonged to Salk replied "Well, the people, I would say. There is not patent. Could you patent the sun."? Although lawyers for the sponsoring foundation did research the possibility of creating a patent for the polio virus it never happened. Salk also tested the vaccine on himself, his wife and his three sons so he certainly was extremely confident that his vaccine protocol was not dangerous.

273

I am free, I am free, I AM FREE

Let's move this thought machine beyond DDT masquerading as polio and move the discussion to the adjuvant. The what? Read on dear reader.

I am free I am free I AM FREE

Adjuvants

Dun! Dun! Dun! It came crawling out of the veiled darkness of the night. Dripping unknown toxins from its sharp pointed needle.

Ok seriously adjuvants don't get enough recognition in the vaccination talk permeating out there, so I have done some reading and would like to present you with the ugliness that is the adjuvant.

But first what the heck is an adjuvant you may ask? I know I did.

When someone tells you that they are putting aluminum in the vaccines they are referring to the adjuvant. Many vaccines use aluminum phosphate or aluminum hydroxide as the adjuvant.

Adjuvants hyper stimulate the immune system because a vaccine by itself is not strong enough to stimulate the immune system. If you or your bestie are injected with a vaccine it will likely do very little or nothing to you without the assistance of the adjuvant.

Vaccines only contain the viral antigen to the viruses they are targeting. Being injected without the adjuvant would create a situation in which only a few immune cells would respond which would not be enough to develop "immune memory" within your body.

With the assistance of the adjuvant several immune cells will respond to the vaccine where you were injected and become "immune memory cells".

So far at this point adjuvants sound good and necessary but alas there's a catch and it's not a good one.

The adjuvant indiscriminately hyper activates your immune system so it can get the proper response to the antigens contained within the vaccine.

Problem here. Since the adjuvants are indiscriminate in their behavior your body will have a systemic response. This is why a small body such as that of a child's can break out in fever. The cats in the white coats are not able to target their hyper response which means the entire system is a target.

A systemic response is normal behavior for the body when the entire body gives an inflammatory response to a threat. Blood is increased to the area of damage. This excess blood is to bring

275

I am free, I am free, I AM FREE

nutrient-laden fluids and white blood cells to the area to heal the damage or defeat the invasion. If the systemic response continues over a period, the body can start to harm itself.

We are now, via the adjuvants artificially stimulating the entire immune system and doing it to very small infants and children. In the 1960's this was done with 5 doses for polio, smallpox, and DTP. Currently we are at 72 and counting. That's 72 times for the immune system to be artificially hyper stimulated. This is the entire purpose of the adjuvant as the vaccines would not work without the adjuvant. The pharmaceutical companies utilize the adjuvant for this specific purpose. There is no conspiracy about this it is the process and the way that vaccines currently function. This happens when the body and minds of our children are in a hyper state of development.

Autoimmune Disorders

Autoimmune diseases have skyrocketed. This is basically the body attacking itself dealing directly with the immune system. We can see a potential correlation here. We input adjuvants that hyper stimulate the immune system while our children are still in the early developmental stages of life. Autoimmune diseases rise in conjunction, and autoimmune diseases have a direct link with the immune system.

But perhaps that is just a coincidence. How can we possibly prove a link between the two? This is difficult since due to ethical reasons it is not possible to conduct a double-blind placebo test for vaccines as is done for pharmaceuticals.

There is however one study I was able to dig up that did perform a comparison of vaccinated vs unvaccinated on 6 to 12-year-old children in the U.S. Although this is but a single study over a short period the numbers are still something that should make you sit up and take notice.

The premise of the study is concentrated on the long-term health outcomes of children on the current vaccination protocol.

The study aimed to study vaccinated and unvaccinated children on a broad range of outcomes.

It also was looking for an association between vaccinations and neurodevelopmental disorders.

I am free, I am free, I AM FREE

For their study group they focused on homeschooled children in four U.S. States. The sample group consisted of just over 660 children varying in age range from 6 to 12 years old.

This study was funded by grants from Generation Rescue Inc, and the Children's Medical Safety Research Institute. The funders had no role or influence on the design and conduct of the research or the preparation of reports. The authors declared they had no financial interest that had any bearing on any aspect of the conduct or conclusions of the study.

STUDY FINDINGS

Unfortunately, I can't place that information into these writings as I do not have permission. Spoiler alert the non-vaccinated kids fared much better. Do yourself a favor and take an hour out of your day to read through the study. It is time well spent.

The second portion of the study goes into the neurodevelopmental disorders between the vaccinated and non-vaccinated children. Really AMAZING numbers here and the authors consider other factors such as adverse living environments. I am not including any of those findings here but the findings in this study are stunning especially once they account for following a vaccination protocol while pregnant.

You really owe it to yourself to look at this study directly. Although the study group consist of a very small group of individuals the findings are nonetheless powerful.

Journal of Translational Science

Pilot comparative study on the health of vaccinated and unvaccinated 6 to 12-year-old US children.

ISSN: 2059-268X

There are various examples of how some of these vaccines can do damage amongst a populace, but the general public is not made aware.

In 2009 during another influenza pandemic a vaccine named Pandemrix was utilized across European countries. This was during the H1N1 influenza "pandemic" so of course everyone lined up for their shots. Unfortunately, there was a sudden increase in narcolepsy

I am free, I am free, I AM FREE

in portions of the population who got this shot primarily in children between the ages of 4 to 19.   This means that this influenza vaccine caused a chronic neurological disorder which caused peoples brains to stop being able to properly regulate their sleep-wake cycles in a normal fashion. You know that whole thing we talked about regarding your circadian rhythm (total coincidence).

They first discovered that Pandemrix was causing this issue with people in Finland, and then onto other European countries. They also found the link between Pandemrix and the sudden onset of narcolepsy in children in England. The adjuvant used by GlaxoSmithKline the manufacturer of Pandemrix was the AS03 adjuvant. The AS03 adjuvant is made up of squalene, DL-a-tocopherol and polysorbate 80 (probably read that a lot on your prepackaged food items by the way).

The real issue at hand here is not only the fact that this influenza vaccine damaged people it's that the manufacturer does not know how or why. Was it the adjuvant, hyper immune stimulation, immune activation from the H1N1 infection or all of these or a combination of some? Who knows, and that's kind of the point.

Pandemrix was manufactured in Europe during the 2009-2010 pandemic and has not been produced since. It was never licensed for use inside of the United States.

Autism Link

Initially I chose not to write about the link or non-existent link between vaccines and autism but after further digging I decided it's best to present at least one piece of information that should make everyone sit up and pay attention regardless of your current thoughts regarding this subject.

In 2007 there were 5,000 vaccine autism damage claims taken to the little-known Federal vaccine court. One of those cases is of great interest.

This court was setup by congress in 1988 with the cooperation and consultation of the pharmaceutical industry. Vaccine makers do not defend their vaccine products instead that is left to the Federal government who uses Department of Justice lawyers. To be clear your federal tax dollars are utilized to defend pharmaceutical companies' vaccines in a somewhat hidden court that works outside of the norms of traditional courts.

It's the American citizens who pay out for damages not the vaccine companies. Patient fees are added onto EVERY vaccine distributed to help pay for the damages caused by these same vaccines (got get your flu shot every year, cha-ching).

All hearings are closed to the public and the only insight we are given is via the annual reports produced which show the payout amounts. Unfortunately, I cannot place screenshots of those numbers in these writings however I STRONGLY encourage you to take a bit of time to navigate to the following website and download and review the annual numbers from the official HRSA Data & Statistics website. These reports can be found here: https://www.hrsa.gov/vaccine-compensation/data/index.html

The cover page shows that since the inception of this vaccine court they have paid out a total of $4 Billion dollars to individuals. The vaccine court covers all lawyer fees for anyone who brings a case to the court and to date that total dollar amount is $3.8 Million. Subtracting $3.8 Million from $4 Billion and you have your actual total paid out to those that were injured or killed by vaccines. Another note about this $4 Billion in payouts is with regard to how

I am free, I am free, I AM FREE

many people that have been injured by vaccines have even heard of this court much less brought a case to this court? Can you imagine what the actual injured by vaccine numbers must be?

With the link above you can click on the latest pdf report showing updated numbers regarding several data points most of which are regarding payouts per vaccine injury. Check out the DTaP and Influenza numbers for just a bit of shock and awe.

Recently the public has received a tidbit of information with regard to some of the inner workings of this court specifically as to how the court determined that vaccines are not related to autism.

Pause a moment and take a deep breath because what your about to read is rather disturbing.

Dr. Andrew Zimmerman was the chief witness and expert regarding the link or non-link between vaccines and autism. The DOJ lawyers used Dr. Zimmerman as their expert chief witness to determine that there is 100% NO link between vaccines and autism.

Dr. Zimmerman wrote in his official expert opinion witness paperwork:

"There is no scientific basis for a connection between measles, mumps and rubella (MMR) vaccine or mercury (Hg) intoxication and autism. Despite well-intentioned and thoughtful hypotheses and widespread beliefs about apparent connections with autism and regression, there is no sound evidence to support a causative relationship with exposure to both, or either, MMR and/or Hg. *Patient Name Redacted* had a thorough and normal immunology evaluation by Dr. Sudhir Gupta, showing no signs of immunodeficiency that would have precluded her from receiving or responding normally to MMR vaccine."

He went on to state.

"Furthermore, there is no evidence of an association between autism and the alleged reaction to MMR and Hg, and it is more likely than not, that there is a genetic basis for autism in this child."

That seems iron clad however there is an issue here that your keen eye probably already detected.

I am free, I am free, I AM FREE

In September 2018 Robert F. Kennedy Jr. convinced Dr. Zimmerman to write about the events that took place in the court room in 2007 in an official affidavit.

In the affidavit Dr. Zimmerman declares:

On June 15th, 2007, I was present during a portion of the O.A.P. to hear the testimony of the Petitioner's expert in the field of pediatric neurology, Dr. Marcel Kinsbourne. During a break in the proceedings, I spoke with DOJ attorneys and specifically the lead DOJ attorney, to clarify my written expert opinion.

I clarified that my written expert opinion regarding *Patient Name Redacted* was a case specific opinion as to *Patient Name Redacted*. My written expert opinion regarding *Patient Name Redacted* was not intended to be a blanket statement as to all children and medical science.

I explained that I was of the opinion that there were exceptions in which vaccinations could cause autism.

More specifically, I explained that in a subset of children with an underlying mitochondrial dysfunction, vaccine induced fever and immune stimulation that exceeded metabolic energy reserves could, and in at least one of my patients, did cause regressive encephalopathy with features of autism spectrum disorder.

What to do if you're the DOJ lawyers at this point? What governments the world over tend to do when they have a dissenter. Deny, fire and discredit.

Dr. Zimmerman was immediately informed that he was no longer needed as a witness and the DOJ lawyers then misrepresented the information Dr. Zimmerman provided.

On June 18th, 2007 (3 days after Zimmer was fired which covered the weekend) one of the DOJ lawyers that Dr. Zimmerman spoke to addressed the vaccine court:

"I did want to mention one thing about an expert, who did not appear here, but his name has been mentioned several times, and that was Dr. Zimmerman.

Dr. Zimmerman actually has not appeared here, but he has given evidence on this issue, and it appeared in the *Patient Name Redacted* case. I just wanted to read briefly because his name was mentioned several times by Petitioners in this matter. What his views were on

281

I am free, I am free, I AM FREE

these theories, and I'm going to quote from Respondent's Exhibit FF in the *Patient Name Redacted* case, which is part of the record in this case as I understand it.

He then went on to read Dr. Zimmerman's written statement with regard to there being no link with regard to this specific patient. Then went on to state.

"We know his views on this issue."

Dr. Zimmerman was scheduled to testify on that Monday June 18th but was fired over the weekend.

By ensuring that Dr. Zimmerman was not in the courtroom and utilizing his earlier writings regarding the single case patient they made it seem to the court that Dr. Zimmerman was using this as a blanket statement for all children which Dr. Zimmerman specifically informed this DOJ lawyer that he was not.

Seems like fraud to me. Also seems like a Big win for Big Pharma.

If you trust the CDC perhaps you should be scratching your head right now wondering why the CDC did not inform the public that their one-time chief expert used to end the debate and show no link has instead stated that in fact, there is a link to autism within a subset of children? Isn't the CDC supposed to be the official government body that we pay for to ensure vaccine safety?

Pharma owns Capitol Hill. They are one of the most powerful lobbying groups in existence (move over tobacco) because everyone either takes money from them or if they don't, they are hamstrung as nothing can be pushed forward nor any committees formed to investigate these issues. Too many people are on the take and these things never get off the ground.

Again, there are numbers that I cannot place into these writings that detail the amounts of REPORTED money spent in DC on lobbying by Big Pharma. If you want to have your eyes opened head on over to the following website that brilliantly breaks down the spending:

https://www.opensecrets.org/industries/indus.php?cycle=2018&ind=H04

Don't just look at the summary page. Each tab breaks down a deeper dive into lobbying, money to congress and more.

CONCLUSIONS

It's been a difficult road to navigate this land of vaccinations. On the one hand it kind of makes sense to introduce a "dead" virus to an immune system to allow for it to build immunity without having to deal with the actual live virus. On the other hand, introducing a massive number of viruses to a young immune system with little to no studies regarding how the various viruses interact with each other seems a bit like playing Russian roulette with your child's health and wellbeing. If we tack on the fact that no two human bodies or immune/lymphatic systems are the same and that on a cellular level, you cannot separate what is being injected from what medium it was grown in makes it seem like a really suspect way to go about making attempts at protecting the populace from an ever-growing populace of germs. If you buy into germ therapy at a minimum, you must realize that they need to survive so they will mutate and "evolve" to fight any new inoculations. This would simply ensure that we humans help to create a mutant super germ that cannot be contained by any human intervention.

Next, we move into the brave and bold world of attempting to layout some pros and cons regarding the current vaccine climate.

VACCINE PRO

The medical establishment believes that several life-threatening ailments have been nearly or completely eradicated due to aggressive immunization of the populace.

Vaccines are widely considered the greatest public health success in modern human history.
If everyone does it, we will all be safe (but not really).

Looking at the statistics available it appears to make more sense to vaccinate. You of course run the risk of a myriad of illnesses, crippling ailments and death but the numbers before vaccines were much worse and when your distributing millions and millions of shots on an annual basis the death toll is very low (as long as it's not someone you love and care for).

Constant improvements to the vaccine protocol are attempted to help limit the potential damage and death caused in some individuals.

Vaccines are acknowledged to carry a multitude of risks such as chronic severe adverse effects including death. These risks are considered so low in the overall populace that in effect all children are considered virtually safe from vaccine damage or death (again so long as it's not your child).

The majority in the allopathic health care industry such as doctors, nurses, nurse practitioners, etc. genuinely care about saving lives and making people better. In today's environment they have hordes of money and money-making industries behind them to help support the push for additional research into safety and safer distribution of vaccines.

I am free I am free I AM FREE

VACCINE CON

Although common knowledge dictates that vaccines have saved countless numbers of lives when we dig a bit deeper, we find things like SV40 which is a potential catalyst for creating a mega wave of cancer within the human populace.

Most of these "germs" were already on an extremely steep decline prior to the modern vaccine protocol being put into place. Starting in the 1800's infectious disease started dropping rapidly chiefly due to societies ability to create more readily available food to diminish poverty. They also had their own set of healing modalities prior to vaccines but much of this knowledge did not get passed down through the ages. The ability to ensure cleaner living environments also greatly influenced the ability for these societies to keep people in much better overall physical health.

Although nearly all allopathic medical practitioners are concerned with the health and wellbeing of their patients they examine and treat patients from within a learned paradigm that has a hyper focus on needles, lasers, saws and pills. You have symptom X, so I will give you pill A. Pill A will likely lead to symptom Y later but for now we have masked the real problem by turning off the warning sign of something more critical.

Herd immunity doesn't seem to make much sense. It's stated that vaccines do work so long as 80% - 95% of everyone you encounter is fully immunized (with the latest and greatest boosters to boot). This particular scare tactic is interesting. Either get yourself and your entire family vaccinated with all vaccines or you are going to be responsible for putting humanity into a new Dark Ages.

Currently (and historically) we are nowhere even somewhat kinda close to achieving herd immunity. For one, most adults are not vaccinated with most of the recommended vaccines. According to the CDC's own numbers: https://www.cdc.gov/vaccines/imz-managers/coverage/adultvaxview/pubs-resources/NHIS-2016.html

285

I am free, I am free, I AM FREE

Less than 50% of adults are vaccinated (get the real numbers from the link above to see how low these numbers are for some of the vaccines) which means the concept of herd immunity in today's environment is a non-starter. Also, as mentioned above you would still need to get booster shots for many of these vaccines meaning that even with the 50% number presented by the CDC it does not account for adults not getting boosters. All vaccine "protections" dissipate over time. Most within 10 years, but it generally ranges from 2-10 years. This means that our current baby boomer generation have not had protection from vaccines for many, many years unless they have gotten boosters. Keeping in mind that most adults you encounter are not vaccinated why are we not in the Dark Ages right now? We have all lived the last 35 years or so in communities with folks that have no discernible vaccine protection. This herd immunity mythos seems to have nothing to do with science and everything to do with emotion. (i.e. you will be convinced that you are a bad person that will be responsible for the potential maiming and death of others unless you comply).

Finally, on the topic of herd immunity is regarding forced vaccinations for school children. Seems to make sense. You got a bunch of kids in a small box surrounded by 4 brick walls, let's use vaccines to help cull the spread of disease. The problem here is that even if you vaccinate every kid with every vaccine you still have all the adults which are not on regulated vaccine protocols and yes, these adults are within the same school settings. From teachers and janitors to admin staff, kitchen staff and delivery people the schools are still inundated with non-vaccinated adults who are interacting with each other and these children on a daily.

In 1985 they weren't even administering vaccines for 9 of the vaccines that are given today that they demand are necessary. If before 1985 we didn't have pandemics of these 9 infectious diseases, why are they now so important that the threat of outbreak is directly around the corner without them? Below is the list of the 9 vaccines that in 1985 and prior were not given to school children.

Hep B
Hep A
HPV
Influenza

I am free, I am free, I AM FREE

PCV
Rotavirus
Hib
Varicella
Meningococcal

The medium that these vaccines are grown in even today (chicken eggs) pose a potential danger especially if one considers that on a molecular level you cannot separate chicken embryo parts from what is being shot into people. They've known about this since at least the 1960's when they were shooting monkey kidney cells into the populace.

A somewhat secret vaccination damage court exist and within this court not only are the vaccine manufacturers not liable (tax paying citizens are financially liable) they don't even have to show up for court (and they don't).

In terms of morbidity and mortality there exist almost zero randomized trials on any current vaccine given to our children today. This makes sense from an ethical point of view since you can't have a control group of nonvaccinated children if you believe that nonvaccinated children pose a health risk to themselves and the public. There was an exception when several randomized trials in west Africa showed that the high-titer measles vaccine interacted with the diphtheria-tetanus-pertussis vaccine (DTaP) which lead to an incredible 33% rise in child mortality. But hey! What happens in west Africa stays in west Africa.

The system that has been setup should garner little trust from the public. The British Medical Journal had an investigative journalist produce a feature story in BMJ in 2017 by Peter Doshi. The gist of Peter's article is that we the public tend to rely on advocacy groups to help provide information into health issues including vaccines. One such American vaccine advocacy group that Peter researched was Every Child By Two (ECBT).

ECBT was marketing and helping to push for the recent California mandatory vaccines for school children. Peter also investigated two other entities, The American Academy of Pediatrics (AAP) as well as the Immunization Action Coalition (IAC). These are all not for profit organizations that have large followings to help guide both parents and healthcare providers as well as acting as mouth pieces to help champion legislation to present forced immunizations.

While that all sounds fine and good the other thing that these big three have in common is that they receive funding from both vaccine manufactures as well as directly from the Centers of Disease Control and Prevention. Having not for profit companies that garner large portions of their financing directly from vaccine manufactures while they advocate for forced immunizations makes the entire system appear to be as crooked as a question mark and not working in the interest of concerned parents.

Too many times throughout the history of vaccination protocols the numbers and information that reflect negatively on vaccinations has been covered up and hidden from the public creating a level of distrust. Overall trust in all allopathic medicines has come under great scrutiny from having a hand in the current opioid crisis to doctors cutting off incorrect limbs. The level of trust one places in their doctors has seemingly diminished creating a chasm between patient and doctor. Unfortunately, most doctors spend more time working with medical records than their patients. Once people start questioning the doctors they tend to look at all their practices including vaccination of the populace with a hyper critical eye.

Final thoughts.

Vaccines can be extremely dangerous for some and we have no way of knowing how dangerous or to whom until after the shot(s) have been administered. To compound the issue when looking at the potential long-term damage to the immune system and the potential direct link to cancer from portions of the Salk polio protocol it seems like it may be more reasonable to run the risk of actually "catching" a particular virus in the wild.

The vaccine protocol has been around for many years but in recent decades the amount of vaccination shots required to simply interact at a public school is alarming. To compound this concern

I am free, I am free, I AM FREE

new vaccines are being distributed and there are no long-term studies with regard to morbidity and mortality of these vaccines independently and when combined.

If I were an adult in a healthy state I would avoid any and all vaccines (probably worse off getting vaccines if you're in an unhealthy compromised state actually). Although the vaccine protocol has been around for many years and is claimed to have nearly eradicated some illnesses that were smashing through the human population I would concern myself much more with my living/working environment and my spiritual, mental and physical states. When one considers that these vaccinations become useless over time (2-10 years) it makes the entire ordeal a bit of a nonstarter for an adult.

Whether or not you should vaccinate your children is an entirely different ball of wax. Statically speaking the odds of your child being immediately damaged by the vaccine is incredibly low. I believe there are still too many questions with regard to potential long-term damage of vaccines especially when combined with all the other hazards in our world.

For a concerned parent that trust the science, doctors and money hungry medical establishment I believe a reasonable option would be to only vaccinate your children with those vaccines that cover fatal, near fatal or crippling diseases and if possible wait until the child is a bit older and has a fully developed immune system and a stronger, healthier gut biome. To give your child all vaccines in the vaccine protocol in a small window of time potentially poses an unnecessary risk. By keeping the shots down to only those that you deem necessary and spreading out the timeline of the administration of the shots you may limit the potential perceived dangers from the current vaccination protocol.

MONEY

One last item to cover prior to letting this topic be put to bed. What's the deal with the influenza shot and the obscene amounts of money that the flu vax manufacturers are making?

This argument doesn't hold much water. Although flu vax profits continue to grow the percentage of overall profit is low when we consider the Captain Insano amounts of money these manufactures are raking in annually. Let's look at some numbers and then let's look at the inception of trickle-down economics (voodoo economics for all you around in the 80's, thanks Reagan administration).

Let's look at the big guys annual profits.

Glaxo. Doesn't get much bigger than these guys.
Annual Flu vaccine sales: $420 Million
Annual Total sales: $32 Billion
So yeah $420 Mill aint so bad but when one considers that it only accounts for roughly 1.3% of their annual profit it doesn't seem as substantial especially considering they still have the overhead of running the manufacturing process for the flu vaccine.

Novartis.
Annual Flu vaccine sales: $215 Million (are they even trying to make a profit here)
Annual Total sales: $57 Billion
That accounts for less than 1% of their profits.

Although the annual sale rates of the flu vax are skyrocketing (11% from 2014 to 2015) because these same manufacturers make insane amounts of profits from all those other pills the hustlers....uh doctors are pushing they really aren't making much from the flu vax compared to all the other crap they are pushing.

Another issue facing these large pharma companies is expiring patents or intellectual property which leads to their highest selling products to have to compete with an influx of generic brands coming to market. Knowing that the value of their shares can take a hit when

I am free, I am free, I AM FREE

their biggest brands hit their expiration dates for market exclusivity they need to ensure that they come up with crazy new drugs to market to reset new exclusivity dates and/or have a product that is always in demand such as a flu vaccination.

Wait. Didn't I mention voodoo economics? Yep, I did.

How does a small portion of these profits from the flu vax trickle down to your average doctor's office?

You're a doctor and your running your own practice. You love helping your patients and you have, let's say a nice round number like 2,000 patients. You manage to convince 1,000 of them to get the flu vax at your practice. As a doc running your own practice you want to get the best deal on your flu vaccinations to ensure you maximize your profits. You buy directly from the manufacturer which yields you anywhere between a 10% to 25% profit margin. In addition to this nice profit margin for the flu vaccination itself you also receive your vaccine administration fee which can be as low as $10 per or up to $30 per. Multiply by your 1,000 patients that choose to get the shot at your office and you're looking at a nice chunk of extra change between $10,000.00 and $30,000.00 depending on your admin fee. But hhhmmm, you also are concerned about those 1,000 patients and you don't want to just give them this super safe shot. It's been a while since you've had a regular check-up and we should really get one on the books before we give you the shot. Perhaps you convince 60 or 70 of those 1,000 to come on in for a check-up and you've managed to rack up some additional dollars there. Not to mention if your able to pimp other pills to them during the well check exam.

This is one example of how the current millions of dollars in profits taking place within big pharma and vaccine manufacturers trickle down to your local practice. Knowing that the influenza vaccine accounts for a paltry amount of the overall profits for the manufacturers this allows you to extrapolate this scenario out into the larger pill popping populace.

One of the largest sects of pharmaceutical sales is in statins (cholesterol controlling drugs) which sales rake in by the billions year over year. When you work in an industry (health care) that is set up

291

I am free, I am free, I AM FREE

for profit then you are going to have various avenues to make large sums of money via trickle-down economics so long as you push those pills.

Forcing children that attend public schools (*if you have $ for private school no worries*) to get the flu shot every year regardless of the effectiveness rates ensures a set amount of sales which is great business. If you further force every child attending day-care and every nurse to get these shots, you again are building a great set amount of sales year over year which from a business standpoint is rather advantageous. The nice thing is that unlike the poisonous food industry you don't have to spend much on marketing and making crazy color schemes and put colorful, playful characters on your packaging to trap kids into a head full of tantalizing imagery. You simply work with the local and federal government agencies and if a public school doesn't have kids fully vaccinated within a certain period you take money from the school. Having these forced sales every flu season (ever wonder why it's seasonal anyway? Is it on summer vacation the rest of the year) is guaranteed money in hand. You also work with these federal agencies to ensure you get massive amounts of grants to cut down on your R&D costs. From a purely business perspective the flu vaccine is the gift that keeps on giving, season after season, after season.

Have a look at the graphs on the following site which shows the decline of various diseases prior to the introduction of the modern vaccine protocols.

https://childhealthsafety.wordpress.com/graphs

I gotta say this chapter has been a real pain in the ass to write. Speaking of Segway's let's talk ACV.

CHAPTER 11. APPLE CIDER VINEGAR

I would be remiss not to dedicate an entire chapter in these writings to ACV (unpasteurized with the mother). These days it's touted as a miracle elixir and with good reason. The adage of "an apple a day to keep the doctor away" can and does apply when we are referencing apple cider vinegar with the mother.

To be clear regular apples you purchase at your local grocery store are generally loaded with all sorts of harmful chemicals to greatly extend shelf-life. If you love eating apples be sure to spend the extra money and go organic.

It's believed that apple trees were introduced to modern humanity in the Caspian Sea and Black Sea as far back as 6500 BC. They gained popularity in the 16th century as King Henry VIII had his people search the world for the best varieties of apples to create orchards in England.

ACV on the other hand traces back further as trace amounts have been found in urn's in Egypt dating back to 3000 BC.

Much like kombucha, raw organic ACV is like a scoby which is called the mother and is a collection of fermented bacteria that gives ACV it's cloudy disposition.

The key to ACV being an elixir of health promotion for so long is owing to the fact that Non-Pasteurized Organic Apple Cider Vinegar with the mother contains prebiotics from the fermentation process. Prebiotics is essentially a food source for healthy probiotics within your gut and gut lining which is home to about 70% of your immune system. This allows for the "good" gut probiotics to grow in both number and strength. ACV is one of several fermented items you should consume on a regular basis to gain as many varying varieties of good gut prebiotics as possible. Kimchi, kombucha, tempeh and sauerkraut are other fermented foods and liquids to consume for a better overall healthy gut biome.

For internal consumption think of ACV as a cleanser. ACV is not rich in nutrients. You will gain negligible amounts of fats,

I am free, I am free, I AM FREE

proteins and carbohydrates from ACV. Its primary purpose is to help with cleaning your system and to help with breaking down food stuffs in the stomach. Nearly half of Americans over 60 have issues with breaking down food for proper absorption and elimination. If you suffer from a lack of quality stomach acid, you may have a difficult time breaking down calcium's and other difficult to digest minerals. ACV is said to help break down difficult to digest minerals thusly allowing for better breakdown and absorption of minerals from foods.

CONSUMING

ACV has many and far reaching uses all of which generally play the role of a cleanser. From your internal gut biome, to your skin and even to cleaning within your environment proper ACV seems to be the gift that keeps on giving.

Due to the many and various uses of ACV in these writings I have primarily stuck to the external uses for your body.

TYPE

Ensure that the ACV you purchase align with the following standards.

- Unpasteurized
- Unrefined
- Unfiltered
- With the mother

BEAUTY USES

There are several well-known uses for ACV to help clean and brighten the exterior of your body as well as the interior. Let's look at some external uses.

HAIR

ACV has several benefits for your hair and scalp.

- Restore pH balance of your scalp to help avoid frizzy hair and dry itchy scalp.
- Remove nasty product build up in your hair and on your scalp
- Get your shine on.

Restore pH:

Shampoos and conditioners damage the cuticles of hair which causes issues such as dry and frizzy hair.

Simply dilute some ACV with water and rinse through your hair on a regular basis to help restore your hair/scalp pH.

Remove build up:

The acidic properties of ACV allow it to act as a conditioner for your hair since it can help strengthen and seal your hair cuticles.

I am free, I am free, I AM FREE

Shine:

Another great thing about ACV when applied to the hair and scalp is that it will help to make your overall glow shiny creating an overall healthier appearance.

You can cut back on washing/conditioning your hair daily. Most can stick to a 2-3 day a week diluted ACV wash.

CAUTIONS

Although ACV is great for your head there are a couple of items that may be of concern for you.

Long term use of ACV can lighten your hair. That might be beneficial for some and not so much for others.

How To:

There are many recipes available so let's simplify with basic hair application.

Add 4 Tablespoons of ACV to 16 ounces of water.

Pour it over your head trying to get it from the scalp out to your hair. Gently rub your scalp with your fingers for about 2 minutes.

Once the 2 minutes is complete gently rinse your hair under water.

FACIAL TONER/WASH

ACV is popular for controlling acne and other skin care needs. This is partially because ACV has antifungal and antibacterial properties. The acids within ACV can also work to remove dead skin cells helping to present a more overall youthful glow.

CAUTIONS

ACV especially when using it for the first time can be overwhelming in both smell and the physical sting your skin can feel. It's wise to dilute your ACV every time you use it for applying directly to your skin or hair. In this how to the ratio is set low to allow for greater dilution but as you continue to utilize ACV you can adjust this ratio with less water or more ACV.

How To:

Add 1 Tablespoon of ACV with 3 Tablespoons slightly warmed water (preferably distilled).

I am free, I am free, I AM FREE

Pick a portion of your face or forehead and apply a small amount and let it sit for 30 minutes. This is simply to make certain that your skin doesn't go crazy before you apply it to your entire face. Once you know your face is good with ACV you no longer will need this 30-minute test run.

If the test run is good apply the ACV to your entire face.

Splash a bit of warm water on your face.

Dunk a cotton ball into your ACV mix and apply to your face.

Ensure you cover your nose, earlobes, cheeks and neck.

DETOX BATH

There are many natural detox baths to choose from such as clay, ginger, Epsom salts, baking soda and essential oils but since we are focusing on ACV let's discuss what it provides.

An ACV bath is not going to smell nearly as pleasant as an essential oils bath, but the ACV bath is considered greatly superior for its level of detox capabilities. If the smells are too great you can drop in a bit of essential oils to cut the smell of the ACV.

Proper ACV can help create soft supple skin and contains antifungal and antimicrobial compounds.

Easy Peasy How To:
Clean your tub
Get some muscle relaxing warm water into that tub
Pour 1 cup of raw, organic, unprocessed ACV into the water.
Put on some mood music and soak for a good 20-30 minutes or until the water starts to get too cold for comfort.
After your time is up perform a quick shower rinse in either cold or luke warm water.

AGGRESSIVE FACE SCRUB

There are plenty of options for gentle face scrubs such as ACV/Sugar scrub, ACV/Baking Soda, ACV/Green Tea.

These are all great for their various benefits, but this recipe is for those that have aggressive skin issues on the face. It's recommended that you visit a dermatologist first but if you prefer to stick to all-natural healings then check this guy out. Also, side note if you have made significant changes to your diet recently by cutting things out or adding things you normally do not consume, and you are now freshly experiencing skin issues on your face it's a good bet that the dietary changes may be the culprit.

CAUTION

Don't get this in your eyes. ACV is strong and if not diluted it does sting the eyes.

Ingredients:

1 Tablespoon Organic Coconut Oil

2 teaspoons brown sugar

1 teaspoons ACV

How To:

Place melted Organic Coconut Oil into a small ceramic bowl. Add the brown sugar and stir until incorporated.

Lightly scrub face with mix to exfoliate and remove dead skin. Once complete rinse face with slightly warm water.

Using cotton balls apply ACV to face.

All done.

CHAPTER 12. HEALING MODALITIES

L et the healing begin. Within this chapter we are going to provide various healing modalities some of which you can and should incorporate into your lifestyle.

The healing modalities vary with some focusing on specific physical portions of your body and other's such as cold-water therapy incorporate a more holistic "all-in-one" healing practice.

Regardless where you find yourself on your path today make sure to take it slow and don't introduce too much too soon. It's important to incorporate a practice and let it run its course for a bit, so you can determine which healing modalities are the most effective for you right now.

Be well, be blessed be strong.

I am free I am free I AM FREE

Breathing techniques for meditation have been around for thousands of years and currently and historically have existed within many and varying cultures.

Traditional Tao's breathing practices have been around since at least the mid-6th Century BC as one of the earliest forms of using air and energy as a medical therapy was discovered within 12 jade tablets in a Chinese province. From the traditional Tao's perspective proper breathing of air is used for nutrition. The air (prana) you breath is considered more important than food or even water when it comes to supporting and sustaining a high quality life.

In the Tao's traditions there are two primary functions for breathing. One is for cleansing the body, mind and spirit and the other is to energize these same systems.

Automated cleansing breath example.

When you let out a heavy sigh often you can feel pieces of collected "stress" being released from your mind. On the physical level when your body starts to reach higher states of toxicity within the blood this action of a deep gulp of air followed by a somewhat forceful exhalation helps to expel toxins.

Automated energizing breath example.

Remember the last time you felt a bit lethargic and you involuntarily pulled large amounts of air deep into your body in a slow manner? You know a yawn? Usually when we yawn, we either flair our nostrils to allow a larger gulp of air or we inhale through our mouths to garner as much air in one gulp as possible. This deep inhalation and exhalation is an involuntary response your body has started to cool down your brain and get more oxygen to the rest of your organs to wake you up.

For most of the breathing techniques we focus more on the Tao's traditional breath work that helps to calm the mind and spirit and create a stronger connection to the body. These techniques can be

I am free, I am free, I AM FREE

utilized most often during your meditation practices. Other breathing techniques will be outlined in additional chapters because the techniques are for specific applications and sometimes do not follow the principles of the traditional Tao's breathing techniques.

Some of the baseline principles for breathing the Tao's way.

1. Inhalations always come in through the nostrils and never through the mouth.
2. Exhalations can occur through either or both the nose and mouth.
3. Breathing techniques are never practiced while laying down as this does not allow for the proper flow of Chi.
4. The stomach is considered the "Sea of Energy" and nearly every practice will require breathing into the belly.

Basic breathing technique for meditation.

Three keys to successful breath work for meditation.
1. Concentrate all your attention on your breathing.
2. Slow and steady wins the race.
3. Proper belly breathing.

One of the primary purposes to conscious breathing aside from the potential health benefits is to stay calm and relaxed and to allow you to un-focus on the 3D world around us and the social construct. This is one of the most difficult portions of meditation when first starting the practice. Your active societal brain immediately kicks into over drive as soon as you wake up. It immediately projects future events (gotta take a shower, get some food, drop off the kids, oh yeah little Timmy has soccer practice later and I still have to get that TPS report turned in before noon).

Because we have been born and raised inside of this hyper active social construct your brain is nearly always racing along in hyper active mode, constantly thinking about near future events in an attempt to protect you from potential societal pitfalls like forgetting to drop little Timmy off at soccer practice.

Although you can meditate at any time of the day or evening, when first starting the practice you may want to consider incorporating a small 10-15-minute meditation window at the very

I am free, I am free, I AM FREE

beginning of your day. Your social brain will be active but likely less active compared to the rest of the day. Some prefer to meditate in the evening hours just before laying down to sleep at night. This can also act as a good time to start your meditation practice however your social brain may still get stuck in past and future events making it more difficult to gain the state you want to achieve. Further, we already are greatly out of sync with our circadian sleep cycles and adding an additional layer of delay to your natural sleep cycle may not be the most efficient approach. There is a caveat to that. If in the future you start working towards other practices outside of meditation but tie into your sleep cycles like astral projection, lucid dreaming or Merkabah work the evening hours just before sleep are ideal for these practices and having solid, disciplined breathing techniques can be instrumental in achieving these goals at a much faster rate. With that said waking up with the sun and practicing proper breathing and meditation techniques is a more natural approach and tends to be what your body/mind seeks.

BREATHING TECHNIQUE 1: Slow and Steady

This is a baseline breathing technique and is one of the most important ones to use for calming your body/mind and helping you to get into a proper relaxed meditative state.
  Preferred posture:
Comfortably sitting with your back aligned in as straight a line as possible. If you need to press your back against a wall to obtain a comfortable straight spine do it. You can also use a hard-wooden chair with a hard back. If using the hard-wooden chair, ensure that you are barefoot and ground your feet to the floor. You should not be sitting on a couch or cushioned seat. This will greatly disrupt your body's ability to take in the air and properly move your energy.

1. Take a long slow breath in through your nose. This breath should take 4-5 seconds to breath in. You want to focus on breathing into your belly (not your chest). I know we like flat abs but, in this instance, we want to see our stomachs actively rise. A key here is to try to fill your stomach up from the bottom to the top. This might seem like a strange concept but as you practice you will find that you can feel the air rising from the bottom of your stomach and filling up.
2. Once you have your breath hold it for 4-5 seconds.
3. Let your breath out BUT in a slow and controlled manner. You will take 4-5 seconds to slowly let the breath out attempting to let the air naturally release from the top of the stomach to the bottom.
4. Once fully exhaled hold 4-5 seconds with no air in your lungs.
5. Repeat this cycle for as long as you can through your 10-15 meditation practice.

You can practice this one right now while either sitting or standing. This is a very rhythmic calming breath and anytime you feel overwhelmed you can STOP! Take a moment to take inventory of your breathing. When we are stressed or under some sort of pressure our automated breathing tends to increase in speed and becomes shallow. In these moments you can practice the 4 steps

I am free, I am free, I AM FREE
above for a 3-4 breathing cycle and you will find that you have
calmed your body and mind significantly.

BREATHING TECHNIQUE 2: Relaxation

This is one I used years ago when attempting to put myself to sleep. I found I couldn't quite my mind to fall asleep and would spend what felt like hours lying in bed staring at my eyelids hoping for the sweet, sweet nectar of the dream world (although maybe we are already experiencing that). This technique allowed me to focus on breathing and each individual body part. This allows the active social brain to quit down for a bit, so you can fall deep into a relaxed state.
   Preferred posture:
   Laying down on either a hard-wooden floor or on a yoga mat. You can also use this technique for putting yourself to sleep so if your using it for this purpose a comfortable mattress and pillow will suffice.

1. Start taking slow calming breaths similar to the first technique. Slow in, hold, slow out, hold, repeat.
2. Once you have a good breathing rhythm going start to focus on each individual body part. Start at the bottom and work your way up.
3. Start by recognizing your toes. Feel the energy in your toes and start to push that energy up your toes through your feet and into your ankles. Keep the rhythmic breathing going while actively concentrating on the energy you're slowly moving up your body.
4. This can work much like breath work in Yoga. As you are slowly inhaling in you are gathering and feeling the energy at whichever body part you are at. As you slowly exhale move that energy further up the body.
5. Keep this going all the way up your body until you get to the crown of your head. At this point take a nice long slow inhalation. We are looking for a good 7-8 second slow inhalation. A 4-5 second hold, then with your breath push the energy straight out of the top of your head as you breath out.

I am free, I am free, I AM FREE

This is a cleansing breathing technique incorporated to help expel negative energy. It's greatly beneficial in being actively in control of your breathing and creating the mind/body connection.

I am free I am free I AM FREE

BREATHING TECHNIQUE 3: Focused Visualization

This technique can be utilized in many ways. In our Western culture this is largely utilized as future projection to visualize a "dream" into reality. That's good stuff but for our meditation practices the last thing we want to do is focus on the 3D world and the social construct around us. BUT we can create a calm and comforting 3D reality within ourselves.

1. Start the breath work from technique 1.
2. After you have fallen into the rhythmic pattern of the breathing technique start to visualize a comforting environment. As an example, I've always loved the beach. As I visualize the beach it's my own interpretation of a beach. I slowly walk barefoot through the sand towards the sounds of the calming waves. I can FEEL the soft sand between my toes. It's slightly cool because the sun is just starting to come up over the horizon of the endless water. I can hear the seagulls as they fly overhead scavenging for food. Their piercing cries cutting in over the steady, calming crash of the waves.
   a. You get the idea. Your vision may be a forest or a baseball field. Whatever it is you MUST focus on completely being there. Every smell, taste, touch, sight. Really feel that you are present within that location.

This is essentially the 1st technique with some visualization thrown into the mix. Hey, I told you that technique 1 was a key breathing technique for meditation. There are many other breathing techniques such as alternate nostril, breath of fire and dozens of others. Most of these aren't going to focus on beginning the practice of mindful breathing during mediation and some such as the breath of fire have the opposite of a calming effect and instead will work to energize in a forceful manner.

Additional tips

I am free, I am free, I AM FREE

If you can get outdoors, close to sunrise in nature you will incorporate the greatest benefit of breathing in the life healing prana around you.

Doing deep breath work inside of areas of recycled air isn't the greatest but can be better than sitting at a small park located in a downtown city landscape. The air "quality" in most metropolitan US cities is abysmal and should be avoided. Also, not recommended to run or jog in these areas.

It can be frustrating when first starting but like many other things in our lives once we incorporate it as a consistent practice, we get better at it and the results of compound interest kicks in within rather short order to provide life giving energy and healing.

Benefits of active breathing

Improves awareness and connectivity to self.
As outlined in the sex chapter proper breathing techniques will enhance sexual potency.

Helps to calm emotions and shut down the social brain even if for a short period

Improves the power and flexibility of the diaphragm, which improves overall breath control.
Benefits the heart, lungs and overall circulatory system.

You will find that various breathing techniques will present themselves throughout other chapters of this book. This is because these topics have specific breathing techniques to help enhance or improve the practice for that chapter. The sex chapter as well as the cold-water immersion chapters are two examples that have specific breathing and energy control techniques applied to them.

ENERGY BREATH WORK

As discussed earlier in this chapter although there exist many and varying breath work techniques, they all should reside under one of two categories. The breath exercise is for cleansing, energizing or both.

The following sections will review various energizing breath exercises and will also list some of the key uses for them.

Special Attention

All energizing breath work is best performed in the cleanest air you can surround yourself in.

There is an increased risk of becoming light headed while performing energizing breath work. As such you should take precautions to never perform these exercises while standing, operating heavy machinery, swimming, etc.

I am free I am free I AM FREE

BREATH OF FIRE

Alright ya'll let's jump right into the deep end. The coveted Breath of Fire.

I rarely utilize this breathing exercise but within Yoga circles and other....well.... circles the Breath of Fire is considered one of the greatest energizing breath exercises available.

Most people perform the Breath of Fire as a healing modality. It is known to release pent up anxiety, and both strengthens and releases tension from that most import chakra point in the gut. It's also accredited with flushing toxins from the blood stream and massaging some of your internal organs. Pretty good stuff from a single breath exercise.

Don't get too discouraged with this one. It's somewhat difficult to get at first especially if you haven't done any of the slower breathing exercises. The slower breathing exercises can help build the strength of your diaphragm which will make the energizing breath exercises a bit easier to grasp and perform.

Preferred posture:
Sitting comfortably Indian style or a similar comfortable seated position. As with most other energizing breath work you should NOT be standing, operating heavy machinery, going for a leisurely swim, etc.

Rounds:
Entirely up to you. Instead of counting rounds you probably just want to set a timer and once it goes off finish that round of breathing and stop. When you first begin, choose a low time like 1 minute.

Duration:
When first beginning 1 minute is plenty. As you gain power and get more comfortable you can add additional time.

Equipment:
Warm clothing, optional yoga mat, stop watch or stop watch on cellphone.

311

I am free, I am free, I AM FREE

How to do it.

1. Sit yourself down comfortably.
2. Breath in through your nose extremely rapidly pulling the abdomen in.
3. Exhale the air out rapidly through the nose whilst pushing your abdomen out.
4. These breaths are short, rapid and loud. They should be somewhat annoyingly loud. And by rapid we're talking 2-3 cycles of rapid air exchange in and out per second.

That's it. It's an easy breathing sequence but the subtly is in the diaphragm/abdomen work. Once you start to perform this exercise a couple of times a week you may become addicted to the overall feel good vibes you receive from this healing, energizing breathing exercise.

I am free I am free I AM FREE

COLD SHOWER BREATHING PREPERATIONS

This breathing technique pretty much breaks all the normal rules that traditional healing breathing exercises incorporate. Instead of drawing air into your stomach in slow rhythmic sequences through the nose/nasal passages, we will be gulping up large swaths of air via our mouth hole.

Anyone who practices breath work will tell you the many benefits of pulling air through your nose instead of your mouth and they aint wrong.

Two primary reasons why we are not taking this air in through the nose is because we are looking for an energizing charge of oxygen to hyper stimulate various systems within our bodies. We want to force large swaths of air into our systems and our mouth is much larger than our nostrils for intaking large volumes of air. Most breath work done through the nose is for calming as opposed to energizing. We will be missing the cleansing mechanisms of the nasal passages and the warming of the air, however there is another reason to pull air through the mouth during this breathing exercise.

Little known fact but when you pull air through your sinuses, they produce nitric oxide when you perform nasal breathing, humming and breath retention. We don't want this nitric oxide hitting our bloodstream because nitric oxide produces a feeling of euphoria and is a relaxant. This is great when doing yoga and/or hitting your low humming OOOOHHHMMSSS, but not so great for what we are attempting to achieve with this breath work.

Because we lose out on the benefits of nose breathing such as effective temperature control, filtration and effective dehumidification we want to perform this energizing breath work in the cleanest air quality surroundings we can find. It would be idyllic to be in a meadow in the middle of nowhere surrounded by that good ass prana but since this isn't available to many of us do the best you can. If you can get outside away from a city landscape, it's probably better than doing it indoors with recycled air.

This breathing routine can be performed anytime for a boost of energy and to create a connection with mind/body however I tend to

313

use it in the mornings prior to my cold showers. I don't do it every day, but I do it most days and it helps to give me a boost when I perform the exercise.

Preferred posture:
Sitting comfortably Indian style or laying on your back. Might be a good idea to toss a hoodie and sweats on to create additional warmth around your body.

Rounds:
As little as 3 or up to 5. When you get to rounds 4 and 5 the technique changes. If you want to keep it simple do 3 rounds but rounds 4 and 5 are the rounds that create the big boost you're looking for.

Duration:
There is no set time as you are going for rounds.

Equipment:
Warm clothing, optional yoga mat, stop watch or stop watch on cellphone.
   In this exercise you are still breathing into your stomach. Instead of slow breaths through the nose you will be taking large gulping breaths through your mouth. On the release you don't need to forcefully push the air out, but you don't want it to be slow either.

1. Either lay down or sit down in a comfortable fashion such as with your back against the wall. Under no circumstances should you be standing, driving, swimming or doing anything that can jeopardize your well-being should you become light headed.
2. Take a sharp deep breath into your belly pulling the air in from your mouth (warning when you first start doing this exercise your throat will feel dry. After time this will no longer occur).
3. Do not hold the breath simply allow it to naturally release giving it a slight push out.
4. Repeat this in and out air exchange for 30 breaths. Close your eyes and concentrate on the energy in your belly and head as your performing the 30 breathes.

I am free, I am free, I AM FREE

5. When you get to breath 30 on the release you will not take another breath. It's the same as holding your breath but instead of filling your lungs with air and holding it you are expelling all the air out of your body and holding it.
6. Did I forget to mention you need a timer? Hey, you need a timer. When you release your breath on number 30 press a timer and close your eyes.
7. Hold for as long as you can with no air in your lungs. When you need to take a breath stop your timer and take a breath.
8. Hold the inhalation breath for 10-15 seconds.
9. Reset your stop watch.
10. Perform this same 30 breath routine and holding the exhale for a total of 3 rounds.
11. On round 4 we change things up a bit.
12. Don't worry about the stop watch anymore. No timing necessary.
13. Take your 30 breaths as you did in rounds 1-3.
14. On breath 30 after you have expelled all the air from your lungs get on the ground and do as many push-ups with high quality form as you can while your breathe is exhaled.
15. Once you need to take a breath stop your push-ups, get back into your comfortable position and immediately start the same breath cycle but instead of 30 breaths do 15 breaths.
16. Don't worry about timing the hold because it won't be long. Don't hold your expelled breath longer than 1 minute.
17. As soon as you must take in a breath start another round of breath work, but this time go for the full 30 breaths again just like in rounds 1-3.
18. When you expel your breath on breath 30 and are holding with no air in your lungs concentrate on the energy in your head. It's likely that at this point you may be feeling or hearing a crackling like electricity in your head. Are you keeping your eyes closed? I hope so. You may also start seeing many small swirling patterns of various sizes and colors just in front of your vision. Your body is heated up nicely at this point. Once you must take a breath do it and hold the air in for 10-15 seconds.
19. Now your all done and now is a great time to jump in a cold shower.

I am free, I am free, I AM FREE

MEDITATION

Our topic on breathing seems like the best place to start discussing the healing practice of mediation.

What is meditation?

It can be rather confusing and difficult to define the term meditation in today's environment. There are so many varying definitions and theories that often leads to practicing the art of meditation in a very non-efficient manner.

Many will define meditation as a state of deep thinking or contemplation while others define it as a state of being half awake and half asleep, like a dream state.

I'm no guru but I don't believe meditation is either of these things. One of the key factors in meditation is that you are in fact alert and aware. So much so that the outside world slowly fades away from all your senses as you focus on the journey inward.

With so many different marketing products for meditation things can get confusing quickly. Guided meditation, VR headset meditation, visualization meditation, positive affirmations meditation. The problem is none of these are really meditation although some of these can help you in other ways and some may help prep you for attempting to get yourself into the state of meditation.

Meditation should not be looked at as the latest trendy self-healing modality to try out. True meditation is something that may never come your way, or it could take several years, months or weeks to get into a meditative state. When a Yogi is in a true meditative state their energy/awareness is said to move beyond their bodies as they connect to the great divine of the Universe.

One of the oddities regarding meditation is that it is nothing. No. Thing. You are attempting to quite your social brain, so you are no longer aware of anything within our 3D reality. Meditation is really nothing (no thing). You want no single thing to be inside of your 3D reality. Your perceived 5 senses will work to keep things moving inside of your brain. Via kinesthetic you will start to feel your body maybe an itch to distract you or the sensation of hot or cold. Via your audio sensory things, you normally don't hear around your house will start to distract you as you attempt to meditate.

317

I am free, I am free, I AM FREE

Many like to use the practice of meditation to destress. People like to use the process of meditation to achieve the effect of relieving stress. The problem here is that meditation is not a process to achieve an outcome. Meditation IS the outcome. If you can achieve something close to the meditative state that Yogis achieve your outcome is being so connected to your inner self and so far, removed from your ego and social brain that you become connected to Universal bliss.

So how do we journey inward to achieve a state of meditation?

I struggled with this for a long time. Most of the advice I was given centered around clearing my head, thinking of nothing or trying to picture just a lightbulb or beach in my head. None of these techniques worked to move me deeper into a meditative state. Then one day someone gave me the best advice for moving inward towards a meditative state.

He told me that attempting to think of nothing was silly and pretty much impossible. As soon as you relax and close your eyes and tell yourself think of nothing your brain kicks into overdrive and starts thinking about everything or the brain becomes laser focused in attempting to think about nothing and starts to strongly focus on one or two items. Instead of trying to think of nothing allow your brain to think whatever it wants just don't hold on to any single thought. Thoughts are just thoughts. There are no good thoughts and no bad thoughts. Just let the thoughts come right in and let them keep moving along. After a period, the brain kind of exhausts itself and things start to become quiet. It is within this moment that your 5 senses will start to pick up things inside of your environment. At this point it can be very helpful to focus on your slow relaxing breathing and the beating of your heart. Continue to allow these things to pass so you do not start a dialogue inside of your head. If you hear the neighbor's dog barking let the sound come in and then go right back out. If you allow it to come in, then start a dialogue in your head (oh man the neighbor's dog is barking again. They probably just got home or maybe someone came to the door, blah, blah, blah). This is what you are trying to avoid. Avoid this self-created dialogue from starting up. Let things come in and flow right on by.

It helps to practice getting to a meditative state while you are already feeling calm. If you are very stressed and you are trying to

318

I am free, I am free, I AM FREE
use meditation to relieve the stress it is likely going to be almost impossible to quite your mind and find a state of meditation.

Meditation can be difficult for many. I know it was for me when I first started and even now I typically do short meditation sessions in the 10-20-minute range. When you are first starting out you should consider meditating for 1-2 minutes at a time. As you continue to practice you will become better and better at not allowing dialogue to start in your head. As this starts to happen you can then start stretching your meditation sessions on longer and longer until you find the timelines that work best for you.

Getting into a meditative state can be difficult and frustrating but don't be hard on yourself. We have been taught since we were children to observe and react to stimulus within our 3D reality but most of us are never taught to turn off outside stimulus and observe our energy and power within. We believe we know who we are but most of us have never been taught to connect to what we truly are, so we define ourselves according to our perceptions of how we believe others are judging us.

Example:

I am Fred, I am a 35-year-old American male. I work as a bank teller and drive a 2 door American made car. I have 2 kids and rent a small 2-bedroom apartment in a part of town I don't love. This is not who we truly are, but this is how others perceive us, so we perceive ourselves as our names, jobs, careers, cars, houses, education. None of these things truly define who we are they are only the social construct of the avatar we have chosen to show to the rest of society. We are so good a chameleon we can even pull the wool over our own third eye and convince ourselves that we are this person based on the sum of these qualifications.

And why not? We have been taught this our entire lives by simply living and surviving inside of this society. If we never received guidance to show us how to reflect on the internal to find our true power and we have academia that exist to drill it into our heads that life exist by accident and we are merely here to survive and procreate it's no wonder many of us have such a difficult time finding the guiding light of meditation.

Another thing that can be frustrating is although you are trying to get into a meditative state your intention should not necessarily be

I am free, I am free, I AM FREE
to get into the meditative state. I know that sounds counter intuitive, but intentions are important. If your intent is to achieve the meditative state and you keep coming up short your likely to get frustrated which will greatly hinder your ability to achieve the meditative state. Your primary intent should be to simply attempt to achieve a state of nothing.

Tips for meditation.

1. Sit up with a comfortable straight back and head. You need to be comfortable but it's very important that you keep your back straight.
2. Preferred practice is in the morning but whatever time of day you chose try to be consistent with cultivating the practice of stillness during the same timeframe every day.
3. Relax your body.
4. Relax your breathing and practice some slow controlled belly breathing. Listen and feel your breath and your heart.
5. Your breathing is a key to help you let thoughts pass. As thoughts come in witness the thought but do not judge or emotionally connect to the thought. Recognize it, then focus back on your breathing and let the thought exit.

Progress

It can be difficult to judge the progress of your meditation. If you start a workout program you may see a physical change rather quickly and you can track progress visually, but how do you judge your progress when it comes to meditation?

One way I have found is via a journal and progress tracker. Because I couldn't find anything I loved I created my own which handy enough is available for sale.

Your unconscious mind is millions of times more powerful than your conscious mind. Every time you practice getting into the meditative state you are adding coin to the bank of unconscious positive programming. Our brains and egos are like Lord of The Flies. They are unruly, untamed and the fans of thought and ego chaos are inflamed inside of this society with the mass media marketing outlets amongst many other distractions. Your brain is

I am free, I am free, I AM FREE
getting smashed with symbolism and attempts at unconscious programming everywhere you look and go on a 24/7 basis. Taking these moments to practice stillness helps to quite the conscious brain and allows for you to connect to your unconscious consciousness. If you can continue to practice meditation everyday if possible, you will start to find your path towards your true self.

COLD SHOWERS

I'm not always the most subtle or cautious of people. When I first started doing research on cold water therapy I thought once again that the interwebs was full of trolls manically laughing and rubbing their hands together in the Hollyweird super villainous fashion hoping to get suckers to suffer under the plethora of their cold shower lies.

As such I wanted to find out first hand so decided to jump right in. One hot summer day I cranked the bath knob as far as it would go clockwise and jumped in. And then jumped back out, then back in and shivered and shivered and shivered.

I did this for 3-4 days before I finally got to the point where I could at least stay in the water for a full 2 minutes granted I was shivering like crazy and wasn't exactly having the time of my life. When I stepped out of those showers I did feel insanely invigorated though. My mind felt very clear and my energy levels went way up.

It wasn't necessarily the best way to approach cold water immersion, but it worked for me and it's a very rare occurrence that I have taken a warm shower since. Below are some methods to help ease you into this experience and to calm your mind which will relax your body and allow you to yes embrace and enjoy the healing modalities that come with cold water immersion.

When to start

Depending on your climate and your dwelling you may want to start this practice during the summer months. I started in the summer purely by happenstance and when the winter months rolled around the water was a full 20 degrees colder. One reason for this is due to the pipes running into your dwelling.

I live in a house and as such my pipes are in the ground and run directly from the city pipes in the street/sidewalk through my front yard and into my house. As the ground gets colder so do those pipes and boy can they get cold in the winter time. In my environment we have all 4 seasons and typically in the winter it gets cold but not frigid. Even so those cold showers in the winter were typically in the 55 degrees Fahrenheit realm so know your location.

I am free, I am free, I AM FREE

I also noticed that when I went to different regions, typically getting closer to the equator the cold showers were not cold at all compared to my environment.

Another thing that came up for me was when I showered in hotels, apartments or gym facilities. Those waters never really got very cold likely due to the labyrinthine nest of internal pipes the water is traveling prior to coming out of the shower head. With so much time inside of those insulated internal pipes the water heats up by several degrees which makes for a noticeable difference in overall temperature.

When you're first starting off 70 degrees Fahrenheit will likely feel like an ice bath. As you continue the practice and spend additional time in colder waters 70 degrees will start to feel like slightly warm water.

One thing that happens after a period is that you start to wake up your brown fat. Your body has a large (not really large compared to white fat) deposit around your upper chest and collar bone. As you continue this practice you will start to notice you are going to start generating your own heat and much of the source of this heat will be from the upper chest and breastbone area.

I am free I am free I AM FREE

BEGINNER

When first starting off it's best to start with your regular warm shower then end the last 30 seconds of your shower on full cold mode. If you're in a location where yelling and screaming is acceptable you should not hold it in and go ahead and belt out some guttural screams of joy. When first starting off I would do this every weekend because it felt amazing and I wanted to wake the house up.

Do this every day. Don't let your fake brain tell you to skip a day. It's only 30 seconds BUT you MUST maintain consistency to properly level up.

I am free I am free I AM FREE

INTERMIDIATE

Okay, you got some juice now. You've been in the cold water several times and not only do you know you can do 30 seconds on the coldest setting it's starting to feel pretty damn good.

Before you begin check out the breathing techniques chapter and perform the cold-water breathing technique for at least 3 rounds. This helps to prep you mentally and preps the body.

Find an amazing upbeat song that speaks to you in a very positive way. Crank that shiz up.

Remember the breathing routine you just completed?

Set a timer for 2 minutes on your phone or whatever you got.

No warm or hot water this time. Crank it on cold and put your body in that water.

Slow your breathing down and concentrate on the sensations of the cold water flowing over your body. Don't think about the cold or the time. Concentrate on your breathing, the music and feel your upper chest heating up, creating its own fire to meet the cold water.

Keep this going until you can work your way up to 5 minutes. Eventually you should be able to choose whether you want to do the breathing technique or not prior to the shower. You also no longer need the music at this point as it's now more of a distraction. You should now be focusing on your body and your calming breaths. The cold will feel cold for the first 10-20 seconds, but your body will now start heating up quickly and after about 20-30 seconds although you register the water as cold it's not cold anymore. It's just water that's not hot.

I am free I am free I AM FREE

BIG BOSS

Now you're wearing your big boy pants (or big girl panties)
Check out the breathing techniques chapter and perform the Cold Shower Preparations breathing technique for at least 3 rounds but preferably include the bonus fourth and fifth rounds for increased strength, connectivity to self and warming the overall core temperature of your body.

For this part, be smart and safe.

After you have completed the breathing technique, bring your cellphone to the bathroom with you to act as your timer.
Do not turn on your bathroom lights as you want to keep it as dark as possible. Remember to be safe and use common sense while the lights are off.
If you need to block light coming through the bottom of your door use a towel to block that light out.
Put the water on the coldest setting and turn it on.
Set the timer on your phone anywhere from 5-10 minutes. 5 minutes should be the daily practice and once a week you should take a 10-minute cold shower.
Once the timer is set hit Start and cover the phone with another towel to block the light from the phone.

Get in that water.

Place both hands behind your back and allow the cold water to hit your chest. Fully embrace the sensation of the ENERGY of the water pounding onto your chest. Fully accept the cold in the silence and absence of light. Feel your chest warming up as it creates its own heat. Once you feel completely at ease and acceptance of the hostile input has taken place (usually 30 - 60 seconds) raise your left arm above your head and allow the water to pound on your left armpit and ribs. Do this for as long as you want but don't make it too short. At least 30 seconds. Repeat on the right side.
Ensure you individually get both legs covered in water for at least 30 seconds each.

326

I am free, I am free, I AM FREE

Go back to the water pounding on your upper chest. By now the water is no longer cold and has become a friend to grant you strength. Time to bring the pain. Look up and let the water pound into your face and the top of your head.

Tilt your head forward and allow the water to cascade down your entire back.

Keep this routine up until your timer goes off.

Step out of the shower but do not grab for your towel to dry off right away. Feel your chest heating up to warm your body. After you have given it at least 30 seconds grab your towel, dry off and you are done.

I am free I am free I AM FREE
ALTERNATIVE METHODS

There is a practice that has been around since pretty much forever which is a hot/cold methodology. This is available in many spa's but has been in practice for centuries. Back in the day it would be jumping from a hot spring into a cold river which we will simulate via our shower.

Forcing the extremes of hot and cold cause your muscles to expand and contract which is said to allow for a gentle detox of toxins as they are squeezed from your muscles. Remember that heart muscle? Hhhmm, so increasing oxygen input then forcing the heart muscle to put said oxygen throughout the body just might lead to some amazing things.

The hot water is said to draw old blood out of internal organs and the cold water then forces fresh blood back into the organs and the core of the body. The circulation of the entire system is greatly increased as the heart and veins work in tangent to further open and restrict blood flow to various parts of your body including the extremities.

To perform this practice, you can start with a regular warm shower, then turn it over too cold for 30 to 60 seconds, then back over to warm for 30 to 60 seconds. Continue this practice for several minutes ending your shower with 30 to 60 seconds of cold.

!!DANGER WILL ROBINSON!!

If you have a heart condition, it's wise not to jump balls deep into cold water therapy.

If you are currently on chemo or recently underwent chemo treatment you should refrain from flushing blood throughout the body via hot/cold water therapy.

Aside from using hot and cold water for healing some also use items such as hot and cold pads placed in specific regions to stimulate healing within specific organs. We are not looking at that methodology but an obvious potential danger here would be in burning your skin.

Those with high blood pressure should either avoid cold showers or take it very slow. Although it has been found that your blood

I am free, I am free, I AM FREE

pressure can be lowered by cold showers if you have mildly high blood pressure (150/100 and below) it can have a negative impact. The cold water could cause a spike in already high blood pressure.

Once you have obtained a safe zone for your blood pressure consider easing very gently into cold water therapy.

When performing hot/cold water therapy you can start to flush toxins out of the body via the bloodstream. This can cause sensations of discomfort as your blood can become more toxic during these times. Generally, these symptoms are short lived for a day or 3 or 4 depending on the level of toxicity within your body.

I am free I am free I AM FREE
ONE STEP BEYOND

Cold showers are just that. Cold showers. As such they are
limited. They do not allow for total body emersion into waters at or
around the 55-degree Fahrenheit settings that we want to strive for.

If you wish to level up you will be looking for total body
emersion into a cold running river, still lake or perhaps one of those
cold-water holes supplied at various spa's if your so inclined. If you
can get into a river obviously you want to ensure safety first.
Although I love the Ocean, I wouldn't recommend using the Ocean
for these practices. The Ocean can be temperamental, and the
strength of those waters should not be underestimated. Even within a
river know your swimming capabilities and limitations and
understand how fast or slow the current is moving. The last thing you
want is to be swept away in a dangerous rapid while attempt to
implement healing modalities.

When practicing these techniques outdoors keep in mind that
you are no longer in a temperature-controlled environment. Wind
chill (not really a thing by the way) will become a factor in your
ability to perform the cold-water emersion breathing technique and
having your entire body immersed in cold water will be much more
aggressive to your overall senses compared to a cold shower.

As much as I love my morning cold showers time to migrate this
conversation to another healing pattern.

Earlier in these writings we touched upon the wonders of
Intermittent Fasting. Now let's move along into the easy practical
applications of incorporating these healings into our weekly routines.

INTERMITTENT FASTING FOR MEN

"The addition of food should be much rarer, since it is often useful to completely take it away while the patient can withstand it, until the force of the disease reaches its maturity. The man carries within him a doctor; you just have to help him do his work. If the body is not cleared, then the more you feed it, the more it will be harmed. When a patient is fed too richly, the disease is fed as well. Remember – any excess is against nature."
-Hippocreates (the Father of Modern Medicine)

What is intermittent fasting?

Let's start by discussing what IF is not. This is not a diet but rather a systematic way of eating your various foods based on timelines. We are essentially restricting our eating during portions of the 24-hour cycle to take greater advantage of the body's ability to self-repair and to gain the most benefit from the foods we do eat when we decide to eat them.

One of the great things about implementing IF into your lifestyle is that it is not a diet per-se but instead is a very easy to implement lifestyle modification that allows you to continue to eat some of your favorite foods while still allowing your body the necessary time to digest and repair to help keep you lean and in better overall health.

If you are currently carrying around additional unwanted and/or unhealthy visceral/white fat know that you can quickly and easily implement IF into your lifestyle and enjoy the many benefits presented to you by the holistic healing effects of Intermittent Fasting.

Because it is so easy to implement, and you can largely maintain the same food types into your eating window this creates a strategy which allows you to quickly and easily change your "bad" eating habits and allows you to easily maintain consistency to help ensure you avoid the yo-yoing weight gain/loss nature of most fad diets.

THE STATE OF FASTING

It's all about time baby (even though time is an illusion). Most of us growing up in the Western world are programmed to eat 3 large meals a day, and the consuming of endless amounts of snacks and other forms of calorie consumption throughout the day including those empty or negative calories consumed via various liquids such as sodas, sports drinks, latte's, etc.

When you eat in this fashion your body is nearly always working in a state of being fed as opposed to a fasting state. When you consume calories, your body starts the digestion process which can last anywhere from 2-5 hours depending on how much you ate and what type of calories you consumed. This creates a state in which your body cannot burn visceral fat efficiently due to the spiking of your insulin levels.

You might think your good to go after that 2-5-hour window but unfortunately your body then migrates to the processing state. It's not enough to simply digest the calories, now your body needs to do something with the various by-products of the digested content. This process can take anywhere from 6-12 hours which creates another scenario where your body has a difficult time efficiently burning visceral and white fat while it's in a state of processing your last meal.

You might consider it plenty of time of consuming calories between meals for your body to take care of its business but when you start looking at these digestion and processing windows you can see that although you are largely not aware of it your body is busy processing calories while you are sitting down to put more calories in further interrupting your body's natural process' AND making it difficult for your body to finish processing the old calories before consuming additional calories.

When you can place your body into a fasted state it is able to work much more efficiently and aggressively in taking care of burning various types of fat.

BENEFITS

1. Easy to implement, easy to continue to practice.
2. Closer to the natural state of how the body wants to perform.
3. Easy again. I must put it twice because not only is it easy to implement it helps to create ease within your life and day to day routines. Not having to worry about constantly seeking meals and calories gives you time to concentrate on other things in your life.
4. Cost effective. Instead of buying into fad diets that often come with large price tags Intermittent Fasting is the exact opposite. You eat less meals throughout the 24 cycle and can stick to eating foods that you like (within reason). If you combine this with consuming less meals from restaurants and outside of your home, you can save a considerable amount of money.
5. Longer life with higher quality of life. If we could all become breatharians that might be a fantastic thing but it's unrealistic for the vast majority of the human populace. Esoteric knowledge along with more up to date scientific research proves that caloric restrictions can have outstanding health benefits for the human body as a collection of living organisms. The issue is that many people implement multiple day fasting schedules which have proven time and again to be extremely powerful methods of healing but can take a large mental toll for many that are not accustomed to more extreme versions of caloric deficits. Utilizing Intermittent Fasting we are using the same healing mechanisms but spreading it out making it easier to implement and maintain without creating mental anxiety and without fasting in a painful way. Intermittent Fasting also allows you to prep yourself for longer multi day fasting routines if you decide later you wish to implement those on a quarterly or bi-annual basis.
6. Brain function. Studies on animals have shown that Intermittent Fasting may reduce oxidative stress and inflammation. These are well known to be good for the brain.
7. Mind. As your body starts to function in a more efficient manner that it prefers your mind in kind will start to fill itself with positive energies. These positive energies will then feed

I am free, I am free, I AM FREE
back into the cells of your body creating a loop mind/body
positivity which will allow you to move closer to becoming the
free spirit you are.

I am free I am free I AM FREE

PRO TIPS

TIP 1:

You will not be Intermittent Fasting every day. On days that you are practicing your fasting you MUST be as strict as possible with your eating schedule to ensure you gain the most benefit.

Don't' beat yourself up. One of the worse things to do is to create self-doubt, fear or anxiety because this can lead to simply giving up and/or creating a negative outlook on the program. The body has the amazing ability to adapt but when we first try new routines, we can feel pains both physical and psychological. Since we have such strong emotional connections to our foods and food like products it can create a sense of loss and pain going several hours without eating. Although we may feel this largely in our stomach as hunger pains many do not take the time to stop and listen to their emotions. Many times, it is our unchecked emotions that whisper in your ear that eating just a little of this or drinking just a little of that is Ok because you deserve it, or you can really start doing the fasting tomorrow.

This is a moment of challenge. Your conscious, programmed mind-self is attempting to bamboozle you into believing you're not capable of going X number of hours without consuming calories. This can become even more difficult when you eat within your normal eating windows. For example, if you have been eating lunch every day at 11:30 A.M. guess what your body is expecting at 11:30 every day? It's been programmed to start the digestion machine because it knows calories are about to be on their way. For the first couple of days this may be a struggle but again the human body is truly amazing, and you have been blessed with yours and it only wants what is going to benefit you. Work past these fasting windows in the first couple of days and allow your body to reset to the new programming. Once you do this the fasting windows become very easy because they become the new normal for both your body and mind.

TIP 2:

Another critical element is to ensure that your fasting window is at least 16 hours. Short of 16 hours and your body simply will not get the HGH boost or nearly any of the other benefits in an amount to make it substantial. An ideal fasting window is 16-18 hours of consuming no calories. The difference between 16 and 18 hours is also significant. Initially I want you to shoot for the 16-hour window, within 2-3 months you should consider pushing the fasting window to 18 hours to allow for substantially greater benefits.

TIP 3:

DO NOT CONSUME THINGS THAT WILL BREAK YOUR FAST.

That seems obvious but one thing that seems to stump many when jumping on board IF is the consumption of liquids. We tend to forget that many drinks carry calories and once you consume calories even small amounts that may seem innocent you can break your fast and lose all the potential benefits that come with fasting. In this tip I will list items that are SAFE to consume during the fasting window. Pretty much anything else is going to carry calories and thus break your fast if you consume during your fasting window.

Water

Black coffee or Green Tea (nothing added like sugar and cream, and certainly not butter)

special caffeine note: I'm not a coffee guy but in my research, I have seen time and again that adding small amounts of caffeine usually via coffee during your fasting window can both allow for a mental boost and help to suppress your appetite. You can have 1-2 cups of coffee or green tea during your fasting window.

ACV: Apple Cider Vinegar. Doing a small shot of ACV will not break your fast and can help your gut biome.

That's about it. No sugars or artificial sweeteners. This will stop your fasting state and you will not gain the benefits of fat loss.

TIP 4:

Fasting Days. I typically fast Monday through Friday because these are days that I am in the office and can easily keep myself busy and since I food prep when I am ready to break my fast, I have the proper foods available to me in a controlled environment. On Saturdays and Sundays, I do not prescribe to the Intermittent Fasting schedule and instead I prepare a healthy (or not so healthy) breakfast for the family so we can all start the morning together at the table with lively conversation.

Start by incorporating Intermittent Fasting 3 days a week. It does not have to be 3 days in a row, but that is fine to do as well. They key here is we want you focused on getting into the fasted state at least 3 days a week. Within 1-2 months you should bump up from 3 days of Intermittent Fasting to 5 days of Intermittent Fasting per week. You do not have to do a 5-day fasting window but if you find that you are gaining many benefits from the IF schedule you should consider increasing safely to 5 days a week.

TIP 5:

Alcohol. If you can you should avoid alcohol on days that you are fasting. Although you can drink alcohol during your calorie consumption hours you will create a bit of a disadvantage for yourself. Your liver will have a more difficult time breaking down fat if it's busy with the alcohol so if one of your primary goals is to lose fat you should try to avoid alcohol consumption on your fasting days.

TIP 6:

You can create the fasting window for anytime of the day/evening BUT it's advantageous to create a fasting window which allows you to sleep during much of the fasting window. If you average 7 to 8 hours of sleep each day/evening this allows you to complete nearly half of your fasting time while you are sleeping which means your conscious mind while you are awake is only going to complain for 8-10 hours instead of the full 16-18 hours.

PRIMARY BENEFITS

Fat Burner
An animal study conducted by Cell Research found that sticking to at least a 16-week intermittent fasting schedule helps to prevent obesity. Most animals started experiencing benefits within 6 weeks. The published study showed that IF worked to increase the metabolism which helped to burn more fat by generating additional body heat. If you combine this with cold water therapy as outlined in my cold-water therapy chapter you will find that your "good" fat, a.k.a. Brown fat is increased which allows for additional fat loss.
https://www.sciencedaily.com/releases/2017/10/171017110041.htm

Long Life Span
Well that's a bold claim! To support this claim, we turn to our boy's at Harvard who conducted a study which shows that putting yourself into a caloric deficit via IF manipulates the energy producing mitochondria of your cells, which funny enough leads to increasing your lifespan. This study found that the normal process of cell degeneration due to wear and tear on your body shifts once the fasting manipulates your mitochondria. This then leads to your cells being able to maintain normal function for longer periods which helps to promote anti-aging or what the science lab boys would call "healthy aging".
https://www.cell.com/cell-metabolism/fulltext/S1550-4131(17)30612-5

Brain Health
Want to help yourself avoid neurodegenerative diseases such as Alzheimer's and Parkinson's? Good news! According to research from Johns Hopkins School of Medicine neuroscience professor Mark Mattson the fasting state causes the brain to get tricked into believing it needs to protect itself during a caloric restriction crisis. During the fasting state your body will start to burn more fat because it will be forced to. Your body's storage of glycogen will naturally start to drop which forces the body to hit the backup system which is your fat stores. Once the fat burning process is started it kicks off another reaction which is the creation of ketones. Ketones are well known to boost energy levels which helps to eliminate "brain fog".

338

I am free, I am free, I AM FREE

Inflammation Reduction

I tend to spend a lot of time at the gym and with other high impact sports. This tends to create lots of inflammation within the body. Inflammation can lead to unnecessary weight gain. The Obesity has a study which shows that fasting can produce anti-inflammatory effects on the neuroimmune system. The study further shows that a high-fat diet does just the opposite by preventing this process from being able to occur.

https://www.ncbi.nlm.nih.gov/pubmed/21527899

Immune Regulation

When your body is fasting it no longer needs to work to break down food stuffs. This allows the body to free up time to go out and start the job of self-repair. Fasting while consuming distilled water helps for the digestive system to flush which reduces the overall number of natural microorganisms in your gut. Typically, the microorganisms are regulated by the immune system. Freeing up some of these microorganisms gives your immune system the opportunity to divert energy towards other important areas of the body.

I am free I am free I AM FREE

OK. LET'S DO THIS!

For all those talking points the actual fasting regime is incredible
easy and efficient. Typically, you want a 16/8 split or a 18/6 split.
We will start with the easier 16/8 split.
 16/8 Split: 16-hour window consume no calories, 8-hour
window for consuming calories. Fasted state and fed state.
I will layout my schedule as an example.

Consume last meal at 7 PM or 8PM.
Eat nothing and drink only distilled water after this period to
ensure I consume zero additional calories.
Go to bed which will account for 7 of my fasted hours. If I
stopped eating at 7PM and go to bed around 10:00, then wake up at
6am I have already fasted for 11 hours. If I want to go for 16 hours of
being in a fasted state, I only have to skip breakfast and break my fast
around 11:00 am or noon. By simply making my last meal of the
evening around 7 PM or 8 PM I am then able to sleep through most of
my fasted state and when I wake up only must go until about noon
before I start my feeding window.

Fasting Time: 7:00 PM - 12:00 Noon
Break Fast: 12:00 Noon
Fed State: 12:00 Noon until 7:00 PM

When first starting out when you take your first meal at Noon
you should consider having a smaller meal with less calories. You
want to get the body ready for digestion without suddenly slamming
the body full of calories.
 Within an hour have a large meal that can account for about
1,000 calories or so. You might want to shoot for something between
800 and 1000 calories depending on your body composition and level
of activity. You can eat pretty much anything you want but I would
recommend staying away from pounding sugar laden drinks and food
like stuff such as cookies, candies, and foods packed full of
preservatives. Have your sweets every now and then just don't go
crazy with it and keep it within reason.

340

I am free, I am free, I AM FREE

Eat throughout the rest of the feeding window up until 7:00 PM. Although we don't need to necessary count calories you do want to keep it within reason. For most you will want to keep the total calorie count in the 2,0000 range for the rest of this feeding window and you will be in good shape. Once again eat what you want but try to avoid foods that you know may lead to unnecessary health risks such as cancer-causing food stuffs. The less pre-packaged items you can consume in general the better off your going to be. Not all calories are equal so ensure your consuming high-quality calories.

At first you may have a slight drop in energy. This is due to your body now being able to go into a state of self-repair. It probably rarely has this opportunity as this situation is usually only presented when you are sick and not able to consume calories. When you are sick and can't eat the body is telling you STOP putting this shit in me and let me do my job of repairing the damaged goods! When you have a fever, your body is literally heating itself up to burn away infections. This is yet another reason why we want to practice cold water therapy which allows for activation of your brown fat to help during healing crisis. Because your body is in repair mode you can enter a state of what many refer to as a "healing crisis". It's your body killing off and eating away at things that do not belong within your living organism.

For me in the first couple of days my energy seemed a bit lower than usual. By the end of the week my energy levels skyrocketed like crazy. The only times my energy would crash would be when I ate a large meal in a single sitting. I believe my body became much more efficient in the fasted state and would get slowed down once I introduced copious amounts of food like products to it. That is why I suggest above that you take a small meal when first breaking your fast to prep the body for the incoming larger consumption of food.

While I was writing this, it dawned on me that not everyone is going to have a similar schedule to mine. My brother for example tends to spend lots of time entertaining clients late into the evening hours.

I thought it best to present another time window to give you an idea of how this might look for all the night owls out there.

Fasting Time: 2:00 AM - 6:00 PM

341

I am free, I am free, I AM FREE
Break Fast: 6:00 PM
Fed State: 6:00 PM until 2:00 AM

Many prescribe to incorporating expanded fasts on a regular
basis to accompany their Intermittent Fasting. They tend to add one
24 hour fasting day a month which will super charge your bodies self-
repair healing abilities. Other's prescribe to incorporating a 3-7 day
fast on a quarterly or bi-annual basis.

I believe these all to be good options but if you are going to fast
past a 24-hour cycle ensure you do some homework regarding the
proper safe and healthy way to do this. Although I have practiced
these methods these writings do not detail longer duration fasting and
although you can gain a great deal of health benefits from these types
of fast's if you do it incorrectly you can do a great deal of damage to
your body. A couple of resources for longer term fasting are
Gerson Diet
Bragg, The Miracle of Fasting
Fuhrman, Fasting and Eating for Health

Also, as a final note don't neglect good nutrition. Intermittent
Fasting is so easy and if you stick with it you will gain a great deal of
benefits which can lead to becoming more susceptible to eating shit
instead of eating foods for nutrition as well as to satisfy your taste
buds.

Some people have binge eating issues when implementing
Intermittent Fasting into their lifestyles. If you want to avoid binge
eating, I would recommend the following tips.

As often as is realistic prepare and pack foods with you ready for
consumption when you're ready to break your fast.

Take your time, chew slowly and enjoy your food. It takes the
brain in your head 20 minutes to figure out that your belly brain is
full. If you scarf down your food your brain will not understand that
you are full, and this can lead to overeating.

Drink plenty of distilled water during your fasting window.

I am free I am free I AM FREE

INTERMITTENT FASTING FOR WOMEN

If you haven't read the chapter right before this one "Fasting For Men" give it a quick glance as you will likely find some helpful tidbits in that chapter that will not be included in this chapter.

So why have a separate chapter for men and women when it comes to fasting anyway?

In GENERAL, the female form reacts in a different manner to caloric deficit compared to their male counterparts.

All of us are unique when it comes to how our bodies are put together and how they react to input or lack of input for the living organism. As such in this chapter we address some items that can be of GENERAL concern but will not necessarily apply to every female across the board.

One of the key factors is that the female form in general does not respond the same to fat loss and the level of HGH boosting. Also, a key factor in the female life form is that they are the life bringers. As such the body reacts in a much different fashion when it senses potential starvation encroaching. Because the female body has the duty of carrying and nurturing a life form the body will shut down the factors which allow for the creation of life. Once the body receives the information that starvation is afoot it attempts to eliminate the potential for creating a new life to ensure a healthier overall body. Since your body cannot differentiate potential starvation from a short Intermittent Fasting window it defaults to starvation mode.

Don't let this next part scare you but it's important that you have a deeper understanding of what's happening underneath the hood so to speak.

Hormones are a funny thing. You change one up just a bit and Biggity Bam you just started a cascading effect since these hormones are so interpersonally connected and deeply dependent on one another. By simply creating a caloric deficit you kick off a chain reaction of hormones. Because your body went into protection mode for starvation you now have the potential to start a cascade effect including:

I am free, I am free, I AM FREE

Irregular or loss of periods (usually irregular and lower percentage total loss).

Ovary shrinkage

Fertility issues

One of the key take a ways is that if you are trying to get pregnant now or sometime in the very new future you should NOT move into an Intermittent Fasting modality as it can have grave negative impacts with your ability to procreate.

Regardless of the level of your badassary we need to approach this healing modality a little slower than we would others. The reason for this is because we don't want to bombard your body with a massive influx of hormonal changes. Instead we want to ease it in and allow it to slowly incorporate the new changes.

I'm somewhat hesitant to toss this out there but I do know many amazing women in my life and I have more than a couple that would want to give me a hardy double handed shove in the chest at the mere mention of taking it slower or a bit easier. Keep in mind that you should know your body better than any other person on this Earth. There will for sure be a percentage of women who decide to take this path that can and will start straight off with a more aggressive schedule. Nothing wrong with this if you know your body just keep in mind that some things such as natural processing hormones can work outside of our control regardless of how much of a badass, we are.

There are a couple of things we are going to do differently to slowly introduce the Intermittent Lifestyle to the female body.

1. Less: We are going to introduce IF 3 days a week as opposed to 5 or more.
2. Hours: We also compress the fasting window. Instead of the 16-18-hour window we will look to achieve a 12-14-hour window.
3. Uptick: Each week you can uptick just a bit but do not go beyond a 16-hour fasting window and do not go beyond fasting for 5 consecutive days.
   a. In week 2 you may go from 3 days a week to 4.

I am free, I am free, I AM FREE
   b. In week 3 you may go from a 12-hour fasting window to a 13-hour fasting window.
4. You can keep building as necessary or if you find your sweet spot just maintain.

That's about it ya'll. If you want to know about all the various benefits go back one chapter to Fasting For Men where I outline various benefits you will find from the Intermittent Fasting lifestyle.

The key take a ways is about potential large mood swings, or odd menstrual cycles. If you start to experience these phenomena you will want to scale back or stop your Intermittent Fasting schedule.

Let's push along to discussing an easy option for introducing better gut health to your life.

Kombucha Part I

Kombucha is a fermented tea and as such needs at least 5-7 days to maturate. Kombucha has two batch cycles.

The first cycle is the portion to allow the SCOBY to feast and grow in strength and potency. The second cycle is to allow your individual bottles of kombucha to create carbon for that wonderful fizzy flavor. During this second maturation process you can add fruits and other healthy items such as ginger to further flavor your tea.

TOOLS REQUIRED

Water
Use distilled water only. Under no circumstances do you want to use tap water or water of a questionable or unknown source. It could damage your SCOBY and you don't want to consume water full of pathogens.

S.C.O.B.Y.
A SCOBY is a symbiotic culture of bacteria and yeast. It's alive and it is the living organism that does all the work for us in fermenting the tea. Every time you brew a new batch of tea you end up with another SCOBY so if your brewing a gallon a week you will end up with many SCOBY's over a rather short period. If you know someone who is brewing kombucha ask them for a healthy SCOBY. If you don't know of such a person you can create your own SCOBY from scratch but that takes a bit of time. You can also check out online shopping websites like Amazon where you will find people selling SCOBY's with the starter bouche in a sealed bag.

Starter Bouche
Every new batch of kombucha requires a bit of bouche from your last batch. That's no problem once you get going but when you're first starting off just like the SCOBY you need some starter bouche. If you purchase your SCOBY online try to find one that sells it with some starter bouche. If you can't that's ok. Find a local grocery store and purchase a bottle of kombucha ensuring it is NOT flavored just

346

I am free, I am free, I AM FREE

regular non-flavored as all get out kombucha. You can use some of this bouche as your starter bouche for your first brew.

Large Jars

I recommend getting ahold of two larger 1-gallon jars. Many people use large pickle jars. One of the keys is that it needs a large opening on the top. The SCOBY grows to the size of the jar so if it has a small opening at the top you will not be able to get your SCOBY in and out of the jar. The reason for two 1-gallon jars is so you can use one for your weekly brewing and the other can store your extra SCOBY's with some bouche. The nice thing about creating this type of SCOBY hotel is that you always have extra bouche on hand for a new brew and if you accidently destroy your SCOBY you will still have plenty of extra's in the SCOBY hotel. Also, you always have extra SCOBY's around for any friends or relatives that get into brewing their own kombucha.

Cheese Cloth

You can purchase a roll from an online store or sometimes at large box stores. The cheese cloth will be used instead of the lid of the jar. The cheese cloth allows the SCOBY to breath while ensuring you don't get the kombucha inundated with flying insects. These are easily found online.

Thermometer

Once you heat your water and steep the black tea you must wait for the water to cool prior to placing the SCOBY into the tea/water. If you place the SCOBY into the tea/water while it's too hot it will destroy the SCOBY. You can purchase any low-cost run of the mill thermometer which you can also utilize for other things such as checking oil temperatures while cooking and checking the water temperature if your taking your cold showers (as you should).

Plastic Funnel with filter

You will probably need the funnel while getting the tea/water from the pot into the 1-gallon jar and later to pour it from the 1-gallon jar into your smaller bottles you will be using to drink the kombucha

I am free, I am free, I AM FREE

from. It's better if it has an attachable filter/strainer so you can strain out any small particles of SCOBY when you are bottling your bouche.

Bottles

I got my glass jars from when I was purchasing store bought kombucha. Instead of recycling the jars I washed them out and kept them. Now I simply bottle my bouche in these reused bottles. Alternatively, many people in the bouche making world purchase glass bottles that have flip top seals. While these are super fantastic for creating a strong seal and allowing for very strong and fast carbonation you do have to burp your bottles more often to ensure they don't explode on you. If I was purchasing new bottles, I would still opt for the simple twist top making it easier to burp if necessary and risking less chance of having a carbonation explosion when opening the bottle for a drink.

Black Tea

Although many people will ferment with flavored tea this is a bad idea. The oils from the flavored tea can damage the SCOBY. Introduce additional flavors during the bottling process. Use organic black tea. You don't need high-end brands (but also not the cheapest) try to find organic black tea bags. I usually stick with Lipton Organic Black Tea or whatever is on sale.

Sugar

Lots of options here. Although I'm not a fan of big box stores, I do hit up Costco to purchase large bags of white pure cane sugar. Although refined sugar is cheap and doesn't hail from the lands of natural awesomeness keep in mind this sugar is food for the SCOBY. Other brewers seem to enjoy coconut sugar and other natural types of sugars but since the sugar is for the SCOBY and not for human consumption this should not make too much of a difference. If you really want to be super natural and create extremely healthy SCOBY's you can use the juice of organic young coconut's which is going to give you one of the purest forms of sugar for the SCOBY.

Flavor Enhancers (optional)

I am free, I am free, I AM FREE

Once you bottle your bouche into consumer type 16oz bottles you have the option to add additional flavors. When I first started brewing kombucha I always added additional flavors such as strawberries, pineapple, raspberries etc. to sweeten the final product. Over time my palette started to really enjoy the flavor of the bouche without the addition of fresh fruits. In the how to guide to follow I will include information on how to add these flavor enhancers which you may want to try when first brewing bouche. They can also be super fun to experiment with and they are easy to incorporate into the brewing process.

Blender (optional)

If you decide to go the route of adding flavor enhancers you will need a blender to blend down the fruits for preparation for bottling. You could cheat code this and purchase a bottle of a non-pasteurized flavored drink of choice and use this instead of creating your own from purchased organic fruits. If you do use this shortcut, make certain it's non-pasteurized juice (which can be difficult to find).

KOMBUCHA PART II

Let's get down to the nitty gritty.

This process is easy to do but difficult to explain so I will do my best.

There are two instructions I'm putting together.

This first set of instructions is for when you are making your very first batch of fermented tea. The second set of instructions will be how to make all subsequent batches of fermented tea.

The reason for this is because the process is slightly different only when you create your very first batch of fermented tea. From that first batch on you can easily utilize the same steps each week or 2 weeks or 3 if you want to catch a buzz. I generally create a new 1 or 2-gallon batch each week but you can ferment for longer if you want.

FIRST BOUCH STARTER BATCH

YIELD:
1 gallon

TIME TO PREP:
15-20 minutes
Several hours of allowing the tea to cool (hands off so you can just leave it and go about your day).

INGREDIENTS:
1 SCOBY
1 cup or more of non-flavored starter bouch
8 bags organic black tea
4-5 cups distilled water

UTENSILS:
Pot for boiling water

I am free, I am free, I AM FREE

1 gallon glass jar

Cheesecloth to cover lid of jar

Thermometer

Strong tight rubber band or piece of string.

INSTRUCTIONS:

Rinse hands well but NOT with soap. SCOBYS are bacteria and anything that destroys bacteria such as soap will likely destroy your SCOBY. Just rinse hands in cold water prior to handling your SCOBY.

Pour 4 cups of distilled water into a pot and bring to a boil.

Once boiling turn off the heat and add the 8 organic black tea bags.

Allow to steep in the hot water for 8 minutes.

Remove tea bags and pour tea water into 1-gallon glass jar.

Add 1 cup of white sugar (or sweeter of choice) to the 1-gallon glass jar and give it a good stir.

Add additional room temperature distilled water to the jar with the tea until it is nearly full. You must leave room at the top of the jar for both the SCOBY and some of the starter bouche so do NOT fill to the top of the jar. Adding half the necessary water at room temperature allows for the tea to cool faster (pro tip).

Now you wait. You can place the jar in the refrigerator to allow it to cool faster. You need to allow it to cool down below 90 degrees Fahrenheit to ensure you do not damage the SCOBY when added.

Once cooled sufficiently wash hands in cold water no soap and toss in your SCOBY then top off the jar with your starter bouche.

Wrap the top with a cheesecloth to cover and ensure it's tight with a rubber band or a piece of string.

I am free, I am free, I AM FREE

At this point you need to store the jar in a cool dark area for at least 1 week. This allows the SCOBY to eat the sugar and tea. The longer you allow it to ferment the more pungent the kombucha and the more alcoholic it will become. If you go for one week it will likely still be a bit sweet as the SCOBY would not have had enough time to consume the sugar.

As the weather gets colder in my area of the map I wrap my jar in a cheap blanket and place it near my baseboard heaters behind my couch. It's dark, warm and has zero human traffic which is ideal.

After 1 week or longer you can now bottle the bouche.

BOTTLING:

Migrating your bouche from the 1-gallon jar into small separate bottles for consumption.

UTENSILS:

The 1-gallon jar of Kombucha you just fermented
Additional 1 gallon glass jar
Funnel with filter
Organic fruits or unpasteurized fruit juice of choice (optional).

INSTRUCTIONS:

Grab the empty 1-gallon jar

Grab your 1-gallon of newly fermented kombucha.

Remove rubber-band and cheesecloth from top of jar.

Rinse hands in cold water NO soap.

Remove SCOBY from your new batch of kombucha and place into your empty 1-gallon jar.

Pour some of the kombucha into your jar that now holds your SCOBY. Doesn't need to be a lot, about 2 cups or so.

I am free, I am free, I AM FREE

Place the lid on the jar that now has the SCOBY and place in fridge. You now have a SCOBY ready for another weekly batch or you can just toss it in the fridge and make another batch whenever you feel like. Tossing the SCOBY in the fridge with some of the Kombucha slows it's growth and allows you to create your new batch straight away or wait several months if you like.

If you are not adding additional flavors simply use your funnel with the filter and pour the Kombucha from your fresh batch into your jars filling them nearly to the top. Ensure you leave some room at the top to ensure your bottles don't explode. Put the caps on nice and tight and store them in a cupboard for 2-3 days then transfer to your fridge.

FLAVORS

If on the other hand you decide to add flavors you can create your own super organic natural style by following the steps outlined below.

Hit your farmers market or grocery store and buy some of your favorite organic fruits. You can go strawberry's, but I wouldn't recommend going with fruits that do not have protective skins. Something like an organic pineapple is a good choice because it's super sweet and has a protective layer over the fruit itself.

Chop up your fruits and anything else you want to add. If adding ginger go light because it's strong.

Toss these items into your blender and add a bit of distilled water. Blendy, blendy until nice and smooth.

Using your funnel pour some of your newly created organic juice into your empty drinking bottles. About ¼ or less is good to keep the flavor sweet and still retain a good amount of the gut healing kombucha.

Fill each bottle the rest the way with your Kombucha ensuring you are not filling to the very top.

I am free, I am free, I AM FREE

Twist caps on nice and tight, store in cupboards 2-3 days, then into the fridge.

NOTES

Once you bottle you can consume at any time.

The longer you leave them bottled the more carbonation is created. Eventually you hit a point of no return where the pressure is too great, and you get exploding lids or bottles. If you find this happening on a regular basis you can simply burp your bottles. Periodically you can untwist the lids just a bit and let some of the pent-up gasses escape then twist the lids back into place.

I usually start my next weekly brew right after I bottle my weekly brew that just finished. Since you have two 1-gallon jars one can hold all your extra SCOBY's and starter bouche while being kept in the fridge and the other 1-gallon jar can be utilized for the weekly fermentation process.

If your drinking your bottled Kombucha straight from the cupboard drop some ice in a glass, then pour. It tastes much better. You can also use the funnel with a filter when pouring from your bottle to a glass to help trap any small particles from getting into the glass. This is the best way to serve Kombucha to someone who is new to the Kombucha game.

KIMCHEE

Let's keep the DIY gut biome fixing going. Kimchee bitches! Make it once eat it 100 times.

I was never a fan of kimchee until I decided to make my own. There are many writings hailing the benefits of consuming this fermented food that can help your good gut bacteria. The vast majority of kimchee you purchase from a store will have added fish or some other sea life. This vegan version is just as tasty but does not include any of our fishy friends. You can also ensure to purchase organic ingredients to get this as close to healthy as you can.

Note: While your cabbage is resting you can prep the rice porridge and the chili paste.

I love this because it's easy to make and once you make one batch it can last in your fridge for up to a year. Because it last so long you rarely need to make a batch.

YIELD:
A whole mess load that will last you a long time (about 1 gallon).

TIME TO PREP:
Several hours BUT much of that time is waiting not actively doing anything.

TIME TO COOK:
N/A

CABBAGE INGREDIENTS:
1 Purple Cabbage cut in half
1 Napa Cabbage cut in half
2 Ounces Salt of choice

RICE PORRIGE INGREDIENTS:
2 Tablespoons flour (rice flower if going gluten free)
5 1/2 Ounces Water
1/2 Teaspoon maple syrup or sweetener of choice

I am free, I am free, I AM FREE

3-4 stalks of chopped green onion
1 grated daikon radish
1 grated large carrot

CHILI PASTE INGREDIENTS:
1/2 a white onion
6 Cloves Garlic.
Thumb size piece of Fresh Ginger
4 Tablespoons Tamari
1/2 Teaspoon Seaweed Sheets
2 Tablespoons Korean Chili Powder

UTENSILS:
1 large glass jar. 1-gallon jar with a lid tends to be the best option
Blender
Vegetable Knife
Rubber Spatula
Whisk

INSTRUCTIONS:
Chop your two cabbage halves into smaller bite sized pieces and place into a large bowl.
Rinse the cabbage thoroughly and drain out any excess water. Be sure to rinse the cabbage very well.

Add 2 ounces of salt to your cabbage in the bowl.
Using your clean hands massage that salt in there very well. Make sure to cover all the cabbage
It's a lot of salt but don't worry the salt is only used to break down unwanted bacteria before you start the fermentation process.
After the salt massage let the cabbage rest for 30 minutes to allow the salt to break down that bacteria.

After the 30 minutes is up.
Massage it again for a couple of minutes.
Let it rest for an additional 30 minutes

I am free, I am free, I AM FREE

After the second 30 minutes is up massage it again and then rinse the salt off. Get as much of the salt rinsed off as possible so you can avoid salty kimchee.

RICE PORRAGE
While your cabbage is resting make the rice porridge.

Chop your onion and set aside
Grate both your daikon radish and carrot and set aside.
You can use any flour you wish but if you want it gluten free use rice flower.
Heat up a large pot on the stove top on high heat
Add 5 1/2 fluid ounces of distilled water
Add 2 Tablespoons of flour slowly or through a sieve so it doesn't clump
Using a whisk stirry, stirry until it becomes a thick porridge
Add 1/2 Teaspoon maple syrup or sweetener of choice
Add the onion, radish and carrots.
Turn off the heat on the stove top and remove the pot.

You also need to make your chili paste while your cabbage is soaking in its salt bath.

CHILI PASTE
Pull out that blender and add the following
Half a white onion
6 cloves garlic
Thumb size piece of fresh ginger
4 tablespoons tamari
1/2 Teaspoon dried seaweed sheets
2 Tablespoons Korean chili powder
Blendy, blendy
Set mix to the side.

Once the cabbage has finished its final 30-minute salt bath
Rinse off cabbage
Add chili paste to cabbage
Add rice porridge

357

I am free, I am free, I AM FREE

Use your hands to mix everything. Make certain that all the cabbage pieces are covered with the porridge and paste.

Into a large jar and let it sit 3-5 days
Leave the lid slightly open so air can get in.
After 5 days close the lid and put into fridge
Can last for up to a year.

Taste great on toast with avocado.

That's it for the simple fermentation process. If you decide to get into it, you can start jarring all kinds of stuff. I have a couple of favorites but these writings taking up too many pages, so I will leave our fermentation at kombucha and kimchee.

That's a wrap. Onward and upward. Actually downward. Let's journey to your land down unda for an unlikely place to find clues to your internal health.

POO

Ahhh good ol' poo. It has a storied history that I would love to get into but let's focus on how knowing our poo can help us better heal ourselves.

You ever go to the doctor's office and they ask for a stool sample? Not me personally but I've seen it in movies and on those drama medical shows so I'm sure it's real.

Ever wonder why animal trackers and paleontologist are all about the animal poo? At our local zoo once a year they have Zoo Doo for sale and, it's a wildly popular event.

Poop not only can accommodate countless hours of adolescent humor but can also help us to determine the health and wellbeing of some important body processes. Your poo can act as an early warning system regarding digestive issues. If you keep it around and frolic in it your likely to get yourself extremely sick especially if your various internal body systems are already dealing with something or are in ill health. That should get your brain to consider what would happen if you have an impacted colon and the internal pipes that the poo moves through start to clog up with fetid crap. I'm sure it's just a coincidence that colorectal cancer is the third most common cancer diagnosed in both men and women in the US. The O so trustworthy American Cancer Society does say there are ways to help attempt to prevent this from occurring with the first thing being too of course go see an allopathic doctor and get screened. Next up are some important ones.

1. Manage your weight
2. Ensure you partake in regular physical activity
3. Eat more veg, fruits and whole grains. Baby spinach is great to help regulate the poop shoot.
4. Don't drink too much alcohol.

Frustratingly enough I put my hands on a research paper regarding the statistics of bent colons amongst the US populace and the numbers were not good, but alas this was many moons ago and I no longer have that research available. I do recall that the research

I am free, I am free, I AM FREE

found that most of us that use a toilet have our colons miss shaped which can cause a host of ills.

Top 4 Quick Fix To Gain Poo of Envy

1. Eat real food such as leafy greens and fresh fruits. The more local and in season you can get the better.
2. Drink plenty of distilled water. See water chapter for additional detailed info.
3. Take your time and prop your feet.
4. Consume healthy probiotics via natural sources such as kombucha (you can brew yourself see the chapter on that), kimchee (can make your own see the chapter on that) and other fermented foods.

I am free I am free I AM FREE

POO TOP 5 TO STRIVE

Slow down and take your time with your bowel movements. Don't be in such a rush. Relax and enjoy your time on the porcelain thrown.

Do you enjoy your poo time now? I would hazard to guess that most people don't. In fact, most people rush through the waste removal process as quickly as possible pushing and grunting like mad. I don't want to get all new aged about poo because...... well it would be a weird thing to get into in that context, however I would like to point out the fact that while you are clearing your physical body of parasites aside from your skin your booty hole is the greatest place for elimination of parasites and toxins. As such maybe don't think about the oddity of celebrating the release of toxins through your booty but at least acknowledge the fact that your becoming cleaner and lighter via a normal bodily function of elimination. With that said top tips for pooing.

1. Slow down! You're not getting an award for ninja pooing. In fact, you're probably damaging your colon and pushing <------ (see what I did there) your way towards a total blowout of your internal organs. Take it easy. You don't need to time yourself, but 15-20 minutes should be considered pretty normal. A 20 second grunt fest shouldn't be considered at all.

2. Let's do it Indian style. Feet up to relieve pressure on that colon. Toilet seats were a great convenience when invented. First there was the hole in the floor. Then some dude came around and put a bend in the pipe below the waste hole and everyone breathed a desperately needed sigh of relief. Then came the toilet for a nice feeling on the bumm while relieving yourself. That was a great invention but unfortunately it also puts a bend somewhere else, namely at the bottom of your colon. Not good people. Squatting is considered the ideal way to release that poo and keep good colon health or at least to help alleviate severe damage. You can purchase a toilet squatting stool from places like Amazon or you can keep it simple and go to a second-hand store and find a nice-looking wicker magazine holder that is a good height for you to prop your feet on while sitting on the

361

I am free, I am free, I AM FREE

toilet. Now you can read a magazine and help straighten your colon. Ideally you would squat directly on the toilet seat but that could get dangerous in its own right.

3. How often. How often you poo is important. When I didn't give a rat's ass about what I stuffed into my mouthole I was pooping maybe 3-4 times a week. Pretty heinous. Once I started drinking more water my poop routine started to pick up. Before I knew it, I was nearly a once a day regular pooer. Once I started changing my eating habits my body started to work in a good 1-2 daily poos. If you have trouble with lack of poo's I once again recommend stuffing baby spinach into your maw daily.

4. Get proper amounts of sleep. Studies have shown that there is a direct link between poor sleeping habits and constipation issues.

5. The Look! Seems kind of strange to be checking out your poo but you don't have to go in there with a magnifying glass or anything. You're just conducting a quick peek to see what your poo looks like which can be an indicator of various health issues. Conduct a duckduckgo.com search on the Bristol Stool Scale. Docs don't just run diagnostics on your poo they also reference the Bristol Stool Scale which is a chart that shows various types of poo and assigns a kind of classification.

Enough about poop. Let's move on into a new chapter.

In this chapter we will attempt to create one-page info sheets about various objects you likely have around your household now. I will discuss their potential harm and try to relay some alternative options. Note that some alt options require work while others require the expenditure of money. For my own lifestyle I prefer a bit of work over spending additional fake fiat currency but then again at other times I'm busy, lazy and trying to write a book so I shortcut it.

When possible, you should consider purchasing any necessary cosmetic type of items from smaller natural shops. It takes money out of the hands of the giant conglomerates and large corporations and helps to support people that are mostly attempting to keep you from unwittingly poisoning yourself.

I am free, I am free, I AM FREE

Another important note is with regards to researching "beauty" products including soaps, shampoos, colognes, make up, etc. before purchasing. A nice handy dandy way to save yourself some time is to check out the EWG's Skin Deep Cosmetics Database. It's the serious awesomesauce ya'll!

I am free I am free I AM FREE

DEODORANT

Deodorant. What's the deal, seems harmless enough? I was very proud the first time I started using deodorant. After all puberty was hustling its way into my young life and I had a couple strands of pit hairs to show off. It felt great to finally have enough man stank to require the use of deodorant.

Let me pop that bubble. Before we go into the poisons contained within most deodorants (both spray and roll on) let's tackle a bit of information regarding why your armpits and the collective of Lymph Nodes are important. Some of this will be repeat information from the chapter regarding your Lymph Nodes.

Your lymphatic system is important in keeping your body in good running heath as they act as critical clumps of tissue that assist in the body's immune response. What may be more important is its ability in carrying dis-ease fighting cells to various areas of the body.

Your skin being the miracle that it is, is incredibly durable and can expel many toxins from the body but also can absorb toxins into the body. That second part isn't so good for our organisms.

Under your pits (and neck, collarbone and groin) you have bundles of lymph nodes. When you put on deodorant you are doing two terrible things to your body.

First, you're not allowing the toxins that need to be expelled from the pits to be expelled. Instead you have placed a barrier directly on the pit which blocks the ability for the body to naturally expel these poisons as intended by the very nature of your body.

Second you are putting poison directly on your pits and this poison can be absorbed and then BIGGIYTYBAM the lymph nodes located directly under your pits carry those poisons throughout your body.

Now your body must take energy away from other repair duties and figure out what to do with the newly introduced poisons.

If you were to eat some of these toxins it would of course be bad but at least you would have your liver and digestive system to attempt to metabolize the poison before hitting your bloodstream. When poisons are put on your skin they are not always metabolized prior to getting into your bloodstream.

I am free, I am free, I AM FREE

Toxins within most off the shelf deodorants:

Aluminum:
This metal has been linked to causing gene instability in breast tissue. Over half of all breast cancers start in the upper outer portion of the breast which happens to be local to the pits. Aluminum in antiperspirants clog your pores and prevents sweating.

Triethanolamine (TEA) and diethanolamine (DEA):
These are chemicals that are known carcinogens and have already been banned in Europe.

Artificial Colors:
Also known carcinogens that also can cause serious allergic reactions.

Parabens:
A heavily utilized chemical preservative that is known to act as an estrogen blocker which disrupts hormone balances which can also be linked to both breast and prostate cancer.

Triclosan:
The FDA classifies Triclosan as a pesticide and its used as an anti-bacterial agent. In 2016 the FDA finally banned triclosan, but companies simply started utilizing other anti-bacterial chemicals not currently on the banned list. The other problem is that triclosan is also utilized in many other household products that are not regulated by the FDA such as clothing, kitchenware, furniture and toys.

What to do:

Throw away your deodorant.

Shave your pit hairs down so it's less of a fetid sewer in there.

I am free, I am free, I AM FREE

If you must have some sort of fragrance up there (you don't) then use something natural like Jojoba oil spray. You can also make your own deodorant and it's a cheap and easy process.

Take short cold showers after workouts and ensure you cleanse those pits out in the cold water.

Look up your current product in the Skin-Deep Database to find out its level of toxicity
https://www.ewg.org/skindeep#.WI_W7q6nHmE

This DB is great for looking up the level of toxicity for INDIVIDUAL items, but we must remember that the mixing of various contaminants found in nearly all these chemical laden products is of concern.

Homemade Deodorant is easy to make but there is a caveat.

The base ingredient is usually either Coconut Oil or Shea Butter.

Both ingredients are great to use but don't do so well in the heat.

This deodorant will not travel well and will melt in the heat UNLESS you are sure to include bees wax in your recipe.

It also feels wet and runny. To fix this we add melted beeswax which smells good and helps solidify the deodorant for an overall better feel and better shelf life.

I also purchased some empty deodorant containers online. This way it looks and feels exactly like one you would purchase at the store.

You can use either Shea Butter or Coconut Oil as the base ingredient, but Coconut Oil feels better rolling on and smells better. Shea Butter can be a bit crumbly.

Don't skip out on the tea tree oil as this acts as an antibacterial ingredient.

You can purchase bees wax pellets from online outlets.

DEODORANT INSTRUCTIONS

366

Topic Summary

Detox:
    Pit Stank Assistance

What is it:
    Your very own roll-on deodorant.

Objective:
    Create easy to use roll-on deodorant sticks just like the ones you buy at your local store.

Resources Needed:
    Empty deodorant containers (2.5-ounce packs easy to find online)

    ¼ CUP Corn Starch

    ¼ CUP Baking Soda

    3 TBS Coconut Oil

    1 TBS Bees wax

    5-6 Drops Tee Tree Oil

    2 TBS Arrowroot (optional)

    PREPPING

- On a stove top melt the Coconut Oil and Bees Wax pellets together.

    If you don't want to use a pot for this instead use an empty glass jar. Place coconut oil in glass jar, fill pot with boiling water and place jar into the boiling water to allow the melting process. Make sure it's a thick glass jar or just get the water hot enough to melt the coconut oil without damaging the glass jar.

- Once melted remove from heat and add rest of ingredients
- Mix it up nice, before it cools and solidifies.
- Add Tee Tree oil and any other oils you want.
- If this mix isn't already in a glass jar get it into one now.
- Once it has cooled down a bit but hasn't started to harden pour your mix into your empty deodorant containers.
- Put them into the fridge to fully cool and harden.

It can be a bit odd to have your deodorant sticks in your fridge, but they will keep well and as easy as that you have natural deodorant that is not full of potentially poisonous and dangerous metals.

There are several types of recipes available and I have only included one. I no longer use deodorant, but I have made these several times with great success.

I am free I am free I AM FREE

COLOGNE

My body spent several years in my youth layered in an odd combination of funk, deodorant and cologne.

Still being a youngster, I was less concerned with the act of showering to remove the funk and instead relied heavily on the copious use of deodorant and cologne. I couldn't afford cologne, but I could rummage through my older brother's belongings and steal sprays of various coconscious of the day.

Part of the no shower rule came into play on that first day of middle school. Gym class was always my easy A that I greatly enjoyed and that first day of Jr. High I was looking forward to gym class with great enthusiasm. Everyone was taller and more muscular than I, but I was extremely tenacious and quick both of wit and foot.

As the period started to come to its conclusion we headed to the locker room to change back into our street clothes. Our gym teacher informed us that we all had to strip butt arse naked and hop in the showers. Not a one of us did and instead carried our stank through the rest of the day. Eventually I started showering in the school locker room but I along with all my other classmates went at least a good month funking that school up after gym class and it was within this reality I realized I could just place a layer of deodorant and cologne on top of my layer of funk.

Although making alternative deodorant aint so bad cologne is another challenge. You can search for natural oils to discover what works well for your body type. This option isn't bad but does take some work by trial and error to find just the right combination of natural oils that work well together for your specific natural musk.

You could also continue to purchase your cologne of choice but opt to never put it directly on your skin. Although be forewarned that some asthma attacks are specifically triggered by cosmetic fragrances. Instead you can spray your clothes with a modest squirt and be done with it. Lastly you can simply avoid the use of cologne all together (pretty good option).

In our society it seems that a lot of people use strong fragranced perfumes and colognes much too liberally. You don't need or want to splash this stuff all over your skin and even putting it on your clothes

I am free, I am free, I AM FREE

you don't need to go crazy with it. The natural smells of our bodies already work as natures aphrodisiac and is in place to create an attraction between people. Take regular cold showers without soap and shampoo's and forgo the deodorant and colognes. If you have body odor that will creep up during the day, consider finding a way to shower part way through the day. Many office buildings I've worked in have a gym facility available with showers. I love my morning and mid-day cold showers as the mid-day cold shower gives my mind and body a good zap. You can also make a batch of the natural ingredient deodorant as outlined in this chapter and keep some sticks at work and at home, keeping in mind that they do need to be kept in the fridge to keep their solid constitution.

I am free I am free I AM FREE

COLOGNE INSTRUCTIONS

Topic Summary

Detox:
Body odor cover up

What is it:
Your very own essential oils (cologne/perfume).

Objective:
Create your essential oils that after some trial and error can lead you to creating a combination that matches well to your own natural body scents.

Resources Needed:

Small brown bottles with screw on dropper lid.

Various natural oils.

Below is a list of some "masculine" type of natural oils that you can start to blend and play with to find a combo that works for you.

Woods: Cypress, spruce, cedarwood, pine, oak. Very manly.

Spice: Cinnamon leaf, black pepper, nutmeg

Citrus: lemon, lime, grapefruit, tangerine

Floral/Other: Lavender, sandalwood, patchouli, vanilla, peppermint, rosemary

Vitamin E: Adding Vitamin E can help keep the oils from turning.

A bit of Coconut or grapeseed oil is also recommended.

<u>Prep:</u>

Fill your small brown glass bottle nearly to the top with vodka.
Add 2-6 drops of essential oils using a dropper.
Add either a bit of coconut or grapeseed oil and Vitamin E.
Gently shake.

<u>Use:</u>

Place 1 drop on the inside of each wrist. Rub the inside of your
wrist's together and then rub your wrists onto your neck and collar
bone.

<u>WARNING</u>

Test on a small patch of skin on the back of your hand before
putting any oils onto your neck and collarbone or anywhere else. Let
it sit on your hand for 20 minutes before you use the oil for the first
time to ensure that your skin is not irritated by the oils.

Keys to success.

BASE
Create your base first. This is going to be either vodka, jojoba
oil, almond oil or coconut oil. I use cheap vodka and fill the small
brown glass jars nearly to the top with the vodka.

SMELL
Think of smells that you like. If you're having problems with
that you can visit a natural store or wander around your local grocery
store near the natural products section. Smell the various herbs,
spices and flora and try to find smells you dig. This is a good thing to
do before dropping coin on buying various oils that you may end up
not liking.

Purchasing pure essential oils which are easy to find online and
health stores.

Often you can find smaller sampler packs of several different oils at a low cost. This is a good option to start off by getting your hands on several different oil's in small quantities for testing purposes. These oils will last a very long time as the majority of your base is vodka with only small amounts of oil used per fragrance bottled.

You can experiment and have fun with it and create something uniquely you.

TOOTHPASTE

In the ever-present battle for pearly whites and tasty fresh breath there are few things in our society that is more ubiquities than toothpaste. Unfortunately, just about all toothpaste on the market contain fluoride.

Many people will soap box about fluoride in the water but to be fair I would be much more worried about other copious amounts of toxins in your municipalities tap water. Fluoride is typically only contaminated with 1-10 parts per million. Toothpaste is in the 1000 parts per million range. Yikes! Ever wonder why they have poison control information on your toothpaste tube, yet the expectation is for you to put this substance in your mouth and brush 3 times a day? Why do dentist warn that children need to be supervised when using toothpaste? I would guess because they flavor many of those toothpaste to taste like candy or spearmint and kids are swallowing down that poison.

Fluoride
How much toothpaste does my child need to swallow before it's a concern?
You can find the information on the link provided below but a quick sum up.
1-year old: 42% of tube.
2-year-old: 52% of tube.
3-year-old: 63% of tube
4-year old: 67% of tube
http://kidemergencies.com/toothpasteingestion.html

We can see why they put the poison control information on the label. It's for that time when a kid swallows down half the tube of toothpaste in one go. To note there is no antidote available for fluoride poising when this happens. Most symptoms include nausea and vomiting. The scary part is the rapid depletion of calcium and magnesium in the body followed by the potential for cardiac arrhythmia.

I am free, I am free, I AM FREE

As an adult fluoride in your toothpaste is one of those items that will have no noticeable ill effect when used day after day, especially if you're not ingesting the toothpaste. One of the greatest harms it can cause you according to new age philosophy is the calcification of your pineal gland. I suppose this could be true but I'm not certain we have any way to know this for certain.

It is largely surmised that rotten teeth and a fetid mouth hole is caused by food sitting in between your teeth and rotting. This however has never been proven to be true and in fact all signs point to the real culprit being eating terrible foods or food like products.

Early on in my journey for better health I moved away from typical store brand toothpaste and tried several "natural" brands that had a good reputation going for them. After changing over to these natural brands and using them for a couple of months I was busy one day doing some video editing when I noticed a guy that looked exactly like me but had some yellow ass teeth. I checked in the mirror and sure enough somehow my teeth had taken on a not so nice yellow/brownish sheen.

In my quest for vanity I switched back to the potentially pineal gland poisoned fluoride toothpaste for a couple weeks, so I could do some proper research on how to create my own truly natural way of cleansing my mouth hole and keeping my teeth from looking like an extra on the set of Pirates of The Caribbean.

So, I did and now I present it to you. I happen to love this recipe and I only have to make it once every 4-5 months (it's incredibly easy to make to boot). Fair warning it can taste a bit chalky and if you like the flavor of spearmint and such you probably aren't going to like this. My girlfriend tried it for 2 weeks then bailed because she had to have flavored toothpaste. With that said you can purchase flavored Diatomaceous Earth such as chocolate or you can flavor it yourself with ingredients such as peppermint oil.

TEETH WHITENING INSTRUCTIONS

Topic Summary

<u>Detox:</u>
Mouth Cleansing

<u>What is it:</u>
Your very own mouth cleanser followed by wheat grass pulling.

<u>Objective:</u>
Clean your mouth and whiten your teeth without using potentially dangerous chemicals.

Resources Needed:

<u>Small glass jar with lid:</u>
I use a small leftover food jar. Gave it a good wash and it was good to go.

<u>Activated charcoal:</u>
I purchase Activated Coconut Charcoal Powder from EarthShiftProducts.com Sometimes their prices run a bit higher than what you can find on Amazon, but they do have high quality products that I trust.

<u>Natural baking soda (Sodium Bicarbonate):</u>
I got one bag from EarthShift and one bag from "Prescribed For Life". The Prescribed For Life I found on Amazon and they are an American company.

<u>Bentonite Clay OR Diatomaceous Earth:</u>
I chose to go with Diatomaceous Earth instead of the Bentonite Clay. I got my DE from "earths-answers.com". They are a small American based company and have several flavors available at very reasonable prices. Although I do not have any cavities word around the campfire is that Bentonite Clay could bind to metals such as amalgam fillings and over time wear them down. This would be a

376

I am free, I am free, I AM FREE

BAD thing so if you do have fillings you may want to swing towards Diatomaceous Earth instead of Bentonite Clay.

Organic Wheat Grass:
This stuff is made to be mixed in with some water and consumed, which you can of course do as wheat grass has been shown to be a healthy product to consume. For this situation we are going to use it as a teeth puller. Many people use Organic Coconut Oil which you can use but Coconut Oil has one very large downside. If you spit it down your drain especially in the winter months and you live in a colder climate you run the risk of it solidifying and jacking your plumbing up when you spit it down your bathroom sink. I've done both and prefer the Organic Wheat Grass over the Coconut Oil. I purchased my Organic Wheat Grass powder from Amazon. The product is Amazing Grass which is an American Company.

How often:
Once in the morning and once in the evening.

Research:
Most of my research came from various health books from the 1990's.

Testing Protocol

Place 100 grams or so of each ingredient into your glass jar, secure the lid on the jar and give it a shake.

Open the lid (watch out for the powder puff) and sprinkle a bit of it onto the palm of your hand in a straight line. Grab your softhead toothbrush and scrap your mixture from your hand onto your toothbrush. Brush-a-brush-a-brush-a as you normally would. Your mouth and teeth will look black but that's a good thing. After done brushing rinse mouth out with minimal amount of water to get the blackness out of your mouth and off your teeth. When brushing ensure you're not going too fast and too rough. Gentle small circles is a good practice. Be sure to get your gums and the area of your teeth where your teeth meet your gums.

After you are done brushing your teeth put one small scoop of wheatgrass into an 8 oz glass of distilled water. Mix well until not chalky. Drink most of this down but save a small amount for teeth pulling.

Wheat Grass Pulling:
Many use coconut oil instead of wheat grass but there are various issues with using coconut oil. When using oil, it tends to feel weird putting a glob of oil into your mouth. If you spit it down your bathroom sink or toilet it could re-solidify and jack your pipes up.

Benefits of Wheat Grass Pulling:

You can find high quality Organic Wheat Grass powder at very reasonable prices.

You can drink some of it down before the pulling to gain the benefits of the Organic Wheat Grass for your internal system.

It appears to be just as effective as Organic Coconut Oil, so you do not lose any potential benefits for your teeth and mouth you only gain the benefit of drinking it.

Although a bit grainy it has a much better mouth feel compared to pulling with oil.

How to do it:

With the small amount you left in the glass put this in your mouth and swish it around ensuring to pull it through your teeth and swish it all around your mouth. You want to do this for at least 5 minutes. If you're doing the cold-water therapy outlined in the cold-water therapy chapter, then it's easy to start the pulling then jump your naked bum into your cold shower and do the pulling while enjoying the love of the cold water.

Results:

My teeth have been yellow for many years, but I never realized HOW yellow they were. After a mere 7 days of this protocol my teeth turned very noticeably MUCH less brownish yellow. Part of the reason it was so noticeable is because for one I was paying very close attention and for two I found out I wasn't brushing the very top of my teeth where they meet my gums. So, within 7 days the tops of my teeth toward the gum line were a nice canary yellow which would be great if my teeth were a 1969 Chevy Nova but alas, they are not. Although I had a bad brushing technique it turned out to be a very nice measuring tool to see how impressive this small change was. After that I started to slow down my brushing and changed my technique to ensure I was getting the entire tooth footprint.

Another thing I noticed was the back of my teeth. My four front bottom teeth are very crowded together and the backs of them have been a dark nasty looking brown for many years. They still have some light brown discoloration, but they are amazing looking compared to what they used to look like before I switched over to this homemade mouth powder.

Lastly and VERY important. My girlfriend also started this protocol but only saw slight improvements with her teeth. She also follows a pretty dialed in food intake regiment, but she does not perform any other healing modalities as I do. The one healing modality that I believe makes a significant difference is the oil/wheat grass pulling. She decided to forgo this portion of the healing modality, but I believe this is one of the key elements in helping to ensure your teeth move towards glorious whiteness.

She gave up the toothpowder for several months only to find that her teeth reverted back to a more yellowish tint then she decided to journey back into the land of self-made toothpowder.

Additional Notes:

Tongue Scrapper
Get a tongue scrapper. After you get out of the shower and spit out your Organic Wheat Grass run a tongue scrapper over your tongue 3-6 times to get rid of any nastiness on the tongue. This will greatly help your breath. Don't walk into your local grocery store and

I am free, I am free, I AM FREE

purchase a cheap plastic tongue scrapper. Shop around on various websites and purchase a nice titanium tongue scraper. It's better for your mouth, will last longer, is easier to clean and just looks WAY cooler.

Purchase a soft head bamboo black bristled toothbrush. They are made specifically for using with this type of charcoal mouth cleaner.

BONUS ROUND

If you have read this far into my brain thoughts, then you should know I tend to dive deeper than is necessary. Consider this a continuation of the "one pager" for mouth cleaning just to give you a little bit of background of what I'm telling you to put into your mouth on a daily compared to the big boys you've been buying your entire life (brand loyalty anyone).

The primary player in this formula is the activated charcoal. It's odorless, tasteless and is utilized for several purposes including treating intestinal gas and cholestasis during pregnancy. It's not too unlike the stuff you fire up under your grill however large pores are created within the charcoal trapping various chemicals. The pores then bind with the rough portions of your teeth usually the plaque. When the charcoal is washed out of your mouth it can then remove portions of the plague and yellow with it. It also collects small particles of food stuffs and stains. It basically gets rid of surface stains by latching onto the gritty particles of foods. So, if you have deep seated yellowed teeth it's not really going to work BUT if you have slightly yellowed teeth that have trapped particles of various items it will scrub and remove.

Baking soda is the other star of this show. Sodium bicarbonate pops up a lot in self-healing writings including these here writings because sodium bicarbonate along with non-pasteurized apple cider vinegar with the mother are cleansers of our external environment as well as internal when applied properly. Baking soda in the mouth basically neutralizes the acids in the mouth which helps to kill germs. When we combine these two superstars along with DE we create a substance that is superior to our store-bought pastes.

I am free I am free I AM FREE

QUICK PRINT RECIPE

100 grams activated charcoal
100 grams natural baking soda
100 grams bentonite clay or DE

brush once in morning
brush once at night
brush soft and gentle with soft toothbrush
don't kill your enamel and gums

Product Recommendations:

Bentonite Clay Powder:

(USA) Bentonite Clay Food Grade Powder
http://amzn.to/2nz83Jp

(UK) Bentonite Clay Food Grade Powder
http://amzn.to/2AT8PGd

(Worldwide) Bentonite Clay Powder
https://iherb.co/3e8BWizX

Activated Charcoal Powder:

(USA) Activated Coconut Charcoal Powder
http://amzn.to/2x8iLd8

(UK) Organic Activated Coconut Charcoal Powder
http://amzn.to/2xt8UP7

(Worldwide) Activated Charcoal Powder
https://www.iherb.com/pr/Country-Life...

Natural Baking Soda:

(USA) Organic Aluminum Free Baking Soda
http://amzn.to/2uSRzvd

I am free, I am free, I AM FREE
(UK) Aluminum Free Natural Baking Soda
http://amzn.to/2via1NH

(Worldwide) Natural baking soda –
https://www.iherb.com/pr/bob-s-red-mi...

Weight conversions:

100 Grams of Bentonite Clay is 3.53OZ's
100 Grams of Activated Charcoal is 3.53OZ's
100 Grams of Baking Soda is 3.53OZ's

WRAP UP

Here we are at the end of these journeys. I'm simply ecstatic that you stuck around and absorbed some of this information. Hopefully this will lead to some lively conversations amongst the various groups of people you choose to spend your energy with. My hopes are that some of the healing modalities can help you heal various ailments we all tend to suffer from. I think a bit of pain and suffering is just part of the deal with being human and being self-aware. And that's kind of the point of most of this content allowing us to become more self-aware and to question these perceptions of fake authority that inundate the social construct in which we live, love and play.

We have individually and collectively given up so much of the power of ourselves that we are now barely aware of who and what we truly are. Now is a good time to reevaluate how you spend your energy currency. If you find yourself with your eyes staring at various screens on a regular basis it's time to change those habits and replace screen technology with the beauty that is nature. This will give you time to connect and start diving deep into you.

We live in a world where we're all about updating. We update our computers, phones, cars, careers—even our partners. Now it's time to update your personal philosophy and world view. It's time to update you.

Self-help and prevention are intrinsic to homeopathy and the creation of an overall healthy lifestyle. We all must be involved with our treatment and accept that changes in our lifestyle, diet, habits, philosophy, control of stress and the sheer willpower to regain our health are interrelated. In these ways, the natural healing forces within the body are brought back to life and optimized to the highest level within this toxic reality we find ourselves. Baby steps, one day at a time. Do not fear loving yourself fully and then sharing that love with the world outside of yourself.

I am free I am free I AM FREE

Like a River You Will Flow

Physical:
Food - Tantra – Yoga, Physical Activity

Mental:
Meditation – Breathing

Energy:
Nature, Laughter, Smiles, Eye Contact

I am free I am free I AM FREE

ABOUT THE AUTHOR

Anan Rising

Find out more at <u>amazon.com/author/pimrosebooks</u>
Or visit www.pimrosebooks.com

I am free I am free I AM FREE

OTHER BOOKS BY ANAN

Treat Yourself: Thankfulness Goal Setting Journal
Heal Thyself: Self-Healing Journal Companion
Heal Thyself: Cancer Journal Companion

FREE STUFF C'MON AND GET YOURS

Ah how sweet! Check out the Anan Rising YouTube channel for free self-guided meditation audio.

I am free I am free I AM FREE

FAVOR PLEASE

If you enjoyed this book, found it useful or otherwise then I'd really appreciate it if you would post a short review on Amazon. I do read all the reviews personally so that I can continually write what people are wanting.

Thank you for your support!

Made in the USA
Columbia, SC
13 December 2020